MAYFAIR

The Years of Grandeur

MAYFAIR

The Years of Grandeur

MARY CATHCART BORER

W. H. ALLEN · LONDON
A division of Howard & Wyndham Ltd
1975

PRINTED AND BOUND IN GREAT BRITAIN BY RICHARD CLAY (THE CHAUCER PRESS) LTD,
BUNGAY, SUFFOLK
FOR THE PUBLISHERS W. H. ALLEN & CO. LTD,
44 HILL STREET, LONDON WIX 8LB

ISBN 0 491 01645 X

Contents

Foreword

Miss Borer's *Mayfair, The Years of Grandeur* is a fascinating re-creation, through the centuries, of the history of one of London's most famous and illustrious districts. Having had the privilege of reading the manuscript, I so enjoyed the vivid descriptions of the area I know so well today that I found I could picture the panoply of scenes as Mayfair changed from the end of the seventeenth century until the present time.

The research required must have been enormous but the picture is painted in the book so well and in such detail that I could almost see the metamorphosis from the Mayfair of fields and chases at the commencement of the book to the busy Mayfair that exists today.

As President of the Residents Association of Mayfair, I heartily commend it to our members, all those living and working in Mayfair and those interested in the social progress of London over the last three centuries. To read the history of the buildings that still exist or which previously occupied ground where modern hotels, offices or other buildings now stand is fascinating, and, although one considers one knows, it is surprising how much more Miss Borer tells. Furthermore, to realise that many of those whose names feature so prominently in the history of our country over the last three centuries did live there, provides even greater interest in the Mayfair in which we live today.

Indeed, the earlier picture in the book is of the residential nature of the area, of the necessary services which went with that aspect and, throughout, there is the sense of variety and unique values that is Mayfair. Our Residents Association is formed to preserve this in a modern setting, embodying an element that Miss Borer describes in her conclusion: 'As well as the physical reminders of the eighteenth century in the beautiful houses remaining in many of the streets between Bond Street and Park Lane, an intangible personality has survived.' It is indeed this that we must preserve and be grateful to Miss Borer for describing it all so beautifully.

Sir Graham Rowlandson, MBE, JP, FCA

Acknowledgements

I should like to thank Mr Clifford Pestell of Thomas Tilling Ltd for his kindness in showing me Crewe House and giving me a great deal of information about it, Mr C. C. Bishop of Gunter and Company Ltd, for talking to me about the old days, Mr Victor Lownes for arranging for me to be shown over the Clermont Club, Mrs Patricia M. Hayward-Ellen of the Bond Street Association Ltd, the representatives of Thomas Goode and Company, Mallett and Son of Bourdon House and New Bond Street, Asprey's, Tessier's, Cartier's, Elizabeth Arden, the Curzon House Club, the Mirabelle, St George's School and the staffs of the Westminster City Library and the London Library for all their generous help in the writing of this book.

For permission to reproduce photographs which are their copyright, I am indebted to the Trustees of the British Museum, to the Greater London Map Collection and the Greater London Print Collection, the National Portrait Gallery, the National Book League, the Clermont Club and Mr Victor Lownes, and Thomas Tilling Ltd.

MCB

I

Introduction to Mayfair

For more than two hundred years the English aristocracy, as well as politicians and men of affairs, made Mayfair their London home. It was the centre of fashion and elegance, where even after the building of the equally fashionable Belgravia, early in the nineteenth century, people of wit, wealth, intelligence and literary gifts chose to live.

Mayfair is a part of Westminster which has no formal boundaries, but custom has confined its limits to Park Lane in the west, Piccadilly in the south, Regent Street in the east and Oxford Street in the north. In the early seventeenth century, long before these streets were built, it was still a lonely country district of gently undulating fields and farmlands, the home of partridge and pheasant, wild duck and heron, the only buildings being one or two isolated farmhouses and a solitary windmill.

It was watered by the little Tyburn stream, long since converted into a culvert, which rose in the forested heights of Hampstead and meandered gently down through the meadows towards the Thames valley. Following its winding course along the line of Marylebone Lane, the stream crossed the heart of Mayfair in a wide arc, first south-eastwards, where South Molton Street and Avery Row were to be built, and then, turning due south for a stretch, flowing parallel with New Bond Street and a little to the west. During this part of its course it crossed the land where Brook Street, Grosvenor Street and Bruton Street were to arise. Then it flowed south-westwards along the old Lansdowne Passage, crossing Piccadilly just to the west of where the Naval and Military Club now stands, and flowed away across the fields later to become the Green Park to join the Thames at Millbank.

Along what is now Westbourne Terrace flowed a western branch of the stream, a pleasant little brook lined with elm trees, but in medieval times these elms had been used as gallows and were the sinister Tyburn trees.

By early Tudor times the City of London, still enclosed by its Roman wall, had seen many changes. In medieval days it had been a city of a hundred and twenty churches – dominated by old St Paul's, the finest church in all Europe, of churchyards and gardens, monasteries and nunneries, chantries and ecclesiastical colleges, royal palaces and the magnificent town houses of the merchant princes. Here were the splendid halls of the Livery Companies and the beautiful Guild Hall, the busy market of Cheapside, where wares were displayed in booths and sheds, with the poultry, honey, iron, milk and wool markets leading off to the north and the money changing, fish, soap, candles and bread markets to the south.

The building of Westminster Abbey was begun by Edward the Confessor, early in the eleventh century, close to the Royal Palace, and in Norman times the little city of Westminster had grown up round them.

Leading westwards from the City towards Westminster was a lonely, muddy, deeply-rutted track, already known as the Strand, which ran between the slow-flowing marshy Thames and the green fields of Middlesex and ended in the little village of Charing.

With the Reformation came devastating changes in the City. Many of the churches and the monastic buildings attached to them were destroyed. On the site of the Cistercian Abbey near the Tower of London and the Convent of St Clare close by, small cottages were built for the dock labourers. The Priory of the Holy Trinity in Leadenhall Street came down, the stones and monuments being sold for building material. St Mary's Spittal, by Bishops Gate, was demolished and new houses built on the ground. The Church of the Knights Hospitallers was blown up with gunpowder.

Over the pleasant gardens spread crowded courtyards and little twisting lanes lined with houses for the artisans and craftsmen, for London's commerce was growing fast, and with it the population of the City. Soon it was spreading beyond the confines of the square mile enclosed by the walls. Eastwards from the Tower there grew, says Stow, 'a continual street, or filthy straight passage, with alleys of small tenements or cottages builded, inhabited by sailors' victuallers, along by the river of Thames, almost to Radcliffe'.

To the north, the country still came up to the City walls, for Moorfields was as yet undrained and too marshy for building. Here cattle grazed and Londoners took the air on summer evenings. But south of the only bridge, Southwark was developing, with its inns and bear-gardens, and the river was busy with barges, sea-going merchant ships and hundreds of wherries, which ferried people from shore to shore, upstream towards Westminster or down to the docks.

It was during these years that the nobility deserted their palaces in the City of London and moved westwards from the congestion and medieval squalor to build new mansions for themselves along the south side of the Strand. The Savoy Palace had been built by Peter of Savoy in the thirteenth century, but by the end of the sixteenth century and the early years of the seventeenth, the palaces of the Earls of Essex, the Howards of Norfolk, the Cecils, the Villiers and the Percys had been built, as well as the first Somerset House of the Duke of Somerset, Lord Protector of Edward VI.

Building also began among the fields and meadows on the north side of the Strand, on the seven acres of 'fair spreading pastures' which before the Reformation had belonged to the abbots of Westminster. Their burying ground, their convent garden and orchard and the great field – the Long Acre – were now Crown lands and were enclosed by a brick wall; and in 1552 they were granted by Edward VI to John Russell, the Earl of Bedford. Part of the land the Russells let off to neighbouring members of the aristocracy for stabling and pasturage. The gardeners still tended the orchard and garden and marketed their produce. And here the Russell family ultimately built Bedford House, which stood until 1704.

Apart from the second Somerset House, built on the same site as the Lord Protector's house, late in the eighteenth century, nothing remains of the palaces which once lined the south side of the Strand, with their beautiful gardens sloping down to the water steps and the boathouses, except the magnificent watergate of the Duke of Buckingham's house. Now standing in melancholy isolation at the edge of the Embankment gardens, the watergate is a reminder of the splendid style in which these courtiers lived out the brief years of their power and favour.

Cardinal Wolsey had lived farther west still, at York Place, halfway between Charing and the crumbling old palace of Westminster, in a regal magnificence which helped to bring about his ruin.

King Henry VIII, in the year that he married Anne Boleyn, also decided to build. He chose a rural retreat a little to the west of the river, where the isolated hospital of St James stood. This was a medieval religious foundation for the succour of 'maidens who were leprous', which had been supported by gifts of money and land from the citizens of London and a grant by Edward I of the proceeds of a fair, which was 'to be kept on the eve of St James, the day and the morrow, and four days following', in the fields surrounding the hospital.

King Henry pensioned off the sisters of the leper hospital, where by now there were probably no leprous maidens left to be nursed, had the place demolished and built on the site a red-brick shooting-box, which became the palace of St James. The neighbouring fields, where the fair had been held, he exchanged for a grant of royal land in Suffolk to the Foundation, and he enclosed them to form St James's and the Green Park.

Cardinal Wolsey had, in the meantime, fallen from grace and made his last, tragic departure from Whitehall stairs, watched by hundreds of boat-loads of London citizens. Already a dying man, broken-hearted and bewildered, he left behind all his magnificence, the rare books, the tapestries, the gold and silver plate, the large household of yeomen of the barge and yeomen of the chamber, the grooms of the stable, the secretaries and the young resident noblemen – and was dead within a year.

Anne Boleyn had for long cast covetous eyes on York Place and now the King took possession, re-naming it Whitehall Palace and adding so many apartments and new buildings, as well as tennis courts and bowling greens, a cockpit and a tilt-yard, that, with the large privy garden to the south, the palace precincts stretched from the Green Park to the river and along most of the present Whitehall, giving it half a mile of river frontage. The palace was approached from the north by Holbein's massive gate-house and from the south by the King's Gate, which gave on to King Street, a narrow way leading to Westminster Abbey and the old palace. But Anne Boleyn was not spared long to enjoy these splendours. In 1536 she took her last journey by barge to the terrible Traitors' Gate of the Tower of London for her execution. This was the year that saw the beginning of the dissolution of the monasteries, when thousands of acres of Church lands came into the possession of the Crown. Much of this land King Henry sold or granted to especially favoured and useful courtiers, but among the manors which he kept for his own use were those of Hyde and Marylebone.

Hunting was one of his greatest pleasures and Hyde and part of Marylebone were enclosed to become, like St James's, royal deer parks, where the deer were bred and reared. At the same time he issued a proclamation declaring that a large tract of country stretching northwards from Westminster to the hills of Highgate and Hampstead and as far east as St Giles in the Fields and Islington was to be a royal chase. This meant that even on land which he did not own, the game – hare, partridge and pheasant – was to be preserved for his own sport. It gave him a splendid stretch of hunting country on his own doorstep, but it was one of those unpopular decrees which was not observed for long, and by the time of Queen Elizabeth the merchant princes of the City of London were sharing in the sport, hunting the hare at the head of the conduit where Conduit Street now runs and killing the fox at St Giles.

James I was as keen a hunter as any of the Tudors and built a small pavilion for himself in Hyde Park, where he would sometimes dine after a morning's deer hunt, but Charles I opened the park as a pleasure ground for Londoners. It was still enclosed and along its eastern boundary ran the narrow Tyburn lane, leading northwards to the Tyburn gallows.

A corner of St James's Park near the tilt-yard was also made public about this time. It was known as the Spring Garden, because of some natural or artificial spring which was to be found there, and it was one of London's earliest pleasure gardens, being equipped in time with a bowling green and a bathing pool, as well as a small menagerie. But it was expensive. The entrance fee was high and also the price of food and drink, and from time to time it became so raffish that it had to be closed down for a spell. What with 'bibbing and drinking wine all day under the trees' and two or three duels each week, it tended to grow 'scandalous and insufferable'.

A short distance away, where Buckingham Palace now stands, James I planted a mulberry garden, being enthusiastic at the time to establish a silk-weaving industry in England. He imported thousands of mulberry trees, which were established in various parts of the country, but something went wrong with the scheme and nothing came of this first venture into the silk-production business, so, during Charles I's time, the mulberry garden became another pleasure garden and a rival attraction to the Spring Garden.

With the outbreak of the Civil War the pleasure gardens were
deserted, and when the Royalist army seemed to be threatening the
City of London from the west, orders were sent to all ministers of
religion that they should proclaim the danger from their pulpits and
stir up their parishioners to rally to the defence of the City. Ministers
were told to urge their flocks to 'send such of their servants and children as were fit to labour with spades, shovels, and other necessary
tools, to help and assist at raising the outworks of the City, which is
very needful to be finished'.

On the eastern edge of Hyde Park, near where Hamilton Place
now stands, a large square fort with four bastions was built, part of
a defensive earthwork which ran southwards as far as Tothill Fields.
Every Roundhead sympathiser gave a hand to help defend the
western approaches of London and 'even ladies of rank took up
spade and basket, and worked in the trenches'.

> March'd rank and file with drum and ensign
> T'entrench the city for defence in;
> Raised ramparts with their own soft hands,
> To put the enemy to stand;
> From ladies down to oyster-wenches
> Laboured like pioneers in trenches,
> Fall'n to their pickaxes and tools,
> And helped the men to dig like moles

wrote Samuel Butler during the relatively calmer days of the
Restoration.

Other forts, all part of the defence system, were built where
Grosvenor Square, Constitution Hill, Victoria Station and Tothill
Fields now lie and it is from the Cromwellian redoubt, built in 1641,
on the site of Grosvenor Square and known as Oliver's Mount, that
Mayfair's Mount Street, derives its name. But the attack never came,
and after King Charles had stepped bravely to his execution from
Inigo Jones's beautiful banqueting hall in the Whitehall Palace, and
Cromwell began his brief reign as Lord Protector of England, the
forts and defences were removed.

During the Commonwealth, the Government sold Hyde Park to
private owners, who posted porters with staves at the gates to charge
a shilling entrance fee for each coach and sixpence for each horse and
rider. As early as 1647 the repressive mood of Puritanism was frown-
ing again on the Spring Garden, and the keeper was ordered to
'admit no person to come into or walk in the Spring Garden on the

Lord's Day or any of the public fast days, and that no wine, beer, ale, cakes or other things be sold there either upon the Lord's Day or public fast days', and soon it was closed altogether for several years. But the Mulberry Garden survived, for on 10 May 1654 John Evelyn recorded in his diary: 'My Lady Gerrard treated us at Mulberry Garden, now the only place of refreshment about the towne for persons of the best quality to be exceedingly cheated in; Cromwell and his partisans having shut up and seized on the Spring Gardens, which till now has been the usual rendezvous for the ladys and gallants at this season.'

Faithorne's map of this part of London in 1658 shows how rural it still was. London was closely built as far as Charing and both north and south of the Strand were now covered with houses and streets, for during the reign of Charles I the Russell family had developed the Convent Garden and the Long Acre, which had come into their possession nearly half a century earlier, by the grant from Edward VI. Inigo Jones had designed for them a square of noble mansions built round a piazza, with the overhanging first floors of the houses making covered walks. This introduction to the Renaissance style of building, in contrast to the huddled, crooked half-timbered buildings of the City, delighted Londoners, even though the money ran out before the project was completed. The market people, who had been there for years, were also impressed. Some even christened their daughters 'Piazza', to be in tune with the times, but they still kept their stalls there, in cheerful squalor, undaunted by the high-born residents of the new mansions.

Inigo Jones was also commissioned to design, as well as St Paul's Church, four streets of smaller houses leading to the piazza – King Street, Henrietta Street, named after Queen Henrietta Maria, James Street, after the Duke of York, and Russell Street; and behind them rose a network of even lesser streets and still smaller houses, for the trades-people and artisans who served the wealthy inhabitants of aristocratic Covent Garden.

To the north of the Garden, people were already living in Soho Fields, near the brick kilns, although the square and surrounding mansions and streets were not to be built until the Restoration years. But west of Charing and St Giles's Fields London stopped abruptly. From St James's Palace the parks stretched southwards. The only other building shown is Berkshire House, the home of the first two Earls of Berkshire, a country house standing alone in a walled garden, just to the north-west of the Palace gates.

Pall Mall is marked as a country lane with no buildings along it, and it was here that the game of 'pell mell' was played. This was a cumbersome form of croquet, the iron-shod mallet being about four feet long. Towards the end of Cromwellian times the first building began in Pall Mall and play was moved to St James's Park, where a track was cleared, known as the Mall.

On Faithorne's map a lane – the first St James's Street – runs due north from the palace to the east–west road, unnamed but briefly inscribed 'From Knightsbridge unto Piccadilly Hall', and where this road reaches St Giles's Fields is marked The Gaming House. North of this track, where the palaces of Piccadilly, marking the southern fringe of Mayfair, were so soon to arise, the map shows nothing but fields and the lonely windmill. And north again, along the line of Oxford Street, is a parallel track, marked 'The Way from Paddington', which continues eastwards to Holborn.

Ralph Aggas's map of London, published in 1560, is even less specific, for the line of Piccadilly is marked 'The road to Redding' and Oxford Street 'The way to Uxbridge'.

At the western end of Piccadilly there were probably by now a few ale-houses and taverns for the drovers and travellers who had made the risky journey from Knightsbridge, for, like Tyburn Lane, the way to Knightsbridge was infested with footpads and cut-throats.

There has always been a good deal of speculation about the origin of the name Piccadilly and also of the nature of the Piccadilly Hall, which lay well to the east of the present Piccadilly Circus. The fields of Mayfair were originally common land and the Vestry of St Martin-in-the-Fields made it their business to crop the hedges and scour the ditches since 'in these same dyches and hedges theves and harlots do lye and resort unto destruction of the Kynge's subjects in wynter season, and in the somer tyme all the harlots contynew and lye there'. Gradually this land came to be enclosed. Much of the western part came into the possession of the Pulteney family who, since medieval times, had grown immensely wealthy as wool merchants.

The land on which Piccadilly Hall was built was acquired from the parish of St Martin-in-the-Fields in 1612 by Robert Baker, a tailor from the Strand, who enclosed it with a brick wall and built his house. The name by which his house was known was probably a nickname, for 'pickadills' or ruffs had become high fashion for men during the reigns of James I and Charles I and Robert Baker must have sold dozens of them in his time, at his Strand shop. There is said to have been a special kind of cake called a piccadilla, which was sold in the surrounding fields of Piccadilly Hall, but the cake may well have been named after the ruff.

The region first called Piccadilly was a wide one, surrounding the northern part of the Haymarket. After Baker died, in 1623, his wife leased the southern part of her land to Sim Osbaldeston for the building of the Gaming House. It was a large brick building. On the ground floor, which was approached by a short flight of steps, were four dining-rooms. On the floor above were the card- and gaming-rooms for ombre, picquet and hazard, and on the top floor were six smaller rooms, with a flat roof which was used as a promenade. The kitchens and living-rooms for the staff were in a separate building to the north, and may have been part of Mrs Baker's 'Piccadilly Hall', but the gardens, bowling alleys and tennis court stretched right along the eastern side of the Haymarket, being bounded on the southern side by the garden wall of Lord Suffolk's house, where Suffolk Street was to be built.

The Gaming House was very fashionable and fortunes could be won here, though more were lost; and Aubrey has a sad story of the summer afternoon when the sisters of Sir John Suckling visited it in tears, fearing that their brother would gamble away their marriage portions.

Osbaldeston died in 1641 but the Gaming House survived the days of the Commonwealth and in 1664 was bought by Thomas Panton, a notorious gambler who gradually acquired the freehold of all the Baker land and developed it as a building estate. By this time the names of Windmill Street, Coventry Street and the Haymarket had emerged, as well as Panton Street, and building gradually spread westwards as well. By 1662 John Evelyn was recording that he 'sat with the Commissioners about reforming buildings and streets in London, and we ordered the paving of the way from St James's North, which was a quagmire, and also of the Haymarket about Piqudillo (Piccadilly) and agreed upon instructions to be printed and published for the better keeping the streets clean'.

The building of Mayfair began in the early years of the Restoration and many of the streets – Burlington Street, Albemarle Street, Dover Street, Berkeley Street, Stratton Street and Hamilton Place – recall the names of men who returned with the King from exile and estab-lished in London the most cynically licentious Court that England had ever known. The exiles had endured years of penury and in-dignity and now that their former power and grandeur had been

restored to them the reaction bred the most startling excesses. When
Count Gramont arrived in England, in 1662 – having been banished
from France for making advances to one of the King's mistresses –
he said that the 'joy for the restoration of the royal family still
appeared in all parts' and 'the same people who, by a solemn abju-
ration, had excluded even the posterity of their lawful sovereign,
exhausted themselves in festivals and rejoicings for his return'.

Like most generalisations of this kind, it was not entirely true, and
criticisms of the Court were soon being made not only by Parliament and the people, but by some of the men who had been loyal to
the King during his exile and worked selflessly for his restoration.
These criticis included Edward Hyde, his Chancellor, James Butler,
who was created the 1st Duke of Ormonde, and Lord Southampton,
the Lord Treasurer, as well as such men of affairs as John Evelyn and
Samuel Pepys.

Some of the amorous adventures of the Court were as farcical as
the Restoration comedies which were soon diverting Londoners at
the Drury Lane Theatre, but others ended in tragedy, and one of the
victims to suffer most heavily was Edward Hyde, Lord Clarendon,
who was the first important resident of Mayfair and built its first
mansion. In 1658, while still in exile, Charles had made him his Lord
Chancellor, and his daughter, Mary Hyde, had been maid of honour
to Charles's sister, Mary of Orange, at The Hague. Here James, Duke
of York, had fallen in love with her, and in August, 1659 had signed
a secret marriage contract.

After the Restoration, however, the Duke, finding himself so near
the throne, had second thoughts. He had promised himself in marriage to the daughter of 'an insignificant Lawyer', without the knowledge or consent of his brother, the King. Mary was by this time
eight months pregnant, although her father seems not to have
noticed the fact, which is odd, seeing that the monstrous and conceal-
ing farthingales were out of fashion and the equally accommodating
panniers not yet in, but Mary, who was to die a few years later from
cancer, was a compulsive eater and had been overweight since girlhood.

The Duke of York consulted his friends on the best course to take,
but in the end 'the tears and despair of poor Miss Hyde presented
themselves; and still more than that, he felt a remorse of conscience,
the scruples of which began from that time to rise against him'.

The Chancellor had already planned a marriage for his daughter
with a less exalted nobleman, but before this could happen the Duke

came secretly, at midnight, to the Hyde home at Worcester House in the Strand, and with Lord Ossory, a son of the Duke of Ormonde, for his witness, he married her.

There remained the hurdle of announcing the marriage to their families and the Court. The bride's father was shocked and embarrassed. The Queen Mother, Henrietta Maria, was so angry that she tried to have the marriage annulled. But the King took the news philosophically and a week or two later, when Mary's son was born, he created her grandfather, Edward Hyde, the Earl of Clarendon. The boy died and the second child, the future Queen Mary II, was born the following year.

The Duke of York, now relieved of his obligation, 'thought that he was entitled, by this generous effort, to give way a little to his inconstancy', as Anthony Hamilton so neatly puts it, in his *Memoirs of Count Gramont*, and proceeded to complicate still further the tangled web of amorous intrigue, by means of which the royal brothers and their friends conducted the Court.

II

Clarendon House

Lord Clarendon was older and more serious-minded than many of
the Restoration courtiers and was no match for their wit and light-
heartedness, nor had he the gift of making himself popular. As early
as July 1661 George Montague was telling Pepys that 'my Lord
Chancellor is much envied, and that many great men, such as the
Duke of Buckingham and my Lord of Bristoll, do endeavour to
undermine him'; but he added that 'he believes it will not be done;
for that the King (though he loves him not in the way of a companion, as he do these young gallants that can answer him in his
pleasures) yet cannot be without him, for his policy and his service.'

One of Clarendon's most implacable enemies was Barbara Palmer.
As Barbara Villiers she had, at sixteen, been the mistress of Lord
Chesterfield.* Then, during the last years of the Commonwealth, she
had married Roger Palmer, who was already working for the King's
restoration. The marriage seemed to have interfered remarkably little
with her affair with Chesterfield until she and her husband visited the
exiled Charles at Brussels. Then the King succumbed to her undoubted beauty and they became lovers.

As the affair continued after the Restoration, and as Barbara gained
her extraordinary power over the King, Lord Clarendon, who had
been a warm friend of her father, killed during the Civil War, became increasingly antagonistic to her. Although he was virtually the

* Philip Stanhope, 2nd Earl of Chesterfield, 1633–1713.

King's prime minister, she was inducing Charles to make appointments of her own choosing, by which she made large sums of money
that the exchequer could ill-afford. Clarendon refused to recognise
her and at this stage blocked the revenues which the doting King
bestowed on her, so that most of her money – and she was a demanding and avaricious woman – had to come from Charles's personal
resources.

Early in 1661 the first child of Barbara and the King was born –
Anne Fitzroy. In the meantime, the rejected Chesterfield, although
still in love with Barbara, had married Elizabeth Butler, daughter of
the Duke of Ormonde, a marriage negotiated by Clarendon, who
also announced the conclusion of a marriage settlement between the
King and Catherine of Braganza. Neither of these arrangements was
guaranteed to endear him to Barbara, even though the Portuguese
marriage was mainly a political manoeuvre against Spain and in
support of France.

Queen Catherine arrived in 1662, a plain little woman with a
retinue of even plainer Portuguese ladies-in-waiting, who were very
soon packed off home again; but the beautiful little fifteen-year-old
Frances Stewart, sent over from France by Charles's sister Minette,
to be a maid of honour to the new Queen, remained and was to be a
source of infinite troubles.

Whatever Charles may have thought of Catherine when he first
met her – and reports vary – he treated her with kindness during the
first few weeks of their marriage and she had the misfortune to fall in
love with him. Barbara was in the background at this time, not
through any discretion on her part, but because she was awaiting the
birth of her second child by the King.

The people welcomed the new Queen and looked forward to the
birth of an heir to the throne; and for a time the road from the Haymarket to St James's Street and beyond, which was eventually to be
known as Piccadilly, was called Portugal Street in her honour.

However, once Barbara had recovered from the birth of her son,
she was at Court again, demanding to be made a Lady of the Bedchamber. At first the Queen angrily refused, but Charles was cruelly
insistent. Roger Palmer was created the Earl of Castlemaine, but at
this point he and Barbara finally parted and the new Lady Castlemaine was given rooms in the Whitehall Palace.

The Court was still the centre of political power in England and
the cabal which now met in Barbara's lodgings was of formidable
strength. It was led by Sir Harry Bennet, later to become Lord

Arlington, of whom de Gramont said that 'his great earnestness passed for business, and impenetrable stupidity for secrecy . . . no one having leisure to examine him, he was taken at his word, and had been made minister and secretary of state, upon the credit of his own importance. Miss Stewart had a fit of giggles when he first called on her and he was furious.'

As Frances Stewart continued to refuse Bennet's overtures he was so angry that 'he was almost tempted . . . to quit the Court party . . . and particularly to propose an act to forbid the keeping of mistresses; but his prudence conquered his resentments . . . and he sent to Holland for a wife.'

No one knew better than Barbara Castlemaine that not only Sir Harry but also the King was falling in love with Frances Stewart. She was not yet his mistress although, according to de Gramont, who had no means of knowing, and was ever ready to sacrifice the strictest veracity for an amusing turn of phrase, her 'virtue was almost exhausted'.

There is no doubt that Frances Stewart, although brainless and childish, and not remotely interested in the political intrigues of the Court, was exceptionally beautiful and that the King loved her deeply. When the Queen fell desperately ill and seemed likely to die, it was generally thought, to Barbara Castlemaine's fury, that when he was free he would marry Frances. But Charles had a sentimental streak in him and moved to pity for Catherine, as she lay between life and death, he begged her to live for his sake, 'without supposing she would take him at his word'. The unhappy Catherine, transported with happiness at this rare sign of affection in the King, at once rallied, which caused at least Barbara, if no one else, to heave a sigh of relief.

In 1664 Lord Clarendon was granted by the King thirty acres of land on the north side of Piccadilly, and here, with additional land rented on a ninety-nine-year lease from the City of London, where New Bond Street, Conduit Street and Brook Street were to arise, the Earl made plans for the building of the first house he had ever owned in England. At the same time he sold two plots of his land to the west to Lord Berkeley of Stratton and Sir William Pulteney, where Devonshire House and Bath House were in time to be built, and a plot to the east where Burlington House was to rise and beyond it Clarges House.

For the architect of Clarendon House Lord Clarendon chose Sir Roger Pratt, intending to spend about £20,000 on it, the money which had been granted to him with the land.

'He had intended a good, ordinary house, but, not understanding these matters himself, he put the managing of that into the hands of others, who ran him into a vast charge, of about 50,000 l., three times as much as he had designed to lay out upon it,' wrote Gilbert Burnet. And as the plans for his house took shape, Lord Clarendon was watched jealously, for his unpopularity was spreading from the Court to the people.

Queen Catherine had produced no children and it was said that Clarendon had arranged the King's marriage knowing that she was barren, so that his own daughter and son-in-law should succeed to the throne. When he re-established the Church of England, both Roman Catholics and Presbyterians railed against him for his bigotry. The site he chose for Clarendon House was where Albemarle Street now lies, looking straight down the slope of St James's Street on to the old palace, and to those who were looking for trouble this was a further cause for resentment, for they alleged that he was deliberately placing himself above the Court.

Long before the destruction of old St Paul's during the Great Fire of London, Archbishop Laud and Charles I had commissioned Inigo Jones to restore the crumbling, medieval cathedral, which had already lost its steeple. A certain amount of work had been done and stones bought for further building, but the Civil War brought the work to an abrupt end. The stones intended for the cathedral were never used and now Clarendon bought them for the building of his new house, a perfectly legal and honest transaction which yet proved another bone of contention. Later, Clarendon wrote remorsefully that he began building his house in 1664, 'encouraged thereto by the royal grant of land, by the opportunity of purchasing the stones which had been designed for the repairs of St Paul's, and by that passion for building' to which he was 'naturally too much inclined'.

A large part of the dowry which Portugal had promised on the marriage of Queen Catherine was not forthcoming – a fact which did not help her popularity – but among the gifts which were honoured was the port of Tangier. This proved a costly business to maintain and govern, and twenty years later, after several abortive attempts to sell it to France or back to Portugal, it was abandoned as a 'nest of papacy where Irish troops and Roman bastards could dispose themselves unchecked'. But at the time it was hoped that it might prove a useful naval base and an alternative to Dunkirk, which had been captured by Cromwell from the Spanish, but was proving enormously expensive, the costs running at about £120,000 a year.

Moreover, Lord Sandwich had alleged that the harbour was too exposed and liable to silting.

After much deliberation, it had been decided, in 1662, that England should sell Dunkirk to France for 5,000,000 livres, part of the money to be used by Charles to help Portugal in her struggle against Spain and part to develop Tangier. The sale was bitterly resented by many Englishmen, who put all the blame for it on Lord Clarendon, and as the foundations of Clarendon House were laid and the walls began to rise it was referred to contemptuously as Dunkirk House, the implication being that Clarendon had pocketed some of the purchase money.

On 20 February 1665 Pepys and Sir John Minnes rode 'into the beginning of my Lord Chancellor's new house, near St James's; which common people have already called Dunkirke-house, from their opinion of his having a good bribe for the selling of that towne. And very noble I believe it will be.'

The building went on. It was a magnificent house, with grounds stretching from the sites of Dover Street in the west to Old Bond Street in the east and reaching back to where Grafton Street was one day to be built. The house was composed of a central portion, with east and west wings forming three sides of a quadrangle. The entrance was approached by a short flight of wide steps and the house was built on two main floors, with an attic storey surmounted by a balcony and a small, domed tower. Set into the low wall dividing the courtyard from Piccadilly was a massive and impressive gateway, and the wall itself was shaded by a line of trees.

'After dinner', wrote Evelyn on 15 October 1664, 'my Lord Chancellor and his lady carried me in their coach to see their new palace now building at the upper end of St James's Street, and to project the garden.'

Three months later, Pepys recorded: 'To my Lord Chancellor's new house, which he is building, only to view it, hearing so much from Mr Evelyn of it; and indeed it is the finest pile I ever did see in my life, and will be a glorious house.' And about the same time, on 2 January 1665, Evelyn was writing to Lord Clarendon's son, Lord Cornbury: 'Upon Wednesday last I went to London, and spent the whole afternoon in viewing my Lord Chancellor's new *house*, if it be not a solecism to give a palace so vulgar a name . . . I was plainly astonished when I beheld what a progress was made . . . It is, without hyperboles, the best contrived, the most useful, graceful, and magnificent house in England – I except not Audley End; which though larger, and full of gaudy and barbarous ornaments, does not gratify judicious spectators. As I said, my Lord: here is state and use, solidity and beauty most symmetrically combined together: seriously there is nothing abroad pleases me better; nothing at home approaches it . . . when I had seriously contemplated every room (for I went into them all, from the cellar to the platform on the roof), seen how well and judiciously the walls were erected, the arches cut and turned, the timber braced, their scantlings and contignations disposed, I was incredibly satisfied . . . May that great and illustrious person whose large and ample heart has honoured his country with so glorious a structure, and by an example worthy of himself, showed our nobility how they ought indeed to build, and value their qualities, live many long years to enjoy it . . .'

This was not to be. It was during this winter of 1664 that the King and his cabal decided to declare war on the Dutch. It was a war for mastery of the new trading areas of the East, the West Indies, West Africa and New England, against which both Lord Clarendon and the Earl of Southampton consistently advised, but it was urged by the anti-Clarendon party, led by Henry Bennet. As Burnet says, in his *History of My Own Time*, 'The grounds were so slight that it was visible there was somewhat more at bottom than was openly owned . . . The house of commons was so far from examining nicely into the grounds of the war, that without any difficulty they gave the king two millions and a half for carrying it on.'

Henry Bennet was one who stood to gain by a quick victory, for he had a personal interest in the Royal African Company which, in competition with the French and Dutch, was operating on the west coast, dealing in ivory, red wood, gold dust and slaves.

The war party thought it would all be over in a week or two, but many simpler souls were full of forebodings, for a comet appeared that winter, auguring no good.

Early in May 1665 the English Navy put to sea. That same month the first signs of the terrible plague appeared, when forty-three people died in London from a bubonic infection said to have been brought from the Levant, by way of Holland, in bales of merchandise. In June there were six hundred deaths and from then until the climax in September thousands were dying each month, mainly in London, although the plague also appeared in southern and eastern parts of the country and as far north as Sunderland and Newcastle.

The plague 'broke the trade of the nation, and swept away about a hundred thousand souls; the greatest havoc that any plague had ever made in England', wrote Burnet. 'This did dishearten all people; and coming in the very time in which so unjust a war was begun, it had a dreadful appearance. All the king's enemies, and the enemies of monarchy, said here was a manifest character of God's heavy displeasure upon the nation; as indeed the ill life the king led, and the viciousness of the whole court, gave but a melancholy prospect.'

But the war went on, and also the building of Clarendon House. Lord Clarendon moved the Court first to Salisbury and then, when the plague appeared there, to Oxford, which remained immune.

Barbara Castlemaine's children by the King were lodged in the house of Anthony Wood, while Barbara, as one of the Queen's ladies-in-waiting, was given rooms at Merton College, about which she was soon complaining; and it was here that she gave birth to her fifth child. The Duke and Duchess of York were given apartments at Christ Church, where the Duke, in between his naval duties, was beginning his affair with Arabella Churchill, sister of the future Duke of Marlborough, while the Duchess was said to have been falling in love with Harry Sidney, whom the Duke, with male unreasonableness, sent packing as soon as his suspicions were aroused.

The Court remained at Oxford for five months, and when it was at last deemed safe for them to return to London, Oxford was glad to see the last of them. 'The greate sort of the courtiers,' said Anthony Wood, 'were high, proud, insolent, and looked upon scholars no moore than pedants or pedalogical persons ... Though they were neat and gay in their apparel, yet were they very nasty and beastly, leaving at their departure their excrements in every corner, in chimneys, studies, coal-houses, cellars.' They were nothing but 'rude, rough, whoremongers – vain, empty, careless', which is a sharp reminder of the crudeness which much of the elegance of the seventeenth century so thinly veiled.

During the plague year, Clarendon was employing about three hundred men on the building of his house, which he thought, said Burnet, 'would have been an acceptable thing, when so many men were kept at work, and so much money, as was duly paid, circulated about', but the ill feeling towards him was in no way diminished. Some still called the mansion Dunkirk House, but now it was also dubbed Holland House, 'because he was believed to be no friend of the war: so it was given out that he had the money from the Dutch. It was visible, that in a time of public calamity, he was building a very noble palace.'

The battle of Lowestoft, in June 1665, when the plague was

spreading to its dreadful climax, was a technical victory for the English, but by no means decisive. The war dragged on and by now England was also at war with France. On St James's Day, 25 July 1666, the Dutch were trounced off the North Foreland, yet hardly had the sound of the victory cheers died away when England suffered the disaster of the Fire of London, which broke out shortly after midnight on 2 September and lasted until 6 September, destroying more than three-quarters of the City within its walls and sixty-three acres outside them. Although there was no recorded loss of life, eighty-nine churches were consumed in the fire and more than thirteen thousand houses. The disaster was caused, people said, by the Dutch, or the Commonwealth men, or the Papists, but when the panic had subsided, a calmer judgment declared that the fire which spread so rapidly from the baker's shop in Pudding Lane was the result of a series of unfortunate circumstances, coming at the end of an exceptionally dry summer.

In February of that year, Samuel Pepys had taken Mr Hill 'to my Lord Chancellor's new house that is building and went with trouble up to the top of it, and there is there the noblest prospect that ever I saw in my life, Greenwich being nothing to it; and in every thing is a beautiful house, and most strongly built in every respect; and as if, as it hath, it had the Chancellor for its master.' And in July, the month of the St James's Fight, he was there again. 'Thence with my wife and Mercer to my Lord Chancellors's new house, and there carried them up to the leads, where I find my Lord Chamberlain, Lauderdale, Sir Robert Murray and others, and do find it the most delightful place for prospect that ever was in the world, and even ravishing me, and that is all, in short, I can say of it.'

On the occasion of his visit in February 1665 Pepys had mentioned that two more houses were being built in Piccadilly, close to Clarendon House, 'my Lord Berkeley beginning another on one side, and Sir J. Denham on the other', but during the troubles of 1665 and 1666 little was heard of their progress. They were to be splendid mansions, though neither was so grand as Clarendon House nor invoked any such bitterness.

After the Fire of London, with Clarendon House still not completed, Clarendon moved from the Strand to Berkshire House near St James's Palace, and from here he wrote to Evelyn asking for his help in the laying out of the gardens of the new house and also in the selection of a collection of portraits to hang on the walls of the state rooms. On 18 March 1667 Evelyn wrote to him: 'My Lord, your

Lordship inquires of me what pictures might be added to the Assembly of the Learned and Heroic persons of England which your Lordship has already collected; the design of which I do infinitely more magnify than the most famous heads of foreigners, which do not concern the glory of our country; and it is my opinion the most honourable ornament, the most becoming and obliging, which your Lordship can think of to adorn your palace withal.' Evelyn goes on to list, under the three headings of the Learned, Politicians and Soldiers, suitable subjects for the portrait collection, which, when it was completed, contained some splendid work of Van Dyck.

Evelyn was a discriminating judge of a building and while so whole-heartedly admiring Clarendon House, he had a poor opinion of Goring House, built on the site of the old mulberry garden, which came into the possession of Clarendon's enemy, Henry Bennet, who was shortly to be created Lord Arlington. On 29 March 1665, Evelyn went to Goring House, that was now Mr Secretary Bennet's and wrote, rather condescendingly, of it, that it was 'ill-built, but the place capable of being made a pretty villa'.

During these early years of the Restoration, building was also going on to the east of St James's and to the south of Piccadilly. St James's Fair, which had first been held on the fields near the palace, had been moved eastwards, near the ground where St James's Square now stands. It had been closed during the Commonwealth but revived with the Restoration. However, Rugge's *Diurnal* for August 1661 announced: 'This year the Fair called St James's Fair was kept the full appointed time, being a fortnight; but during that time many lewd and infamous persons were by his Majesty's express command to the Lord Chamberlain, committed to the House of Correction.' Each year the Fair grew rowdier and more troublesome and before the end of King Charles's reign it was finally suppressed.

In 1664 Henry Jermyn, the Earl of St Albans, obtained a grant of land from the King and planned St James's Square. There was no love lost between Clarendon and Jermyn, but Jermyn had been loyal to the royal family all through the years of exile, having accompanied Henrietta Maria to France in 1644, and stayed with her, conducting much of her business affairs, until the Restoration, when he was created Earl of St Albans. The Queen Mother loved him dearly and many believed that they had been secretly married. He was immensely rich and at the Restoration received many valuable appointments.

St James's Square was at first, like Covent Garden, called the

Piazza, and plans were made for it to be surrounded by 'thirteen or fourteen great and good houses', with four streets leading from it, which were named King Street, Charles Street, Duke Street and York Street, while his own name lives on in Jermyn Street. He also built a market which was first called St Albans and later St James's Market and stood on the ground where Waterloo Place and Lower Regent Street now lie. On 1 April 1666 Pepys went to see the 'new building and market-house, and the taverne under the market-house, looking to and again into every place of building . . .'

The market was soon flourishing and became famous for its veal, but the building of the houses was delayed for a year or two.

By April of 1667 Clarendon House was nearing completion and Pepys went to have yet another look, 'the first time I have been therein; and it is very noble, and brave pictures of the ancient and present nobility, never saw better'. Like John Evelyn, he preferred it to Audley End, 'particularly the ceilings are not so good . . . being nothing so well wrought as my Lord Chancellor's are'.

Yet the Chancellor's star was setting at an alarming rate.

The King was still infatuated with Frances Stewart and he would dearly have liked to have obtained a divorce from Catherine in order to marry her, had there not been so many difficulties, not the least being his aversion to hurting the Queen so mortally. Unknown to Charles, the Duke of Richmond, a young widower, was also paying court to Frances, with whom he was deeply in love. Barbara Castlemaine was the first to enlighten the King, urging him to go to Frances's apartments one evening, when she knew the Duke was with her.

As Barbara had intended, the King found them together and was at first bitterly angry and hurt, but when he had reflected on the matter he assumed a paternal attitude to Frances, saying he would give his consent to the marriage if the Duke's financial affairs were in a healthy enough state. Knowing full well that they were not, he asked Lord Clarendon to give his opinion on the matter. Clarendon could only agree that they were in disorder but told Frances that a family so nearly related to the King could never be left in distress and advised her to marry the Duke.

When the King heard this, he was deeply angry with Clarendon, reviving the old accusation that he was safeguarding the succession for his own granddaughter, Mary. He offered to make Frances a duchess in her own right and settle an estate on her, if she would remain single, but she declined, and at the first opportunity she and the Duke slipped away from Whitehall and were secretly married. At this news, the King 'fell into a rage that forgot all decency' and Clarendon's doom was sealed.

On 12 June 1667 England suffered her greatest ignominy of the Dutch war. The greater part of the English Fleet, including the flag-ships *Royal Charles*, which had brought the King back to England in such triumph seven years earlier, and the *Royal James*, was laid up in Chatham docks, almost entirely undefended. The Dutch sailed up the Medway, passing the outer defences, and sent fireships ahead into the docks, which destroyed the *Royal Oak*, the *Royal London* and the *Royal James*, as well as several smaller vessels. The English defenders were hopelessly unprepared and when the fireships had done their damage the Dutch sailed away with the *Royal Charles* and the *Unity*. As Burnet said: 'The business of Chatham was a terrible blow; and though the loss was great, the infamy was greater.'

The following day, a crowd of angry Londoners attacked Claren-don House, cutting down the trees in front of the wall and breaking the windows. And a gibbet was 'either set up before or painted upon his gate; and these three words writ: "Three sights to be seen; Dun-kirke, Tangier, and a barren Queene." '

Yet the damage was repaired and the building of the doomed palace continued. On 8 October 1667 Rugge's *Diurnal* reported that 'The Lord Chancellor's House, called "Clarendon House" is now al-most finished. The chapel is quite completed, and was consecrated, when His Honour gave a rich Bible, the cover of which was silver, and the Book of Common Prayer with the same covering, together with bowls and other vessels for the Sacrament, to the value of £1,000. A Sermon was preached that day by a Bishop.'

Clarendon must have known by now that his days as Chancellor were numbered, but he seems to have been bewitched by his new house and up until the very end he lavished loving care on every detail.

As the costly war went on, the King, disregarding the parlous state of the exchequer, seemed as much concerned with his love affairs as Clarendon with his new house. He paid Barbara Castle-maine's debts to the extent of £30,000. He had established Moll Davis in a house in Suffolk Street, from where she was soon to move to St James's Square, while Nell Gwynn was comfortably installed in Pall Mall. And Barbara, seeing her charms failing but anxious, above all, to secure money for herself and her children, hung on grimly, quarrelling with the King and returning, again and again. In between times she was conducting a succession of affairs with an extraordinary variety of men, from little Harry Jermyn, who once had to dive ignominiously under the bed when she was visited by the King, to her running footman and Jacob Hall, the rope-dancer from St Bartholomew's Fair.

Harry Jermyn was the nephew and heir of Henry Jermyn, the Earl of St Albans, a little man with a big head and small legs, who, although he sounds unprepossessing, was renowned for his love affairs. While his uncle was rumoured to have married Queen Henrietta Maria and treated her disgracefully, with never a kind word, the gossips said that Harry Jermyn had married in secret her daughter Mary, the widowed Princess of Orange, which, as Pepys said, 'was worse than the Duke of York marrying the Chancellor's daughter', but it proved not to be true.

'His features were not disagreeable,' said Gramont, 'but he was affected in his carriage and behaviour. All his wit consisted in expressions learnt by rote, which he occasionally employed either in raillery or in love. This was the whole foundation of the merit of a man so formidable in amours,' yet the women all doted on him, failing to see 'that a reputation so lightly established was still more weakly sustained'. The Countess of Castlemaine 'followed the delusive shadow; and though undeceived in a reputation which promised so much, and performed so little, she nevertheless continued in her infatuation to the point of embroiling herself with the King'.

But Jermyn soon tired of Barbara, turned elsewhere for a time and then, to Barbara's fury, married 'a lady of singularly good character'. 'The king is mad at her entertaining Jermin, and she is mad at Jermin marrying away from her, so they are all mad, and thus the nation is governed,' wrote Pepys in July 1667.

The Peace of Breda, manipulated by Louis XIV, came suddenly in that same year and the blame for all the troubles of the previous two years fell squarely on the shoulders of Clarendon. Barbara Castlemaine and her friends, particularly Henry Bennet, now Lord Arlington, persuaded the King that he must go. The Presbyterians, led by Ashley, and the Roman Catholics, led by the Earl of Bristol, were equally anxious for his dismissal. The King hesitated at first but, still angry and hurt over the affair of Frances Stewart, needed little persuasion, and he asked the Duke of York to request his father-in-law to return the Great Seal of Office.

Lord Clarendon had at last moved into Clarendon House, but by this time he was crippled with gout. He asked the King to visit him there, but Charles insisted that Clarendon should meet him at his Whitehall office. During that last painful interview, the Chancellor accused Barbara Castlemaine of causing the mischief between them, but the King took offence at the suggestion and left him.

As the broken old man made his way back to his new house, Barbara Castlemaine watched him, with Arlington and Bab May, and they gloated over their triumph. '. . . When he went from the King on Monday morning,' wrote Pepys on 27 August 1667, 'she was in bed, though about twelve o'clock, and ran out in her smock into her aviary looking into White Hall garden; and thither her woman brought her her nightgown; and stood joying herself at the old man's going away; and several of the gallants of White Hall, of which there were many staying to see the Chancellor return, did talk to her in her birdcage . . .'

A few days later the King sent for the Seal. In vain, Lord Clarendon affirmed his innocence of any charges of corruption or accepting any money to which he had not been entitled by custom. For the next three months he lived on in Clarendon House, for he declared that he was 'too proud of a good conscience. He knew his own innocence and had no kind of apprehension of being publicly charged with any crime.'

John Evelyn remained a loyal friend to him during these weeks. He visited him on that same night, 27 August, that he had had his final interview with the King and 'found him in his bed-chamber very sad . . . he had enemies at court, especially the buffoons and ladies of pleasure . . .' A week or two later Evelyn dined with him, finding him 'pretty well in heart, though now many of his friends and sycophants abandoned him'.

But the men who had brought about his downfall were determined to bring him even lower and he was finally impeached for high treason. His only alternative to possible execution or a long term of imprisonment was to flee the country.

At the end of November the loyal Evelyn paid him another visit. 'I found him in his garden, at his new-built palace, sitting in his gout wheelchaire, and seeing the gates setting up towards the north and the fields. He looked and spake very disconsolately. After some while deploring his condition to me, I took my leave. Next morning I heard he was gone.'

Lord Clarendon had escaped into exile, never again to return. Sending his carriage and servants to York House, Twickenham, to

mislead his enemies, he made a secret journey to Erith and crossed to
France, eluding the watch on the sea ports, which had been ordered
by the King, to try and prevent just such an escape. And before he
sailed he affirmed his innocence once more to his two sons, who had
ridden down to Erith with him, saying that 'if friends would excuse
the vanity and folly of the great house he could answer for any other
charges that could be levelled against him'.

For a time his son, Lord Cornbury, lived in Clarendon House, and
here on 20 December 1668 John Evelyn visited him. 'I din'd with my
Lord Cornbury at Clarendon House, now bravely furnished, especially with the pictures of most of our ancient and modern witts, poets,
philosophers, famous and learned Englishmen; which collection of
the Chancellor's I much commended, and gave his Lordship a catalogue of more to be added.'

Shortly after this, Lord Cornbury let Clarendon House to his
father's old friend, the Duke of Ormonde, who was living here when
Colonel Blood tried to kidnap him.

Thomas Blood was that most intractable of human beings, an
Irishman with a grievance. During the Civil War he had at first been
a Royalist, but when things went badly he changed sides, and during
the Commonwealth received English Crown lands in addition to his
modest Irish possessions, and assumed the role of an English country
gentleman. He was furious when, at the Restoration, his English
lands were handed back to the Crown and he had to return to Ireland. The Duke of Ormonde was at that time Lord Lieutenant, and
Blood tried to storm Dublin Castle and seize the Duke, whom he
had vowed to string up on a gibbet. This, like all his plans, including
the attempt, in 1671, to steal the Crown jewels from the Tower of
London, showed imagination but was singularly inept in its execution. He had tenacity of purpose, however, and was still after the
Duke, whom he followed to London.

In the winter of 1670 the Prince of Orange paid a state visit to
London, which was celebrated by elaborate and expensive junketings, including a feast at the Guildhall to which the Duke, now in his
sixtieth year and suffering from gout, was invited. It was in the small
hours of a dark December night that he left the City to drive back to
Clarendon House. His coach had just turned from Pall Mall into St
James's Street when six riders emerged from the shadows, surrounded
it and brought it to a halt. One man showed a pistol to the coachman's head while the others dismounted, quickly dragged the Duke
out of his coach, lifted him on to one of the horses, tied him to the

rider and rode off with him, into Piccadilly and westwards towards Knightsbridge.

Blood was the leader of the party and, with characteristic inefficiency, had forgotten to order the men to tie up the Duke's coachman. The man promptly drove off after them, giving the alarm to the steward of Clarendon House on the way. The chase went on for a mile or two, during which the Duke managed to loosen his bonds. The other members of the party had outstripped the Duke and his captor by now, so they were bringing up the rear, but the captor was still carrying his pistol in one hand. The Duke managed to grab it, put his foot under the man's stirrup and levered him off his horse, so that they both rolled down together into the wintry mud.

After a fierce fight, and with the rescue party well on the way, the kidnappers abandoned the game old Duke, and galloped away, ultimately making their escape by way of Fulham ferry. The Duke's servants found the Duke and carried him back to Clarendon House, where, after a few days in bed, he completely recovered from his injuries, which his doctor described as 'bruised in his ey, and a knock over the pate with a pistoll as he ghessed, and a small cutt in his head, after all which he is like I thanke God to do well'.

When Lord Clarendon died, in 1674, his sons sold Clarendon House to the young Duke of Albemarle for £26,000, about half its initial cost, and the Duke of Ormonde moved to his new house in St James's Square.

The Duke of Albemarle changed the name of Clarendon House to Albemarle House and lived there in great state for a few years but he quickly ran through all the money his father had left him and ruined his health with excessive drinking, being 'burnt to a coal with hot liquor'. He sold Albermarle House to the highest bidder – a syndicate headed by John Hinde, a rich goldsmith and banker, whose place of business was at the sign of the Golden Ball in Fenchurch Street.

The sale fetched £35,000 and the Duke of Albemarle departed with the Duchess for Jamaica, where he had been appointed governor. His main purpose in accepting the post was to recover the treasure from a Spanish galleon which was known to have been sunk near the island. This venture was successful, but shortly afterwards the Duke died. The young Hans Sloane had accompanied him to Jamaica as his physician and now he escorted the widowed Duchess back to England, bringing with him many specimens of tropical plants and a few interesting tropical fauna. On the voyage home, the alligator died, the iguana, frightened by a sailor, jumped overboard, and the snake escaped from its water jar, causing so much panic that the Duchess's footman shot it, but these were the least of the young doctor's troubles, for the Duchess, always a little odd, went completely off her head.

She had cheated the men who had partnered the Duke in the scheme for reclaiming the galleon and brought all the loot home with her, so financially she could have been regarded as a highly eligible widow, but she was so mad by now that she declared that she would take no one for her second husband but the Emperor of China. Ralph, the 1st Duke of Montagu, overcame this difficulty by assuring her that he was himself none other than the Emperor, and they were duly married, whereupon he locked her up and built the second Montagu House, which was one day to become the British Museum. But this is another story in another parish, and Albemarle House was still a far-flung outpost of the parish of St Martin-in-the-Fields.

Hinde and his partners proceeded to demolish Lord Clarendon's palace. On 19 June 1683 Evelyn drove past it with the new Earl Clarendon and saw that they were already pulling it down, less than twenty years after the first stones had been laid. 'I turned my head the contrary way till the coach was gone past it, lest I might minister occasion of speaking of it, which must needs have grieved him that in so short a time their pomp was fallen,' he wrote; and on 18 September he 'went to survey the sad demolition of Clarendon House, that costly and only sumptuous palace of the late Lord Chancellor Hyde, where I have often been so cheerful with him, and sometimes so sad.' He continued:

> They design a new town as it were, and a most magnificent piazza. 'Tis said they have already materials towards it, with what they sold of the house alone, more worth than that they paid for it . . . I was astonished at the demolition, nor less at the little army of labourers and artificers levelling the ground, laying foundations, and contriving great buildings, at an expense of 200,000l if they perfect their design.

Associated with John Hinde in this venture were Cadogan Thomas, a wealthy timber merchant and land speculator, and Richard Frith, a building contractor who had already been concerned with much of the new building in St James's Square. The syndicate's first step in the development of the Clarendon House site,

which came to be known as Albemarle Buildings, was to grant
building leases of certain parts of the land, and three of the major
leaseholders were Sir Thomas Bond, Harry Jermyn and Margaret
Stafford.

Sir Thomas Bond had been comptroller of Queen Henrietta
Maria's household in France and was connected by marriage with
Harry Jermyn, and Jermyn was related to the Berkeleys, while
Margaret Stafford, a wealthy spinster, was a relative of Sir William
Pulteney, who had bought Lord Clarendon's land to the west of
Berkeley House in 1664, at the time that Lord Clarendon had been
granted it.

The work on Albemarle Buildings began in fine style but was soon
to run into financial troubles, and it was to be many years before even
a part of the syndicate's plans was realised.

III

Burlington House and Berkeley House

During the short life of Clarendon House, Sir John Denham's house, soon to be known as Burlington House, was built to the east and Berkeley House to the west.

The story of Sir John and Lady Denham, though it ended in tragedy, has elements of farce in it good enough for any Restoration comedy; and people whose names have become part of Mayfair – Colonel Hamilton, after whom Hamilton Place is named, and Lord and Lady Chesterfield – all played their parts, along with the Duke of York.

About 1665 Margaret Brook was introduced to King Charles by her kinsman George Digby, the Earl of Bristol. She would gladly have become one of the royal mistresses, but Barbara Castlemaine intervened and Miss Brook 'was obliged to discontinue her advances to him'. However, the Duke of York offered his heart to Margaret, in place of his brother's, until Sir John Denham, the King's Surveyor, 'loaded with wealth as well as years', persuaded her to marry him. Count Gramont says that Sir John was seventy-nine at the time and Miss Brook only nineteen, but in fact Sir John was only fifty, and it was his second marriage.

The Duke of York had been enjoying a passing fancy for Elizabeth, Lady Chesterfield, the daughter of the Duke of Ormonde, who was also having an affair with her cousin, Colonel Hamilton. Her marriage to Lord Chesterfield had begun disastrously, for he had for a long

time been enamoured of Barbara Castlemaine, and had given her up
only when she became the mistress of the King. He was still in love
with her when he married Elizabeth and treated his young bride
abominably, although she was infinitely more attractive than the
bad-tempered Castlemaine. At length he had the misfortune to fall
in love with her, whereupon 'she had the pleasure of convincing him
of her indifference'.

The affair between the Duke of York and Lady Chesterfield blew
hot and cold and was beginning to warm up again just when Margaret Brook married, but the effect of her marriage with Sir John was
to re-kindle the Duke of York's ardour for her. Margaret longed to
be a member of the Court and the Duke promised that she should be
made a lady of the Duchess's bedchamber, but now Lady Chesterfield, though closely watched by her husband, who had by this time
become madly jealous of her, intervened and exerted herself to
charm the Duke all over again.

Margaret Denham was outraged and 'railed against Lady Chesterfield with great bitterness', while Chesterfield, not knowing that
Colonel Hamilton was also having an affair with his wife, and in the
fond belief that the Duke of York was her only lover, poured out his
troubles to him – which was as good a dramatic situation as you
could wish for.

Lord Chesterfield took Hamilton for a walk in Hyde Park and told
him an intriguing story. 'Lady Chesterfield is amiable,' he began,
'but she is far from being such a miracle of beauty as she supposes
herself; you know she has ugly feet; but perhaps you are not acquainted that she has still worse legs . . . Her legs are short and thick;
and, to remedy these defects as much as possible, she seldom wears
any other than green stockings.'

Colonel Hamilton, thinking he had been invited to walk in the
Park to be taken to task for his own affair with Lady Chesterfield,
became increasingly puzzled. 'I went yesterday to Miss Stewart's,
after the audience of those damned Muscovites,' continued Lord
Chesterfield. 'The King arrived there just before me; and as if the
Duke had sworn to pursue me wherever I went that day, he came in
just after me. The conversation turned upon the extraordinary
appearance of the ambassadors. I know not where that fool Crofts
had heard that all these Muscovites had handsome wives; and that
all their wives had handsome legs. Upon this the King maintained
that no woman had such handsome legs as Miss Stewart; and she to
prove the truth of his Majesty's assertion, with the greatest imagin-

able ease, immediately shewed her leg above the knee. Some were ready to prostrate themselves, in order to adore its beauty; for indeed none can be handsomer; but the Duke alone began to criticise upon it. He contended that it was too slender, and that as for himself he would give nothing for a leg that was not thicker and shorter, and concluded by saying that no leg was worthy any thing without green stockings: now this, in my opinion, was a sufficient demonstration that he had just seen green stockings, and had them fresh in his remembrance.'

Hamilton, by now tortured with the same suspicion and jealousy as Lord Chesterfield, managed to find some halting words of reassurance and comfort, arguing that there was no reason to suppose that Lady Chesterfield had permitted any further liberty than to show the Duke the colour of her stockings. Nevertheless, at the earliest opportunity, he taxed her bitterly with infidelity to himself, for, as St Evremond once remarked: 'However docile the English may be with respect to their wives, they can by no means bear the inconstancy of their mistresses, nor patiently suffer the advantages of a rival . . .' and Hamilton considered that he had been far worse used than Chesterfield, 'for he could never bring his mind to think that the injuries of the husband could be placed in competition with those of the lover'.

Elizabeth reassured him that his fears were groundless, but she, alas, was 'neither scrupulous in point of constancy nor nice in point of sincerity'. Her affair with the Duke of York continued and it was Margaret Denham, beside herself with jealous fury, who brought matters to a climax.

One night in the Queen's card-room several members of the Court were at play. The Duke of York had little subtlety, and Margaret saw him engaged in the most flagrantly amorous dalliance with Elizabeth Chesterfield, as they sat together at the card tables. The moment Lord Chesterfield entered the room, Margaret hurried over to him and gave him some whispered advice to see for himself what was happening.

'Your cousin was at play,' said the infuriated Chesterfield to the unhappy Hamilton. 'The Duke was sitting next to her: I know not what had become of his hand; but I am sure that no one could see his arm below the elbow: I was standing behind them, just in the place that Lady Denham had quitted: the Duke turning round perceived me, and was so much disturbed at my presence, that he almost undressed my lady in pulling away his hand. I know not whether they perceived that they were discovered; but of this I am convinced, that Lady Denham will take care that every body shall know it.'

Swallowing his personal and private rage as best he could, Hamilton advised Chesterfield to take his wife out of London, and this he did, warning her to be ready to depart for the country in two days' time. It was midwinter and she could not believe he was serious. Not knowing that Hamilton knew all and had advised her banishment, she sent him a note asking him to help her, but he ignored it, and she was duly carried off to the depths of Derbyshire.

However, so far as Hamilton was concerned, Lady Elizabeth had the last word, and the end of the affair is pure farce. She smuggled a letter to him by a relative who had accompanied her into exile, in which she gently reproved him for his lack of faith in her and assured him that she still loved him to distraction and was suffering in the most horrible of prisons, surrounded by rocks and precipices and guarded by a jealous husband whom she loathed.

But, she said, Lord Chesterfield would be away from home the following week and she begged him to come down and visit her. She sent him detailed instructions for finding her and he duly set forth. After riding for a hundred and fifty miles he arrived, in the middle of a cold, dark night, at a small hut built against the park wall of her prison.

With only a peasant to look after him, he waited there for twenty-four hours, until the following evening, when a servant arrived to guide him through the muddy park to a garden gate. Here the servant told him to wait and left him. All night long he waited, with never a sign from door or window of the house, and as dawn broke he took himself back to the hut, cold, bedraggled and hungry, and laid himself down 'on one of the worst beds in the world'.

Two hours later he was awakened by the sound of a hunt passing close by. The peasant told him it was the Earl of Chesterfield hunting a hare in his park. Hamilton scrambled out of bed, assuming that the Earl had returned sooner than was expected, but while he was dressing a servant brought him a note from the cousin who had arranged the venture, apologising abjectly for the way both she and the Colonel had been treated by Lady Chesterfield. 'She triumphs in the trick she has played on you,' ran the note. 'Her husband has not stirred from hence, but stays at home, out of complaisance to her: he treats her in the most affectionate manner and it was upon their reconciliation that she found out that you had advised him to carry her into the country.'

Enraged and mortified, the elegant Hamilton had no option but to return quietly to London, carrying with him 'a severe cold, instead of the soft wishes and tender desires he had brought with him', and as he set forth he was able to see that the prison 'surrounded by rocks and precipices' which the perfidious Lady Elizabeth had described to him, was, in fact, Bretby Park, seat of the Earls of Chesterfield, and one of the most beautiful houses in the county.

The Duke of York, 'not being in the way of seeing Lady Chesterfield, easily forgot her' and Lady Denham 'thought proper to renew the negotiation which had so unluckily been interrupted', but in 1665 the beautiful Elizabeth Chesterfield was, in any case, removed from the arena, for in mysterious circumstances she died. Rumour had it that she had been poisoned by her husband but there was no evidence for this and she probably died of the plague or some similar contagion.

By the summer of 1666 Pepys was recording that 'the Duke of York is wholly given up to his new mistress, my Lady Denham, going at noon-day with all his gentlemen with him to visit her in Scotland Yard (then part of Whitehall Palace); she declaring that she will not be his mistress, as Mrs Price, to go up and down the Privy stairs, but will be owned publicly; and so she is.' And in September: 'At night went into the dining-room and saw several fine ladies; among others Castlemaine, but chiefly Denham again, and the Duke of York taking her aside and talking to her in the sight of all the world, all alone; which was strange, and what also I did not like. Here I met with good Mr Evelyn, who cries out against it and calls it bickering; for the Duke of York talks a little to her, and then she goes away, and then he follows her again like a dog!'

But three months later Margaret Denham was also dead. Again there were rumours of poisoning, either by Sir John in a jealous rage or even by the Duchess of York putting poison into her chocolate, but at the post-mortem no trace of poison was found.

Due no doubt to the appalling way in which his wife had treated him, Sir John lost his reason for a time, on one occasion seeking an audience of the King and assuring him that he was the Holy Ghost. He recovered and took to writing good poetry again, for he was ever considered a better poet than architect, but he did not survive his wife for long, dying in 1667, broken-hearted that his position as Surveyor-General had been taken from him and given to Christopher Wren.

Neither did the handsome and elegant Colonel James Hamilton

live many more years, for he was killed in 1673, during the third
Dutch war. He was, said Gramont, 'the man who of all the court
dressed best: he was well made in his person, and possessed those
happy talents which lead to fortune'. With his uncle, the Duke of
Ormonde, and his cousins, he had been in exile with the King, and
soon after the Restoration Charles had given him the Rangership of
Hyde Park and the triangular piece of ground between the lodge,
where Apsley House now stands, and the present Park Lane. Here a
row of houses had been built during the days of the Commonwealth,
along with the Fort, of which he was granted the leases, and the row
came to be known as Hamilton Place.

Whether Sir John Denham planned Burlington House for the reception of his bride or indeed ever lived in it himself is not clear
from the records. It seems to have been conceived on too noble a
scale for a man in his position and it is more likely that it was intended from the outset for Richard Boyle, the 1st Earl of Burlington.
John Webb, the pupil of Inigo Jones, certainly had a hand in the
design and may have been the principal architect, working under the
direction of Denham, who undoubtedly had many other things on
his mind at the time. By 1668 Lord Burlington was living there with
his wife, Lady Elizabeth Clifford, and this was his London home until
his death thirty years later.

It was originally a red-brick house, built on two main floors and an
attic floor, and had two slightly projecting wings on either side of the
main block. It was set back from Piccadilly and additional low buildings flanked either side of the courtyard, which were probably
coach-houses, stables and other domestic offices, while a high brick
wall, with a row of trees planted on the outside, protected it from the
public gaze. The walled formal garden behind, composed of lawns
and avenues and stiff-looking, triangular flower beds, stretched back
to the hills and fields of Conduit Mead.

On 28 September 1668 Samuel Pepys paid a visit to Burlington
House, 'the first time I ever was there' ... 'Here I first saw and
saluted my Lady Burlington, a very fine-speaking lady, and a good
woman, but old, and not handsom; but a brave woman in her
parts.'

For Pepys the evening nearly ended in disaster, for his periwig
caught fire 'which made such an odd noise, nobody could tell what
it was till they saw the flame, my back being to the candle'.

It was not for another fifty years, during the occupation of the 3rd
Earl, that the old house was faced with stone, and it was at this later

stage in its history that William Kent painted his interior decorations and Colin Campbell built the arcade.

The third great house in Piccadilly during the second half of the seventeenth century was Berkeley House, just to the west of Clarendon House, built on land which had once been part of Hay Hill farm and which, like the Burlington House site, had been bought from Clarendon. Building began for Sir John Berkeley, who later was created Lord Berkeley of Stratton, in 1665, and the architect was John Evelyn's friend Hugh May.

It is not until 25 September 1672 that Evelyn gives us his description of the mansion. 'I din'd at Lord Berkeley's, newly arrived out of Ireland, where he has been Deputy; it was in his new house, or rather palace, for I am assur'd it stood him in neere £30,000. It is very well built, and has many noble rooms, but they are not very convenient, consisting but of one *Corps de Logis*. They are all roomes of state, without clossets. The staire-case is of cedar, the furniture is princely: the kitchen and stables are ill-plac'd, and the corridors worse, having no report to the wing they joyne to. For the rest, the fore court is noble, so are the stables, and above all the gardens, which are incomparable by reason of the inequalities of the ground, and a pretty picina. The holly hedges on the terrace I advised the planting of. The porticos are in imitation of an house described by Palladio, but it happens to be the worst in his booke, tho' my good friend, Mr Hugh May, his Lordship's architect, effected it.'

It was a brick house with stone pilasters and a Corinthian pediment. The kitchen and laundry on the east side of the courtyard and stables and other offices on the west side were joined to the main building by 'brick walls, and two circular galleries, each elevated on columns of the Corinthian order, where are two ambulatories'. The effect was of two curved wings, which made the house look very impressive even though it may have been uncomfortable to live in.

That was a common fault of most of the Palladian mansions built at this time and early in the eighteenth century, when designs were taken from a book and little consideration was given to creature comfort or the rigours of the English winter.

> Thanks, sir, cried I, 'tis very fine,
> But where d'ye sleep, or where dy'ye dine?

Alexander Pope was to exclaim, after experiencing one.

Evelyn gives no details of the furniture in these first Mayfair mansions, but he did describe some of the furnishing of Arlington House

– the former Goring House – when he paid a visit there in April 1673. The Countess of Arlington showed him and Lady Tuke her new dressing-room, which he described as having 'a bed, two glasses, silver jars and vases, cabinets, and other so rich furniture as I had seldom seen', adding disapprovingly, 'to this excess of superfluity were we now arrived, and that not only at court, but universally, even to profusion'.

Eighteen months later the house was burnt to the ground and on 21 November 1674 Evelyn wrote that he went 'to see the great loss that Lord Arlington had sustained by fire at Goring House, this night consumed to the ground, with exceeding loss of hangings, plate, rare pictures, and cabinets; hardly anything was saved of the best and most princely furniture that any subject had in England. My Lord and Lady were both absent at Bath.'

Lord Berkeley died in 1678 and seems to have been unlamented. He had been a gallant Royalist officer during the Civil War, and Burnet said of him that from small beginnings he 'had risen up to the greatest post a subject was capable of', for he was Lord Lieutenant of Ireland for a time and then ambassador to France and plenipotentiary to Nimegen. 'He was a man,' said Burnet, 'in whom it appeared with how little true judgment courts distribute favours and honours. He had a positive way of undertaking and determining in everything, but was a weak man, and not incorrupt'; while Pepys described him as 'the most hot, fiery man in discourse, without any cause, that ever I saw, even to breach of civility . . .' and on another occasion as 'a passionate and but weak man as to policy . . . and the greatest vapourer in the world . . .'

By 1684 Berkeley's widow was writing to John Evelyn about selling some of the gardens of Berkeley House to building developers, and on 12 June Evelyn wrote in his dairy:

> I went to advise and give directions about the building of two streets in Berkeley Gardens, reserving the house and as much of the garden as the breadth of the house. In the meantime I could not but deplore that sweete place . . . should be so much straighten'd and turn'd into tenements. But that magnificent pile and gardens contiguous to it, built by the late Lord Chancellor Clarendon, being all demolish'd, and designed for piazzas and buildings, was some excuse for my Lady Berkeley's resolution of letting out her ground also for so excessive a price as was offer'd, advancing neere £1,000 per ann. in mere ground-rents; to such a mad in-

temperance was the age come of building about a city, by far too disproportionate already to the nation: I having in my time seene it almost as large again as it was within my memory.

The piazzas and buildings planned on the site of Clarendon House had not yet materialised and in the following year, 1685, Sir Thomas Bond died. However, the rest of the syndicate now began their building. When Henry Jermyn, the Earl of St Albans died, in 1684, at his house in St James's Square, the title lapsed and Charles Beauclerk, the son of the King and Nell Gwynn, was created the Duke of St Albans the following year, while little Harry Jermyn was made the 1st Baron Dover.

In 1686 the short stretch of Old Bond Street was built, running into open country where New Bond Street was later to be laid out, and to the west Albemarle Street was built, and west again Dover Street, with the short Stafford Street, named after Margaret Stafford, cutting across all three at right-angles. The syndicate had also planned a three-acre square, to be called Albemarle Square, at the top of Dover Street, Albemarle Street and Old Bond Street, but at this point the money gave out and they had to abandon the idea.

Lady Berkeley's grounds stretched northwards to where the four acres of Berkeley Square and many of the surrounding streets were to arise, and after her talk with Evelyn she sold some of this land to builders but continued to live in the house for a time. By 1693, Stratton Street appeared in the rate books and, by 1698, Berkeley Street.

Princess Anne had quarrelled with her sister and brother-in-law, Queen Mary and William III, over the question of her allowance, which, since it had been agreed that she should succeed only after the death of King William, she determined to have settled by an Act of Parliament. When Parliament agreed that she should be paid £50,000 a year William and Mary were mortally offended, alleging that Sarah, then Countess of Marlborough, was behind the move. The Earl was dismissed from office and Sarah forbidden the Court. Princess Anne protested, but in vain, and when Mary proved adamant she departed with her husband, Prince George of Denmark, from their lodgings by the Cockpit in the Whitehall Palace.

They needed somewhere to live and Lady Berkeley having shown signs of being willing to let Berkeley House, it presented itself as a suitable residence.

'I was yesterday at Berkeley House, which I liked very well,' the

Princess wrote to Sarah, 'but my Lady looked so mightily out of humour that I did not go into all the garrets nor the wings as I intended, and until she goes out of the house it will be impossible to order anything or see it at one's ease; and when she be pleased to remove God knows.'

But a little later, on 22 May 1692, she wrote to Sarah again, from Sion House: 'Some time next week, I believe, it will be time for me to go to London, to make an end of that business of Berkeley House.'

She and the amiable though alcoholic Prince George moved in, having taken a three-year lease at £600 a year, but less than three years later Queen Mary died. Princess Anne was now heir to the throne and could no longer be ignored, as she had been since she had left the Whitehall Palace. Although he had little regard either for the Princess or Prince George, King William made overtures of friendship to them. He offered Princess Anne St James's Palace for a home and in the spring of 1696 she departed from Berkeley House.

In the following year Berkeley House was bought by William Cavendish, the 1st Duke of Devonshire, who had married Lady Mary Butler, younger daughter of the 1st Duke of Ormonde and sister of Lady Chesterfield; and the mansion was soon to be called Devonshire House.

The Duke of Devonshire, says Burnet, was 'ambitious, and had the courage of a hero, with an unusual proportion both of wit and knowledge' but 'was too much a libertine both in principle and practice', being much addicted to women and wine. Macky, however, considered that he was 'the finest and handsomest gentleman of his time'.

The Marquis of Normanby, who later became the Duke of Buckingham, had been anxious to buy Berkeley House, but at the time of the sale there was a great deal of confusion, owing to the ineptness of Lady Berkeley's second son, the 3rd Lord Berkeley, who seems to have sold the house twice over. After long debates before the Lord Chancellor and the Chief Justices, the sale went to the Duke of Devonshire for £11,000, so the Marquis, a few years later, bought the site of Arlington House and here built the red-brick Buckingham House, which was one day to be Buckingham Palace.

During the 1st Duke of Devonshire's lifetime his house became an important resort of fashion and lavish hospitality where kings and ambassadors were entertained. The Duke died in 1707, but the 2nd Duke continued the tradition of pomp and splendour until his death in 1729. It was in 1733, during the time of the 3rd Duke, that the mansion was utterly destroyed by fire and the Devonshire House which survived into the present century was built in its place.

Fifty years earlier, when the first streets of Mayfair were appearing – Old Bond Street, Albemarle Street, Dover Street, Stafford Street, Berkeley Street and Stratton Street – Curzon Street and Berkeley Square were not yet planned, nor was Bath House yet built, but there were other buildings going up in Piccadilly.

Eastwards from Burlington House there were five houses: those of Jeremiah Clarke, Sir Thomas Clarges, Sir Thomas Ingram, Lord Townshend and Sir William Petty, the sailor turned doctor who was so often mentioned by Pepys and was one of the first Fellows of the Royal Society.

By the early years of the eighteenth century there were only two houses left of any importance in this stretch of Piccadilly, the grounds of the others having presumably been absorbed into them and the buildings destroyed. These two houses were Clarges House and Townshend House.

Thomas Clarges was an army physician who had been created a baronet in 1674 and his sister married George Monk, the 1st Duke of Albemarle, whose son bought Clarendon House. Both Thomas Clarges and his son, Sir Walter, acquired land in and around Piccadilly and it was Sir Walter who engaged Neale, the planner of the Seven Dials, to develop some of his land to the west of Devonshire House, but Neale failed to fulfil his commitments and after a great deal of trouble Sir Walter regained the lease and, early in the eighteenth century, himself engaged in the building of Clarges Street.

By 1696 Lord Townshend's house was inhabited by the young Charles Spencer, that 'monster of treachery . . . who, by his destructive advice, premeditatedly brought ruin on his unsuspecting master, James II'. 'At the very time that he sold him to the Prince of Orange,' says Pennant, 'he encouraged his Majesty in every step which was certain of involving him and his family in utter ruin.'

Charles Spencer married Anne Churchill, daughter of Duchess Sarah, and when his father died in 1702 and he became the Earl of Sunderland he gave the house over to his mother for a time, a woman who, according to Queen Anne, was 'the greatest jade that ever was'. By 1709 he was back in Piccadilly. He bought the freehold of Clarges House for £4,600 and incorporated it with his own, building a room at the back to house his famous library.

The Sunderland family lived here until 1745, when the 5th Earl, who was also the 3rd Duke of Marlborough, sold out to the Duke of

Bedford. It passed through several hands after that, eventually being bought by the Lamb family, who lived there until they exchanged it with the Duke of York and Albany for the Duke's mansion in Whitehall, which became known as Melbourne House. It was during the Regency that the old Sunderland House, renamed York House, was altered and enlarged and let out as bachelor's chambers, being known as Albany.

IV

Shepherd Market and the May Fair

In 1688 James II granted to Edward Shepherd a licence to hold a
cattle-market on one of the fields to the west of Devonshire House
called the Brook-Field, through which ran the Tyburn stream. The
London Gazette for September 1688 announced that 'His Majesty
hath been graciously pleased to grant a market for live Cattle to be
held in Brook-field, near Hyde Park Corner, on Tuesday and Thursday in every week. The first Market Day will be held on the first
Thursday in October next, and afterwards to continue weekly on
Tuesdays and Thursdays – the Tuesday market in the morning for
cattle and in the afternoon for horses.'

Within a few years a fair was held here, too, the *Gazette* of 28
February 1695 announcing: 'There is a Fair granted to be kept in
Brookfield Market Place, near the east corner of Hyde Park in
Middlesex, for all sorts of goods, and the first two days will be for
live cattel. The fair will begin on the first day of May next, and continue till the sixteenth day, and so will be held yearly at the same time
and place.'

According to a tract published in 1709 the original grant was made
during the short reign of King James. 'The fair . . . was granted by
King James under the Great Seal, in the Fourth Year of his Reign, to
Sir John Coell and his Heirs for Ever, in Trust for the Right Honour-
able Henry Lord Dover, and his Heirs for Ever; to be held in the
Field call'd Brookfield, in the Parish of St Martin's, Westminster, to

commence on the First Day of May, and to continue Fourteen Days after it Yearly for Ever, for the Sale of all manner of Goods and Merchandise.'

This was a valuable perquisite for little Harry Jermyn, but after the Revolution, during which he remained loyal to King James II and helped him escape to France, he was under a cloud for several years and, being outlawed, was obliged to live abroad. It was not until 1692 that he made his peace with King William and returned to London, and it was after this time that the Fair became famous.

The old St James's Fair had been suppressed since 1664, as it was considered 'to tend rather to the advantage of losseness and irregularity than to the substantial promoting of any good, common and beneficial to the people', but the market was flourishing and growing.

By 1683 Sir Christopher Wren had completed, mainly at the expense of Henry Jermyn, the Earl of St Albans, the Church of St James in Piccadilly, which he said he liked the best of all his churches, having designed it to be 'so capacious as with pews and galleries to hold two thousand persons, and all to hear the service and see the preacher'.

King Charles II had presented Berkshire House to Barbara Castlemaine, in an attempt to be rid of her, at the time when Frances Stewart, now the Duchess of Richmond, at last succumbed to him; and after the Treaty of Dover, when he had met and fallen in love with Louise de Kérouaille whom he made the Duchess of Portsmouth, the indomitable Barbara, not to be outdone, became the Duchess of Cleveland. Berkshire House was now known as Cleveland House and she sold a large part of the grounds, which reached up to Piccadilly, for building development.

The first mansions had been built in St James's Square. The Duke and Duchess of Ormonde had moved into their mansion in the north-east of the Square. The Norfolks were in the magnificent Norfolk House. Moll Davis was installed in a house there. Yet according to Macaulay, St James's Square in 1685 was 'a receptacle for all the offal and cinders, and for all the dead cats and dogs of Westminster. At one time a cudgel-player kept the ring there. At another time an impudent squatter settled himself there, and built a shed for rubbish under the windows of the gilded salons in which the first magnates of the realm, Norfolk, Ormonde, Kent and Pembroke, gave banquets and balls. It was not till these nuisances had lasted through a whole generation, and till much had been written about them, that the inhabitants applied to Parliament for permission to put up rails and plant trees.'

This mixture of elegance and squalor, cheek by jowl, was also to be found in the new buildings north of Piccadilly; for behind the mansions on the Albemarle House site, still known as Albemarle Buildings, the new houses of Bond Street, which Macky, fresh from the remoteness of Scotland, described as palaces, and the houses in all the other new streets, there arose a network of small houses and crooked streets, occupied by the artisans and shopkeepers who served the wealthy nobility surrounding them.

Shepherd Market was well-established by the 1690s, with a substantial two-storey market-house; and the Fair spread over the land where White Horse Street, Shepherd's Court, Sun Court, Market Court, Chapel Street, Shepherd Street, Market Street, Hertford Street and Carrington Street were coming into existence, and over the open ground to the west, reaching to Tyburn Lane.

During the Fair, the ground floor of the market-house, which was usually full of butchers' stalls, was given over to the sellers of toys and gingerbread, and the upper storey was converted into a theatre. In the surrounding fields and streets went up the booths for jugglers and prize-fighters, wild beasts and mountebanks, all among the merry-go-rounds and swings and the stands for the fire-eaters and rope-dancers, the dwarfs, giants and albinoes, the strong men and bearded women, the performing animals, the trapezists, tumblers, wire-walkers and acrobats, the mermaids and monstrosities, fiddlers and freaks and cannibal chiefs, pig-faced ladies and fat boys and all the rest, with sausage stalls and gaming tables and ale-houses by the score, while some of the first-floor windows were turned into stages for puppet shows.

In April 1696 a newspaper carried this announcement:

> In Brookfield Market, at the East End of Hide Park, is a Fair to be kept for sixteen days; the first three days for leather and live cattle, beginning on the first of May; where those that bring leather have their ground this year *gratis*. This Fair continues yearly at the same time and place, where there is a droll called King William's happy Deliverance and glorious Triumph over his Enemies, or the whole form of the Siege of Namur.

This show was put on by Miller, an impresario who, like many show-business people, went the rounds of all the London fairs held at this time – Southwark, Tottenham Court, Mile End Green, Camberwell, Peckham, and the oldest and most important of all of them, St Bartholomew's at Smithfield. Another of Miller's favourite shows was *Crispin and Crispianus*, which was performed at the May Fair in 1702.

'At Miller's booth in May Fair, the second booth on the right hand coming into the Fair, over against the famous Mr Barnes, the rope-dancer, will be presented an excellent droll, call'd Crispin and Crispiana; or a Shoemaker's a Prince: with the comical humours of Barnaby and the Shoemaker's Wife,' ran the announcement. 'With the best machines, singing and dancing, ever yet in the Fair. Where the famous ladder-dancer performs those things upon the ladder never before seen, to the admiration of all men.'

Another attraction of the May Fair that year was Her Majesty's Company of Ropedancers, who were to be found 'at Barnes and Finley's Booth, at the lower end of Brookfield Market, over against Mr Penkethman and Mr Simpson's, and next to Mrs Mills and Mr Bullock's, with as large a Company as they had last Bartholomew Fair; exceed all whatever they have done before. "Vivat Regina." '

In 1701 Brian Fairfax was writing: 'I wish you had been at May Fair, where the rope-dancing would have recompensed your labour. All the nobility in town were there; and I am sure that even you, at your years, must have had your youthful wishes to have beheld the beauty, shape and activity of Lady Mary when she dances. Pray ask my Lord Fairfax after her, who, though not the only lord by twenty, was every night an admirer of her while the fair lasted. There was the City of Amsterdam, well worth your seeing; every street, every individual house was carved in wood, in exact proportion one to another; the Stadthouse was as big as your hand; the whole, though an irregular figure, yet that you may guess, about ten yards' diameter. Here was a boy to be seen, that within one of his eyes had DEUS MEUS in capital letters, as GULIELMUS is on half-a-crown; round the other he had a Hebrew inscription; but this you must take, as I did, on trust.'

Lady Mary, the rope-dancer, was said to have been the daughter of a Florentine nobleman who had left her wealthy home to elope with Finley, the showman. He had taught her to dance on the tight-rope and her performance was immensely popular, both at St Bartholomew's Fair and the May Fair, for she had wonderful grace and skill, but she attempted to continue with her act after she was pregnant and one day she overbalanced and fell. She gave birth to a stillborn child and died almost at once.

Jacob Hall was another rope-dancer famous in his day, with a tremendous following. He was extremely handsome and had a magnificent figure, which attracted both Nell Gwynn and Barbara Castlemaine, and Barbara, being generous with her lovers, gave him a pension.

The fairs were often the training grounds for actors who were to end up on the legitimate stage, and many found they could earn more at the fair-grounds even after they were successfully established in the theatre. Doggett, the comedian who in 1715 established the annual Coat and Badge race to be rowed by young Thames water-men from the Old Swan at London Bridge to the Swan at Chelsea, had a booth at St Bartholomew's Fair when he was already manager of Drury Lane, and the theatre was shut while the Fair was being held. Henry Fielding who, despite his aristocratic connexions, was always short of cash in his early days, was also a Fair showman for a time, after his father's allowance failed to materialise on one occasion, and set up a theatrical booth at St Bartholomew's. There is no evidence that he was ever at the May Fair, but Woodward, who became a popular comic actor at the Covent Garden Theatre, first appeared as Merry Andrew on a mountebank's stage at the May Fair, opposite the Jolly Butchers, on the east side of the market.

Among the varied delights of the May Fair was the Frenchman who, in the front-room of a house in Sun Court, displayed the astonishing strength of his young wife.

A blacksmith's anvil being procured from White Horse-street, with three of the men, they brought it up, and placed it on the floor. The woman was short, but most beautifully and delicately formed, and of a most lovely countenance. She first let down her hair (a light auburn) of a length descending to her knees, which she twisted round the projecting part of the anvil, and then, with seeming ease, lifted the ponderous weight some inches from the floor. After this a bed was laid in the middle of the room; when, reclining on her back, and uncovering her bosom, the husband ordered the smiths to place thereon the anvil, and forge upon it a horseshoe. This they obeyed; by taking from the fire a red-hot piece of iron, and with their forging hammers completing the shoe, with the same might and indifference as when in the shop at their constant labour. The prostrate fair one appeared to endure this with the utmost composure, talking and singing during the whole process: then, with an effort which to the bystanders seemed like some supernatural trial, cast the anvil from off her body, jumping up at the same moment with extreme gaiety, and without the least discomposure of her dress or person.

For a husband and wife team, this seems an extraordinarily unfair division of labour, but this account of the show was published in the *Gentleman's Magazine* for March 1816, written by an old man, John Carter, who had seen it all for himself as a boy, and was completely satisfied that there was no trick or collusion about it.

During that hilarious fortnight of the Fair you could try your luck at donkey racing, bull baiting, grinning for a hat, running for a shift and diving for eels. The ducking pond was always an attraction. This was a pool some two hundred feet across, which lay behind the old Dog and Duck inn, where Hertford Street now runs. The pond was surrounded by willows and protected by a low boarded fence, to prevent people falling in with excitement as they watched the butchers' favourite sport of duck hunting.

It was a barbarously cruel sport but popular throughout the seventeenth century with all manner of people from King Charles and his Court to the higglers in the market. The duck was placed in the middle of the pond by the master of the hunt and then the dogs were let loose by their masters to try and seize it, the duck taking evasive action by diving under the water, time and time again, until it was exhausted.

This senseless and unsporting pastime went on well into the eighteenth century, for on 27 June 1748 a duck hunt was announced at May Fair Ducking Pond, when 'Mr Hooton's Dog, Nero (ten years old, with hardly a tooth in his head to hold a duck, but well known for his goodness to all that have seen him hunt), hunts six ducks for a guinea, against the bitch called the Flying Spaniel, from the Ducking Pond on the other side of the water, who had beat all she has hunted against, except Mr. Hooton's Good-Blood. To begin at two o'clock.'

The announcement continued: 'Mr Hooton begs his customers won't take it amiss to pay twopence admittance at the gate, and take a ticket, which will be allowed as cash in their reckoning. No person admitted without a ticket, that such as are not liked may be kept out. Note – Right Lincoln Ale.'

After the accession of the Hanoverians, one of the favourite puppet shows was the execution scene, one of the simplest and most childish of entertainments, which in one form or another has lingered on in the amusement arcades and sea-side piers to the present century. In the May Fair one of these executions was shown to an admiring audience in a coal shed adjoining Mr Fritti's grocer's shop, where a shutter was fixed horizontally, on which a puppet laid its head, while another puppet appeared on the scene and chopped it off with an axe. A similar show was to be seen at the north end of Sun Court, where, at a circular staircase window, a puppet laid its head obligingly on the sill, for the executioner to cut it off. There was no excitement or drama here – only a fleeting moment of mild amusement – but these little execution scenes had a political significance, for the condemned man represented Lord Lovat, the gallant Jacobite, who was executed on Tower Hill after the failure of the '45 rebellion. The portrayal of his grisly end and the murmurs of approval by the spectators were regarded as an act of loyalty to the Hanoverian régime.

Although the May Fair lasted for only a fortnight, it was a noisy, boisterous, rampageous affair, with eating and drinking, quarrelling and brawling going on far into the night. The younger sons of some of the surrounding noble households may have enjoyed it all and often joined in, but to many living within earshot of it it was an intolerable nuisance, and this applied particularly to Princess Anne and Prince George of Denmark, during their tenancy of Berkeley House, for the back windows looked on to the Fair, and with the gardens curtailed to east and west, many of the Fair people must have streamed down Berkeley Street and Stratton Street, where the dust and confusion of the builders added to the general commotion and disorder.

When Queen Anne succeeded to the throne, she spent much of her time at Kensington Palace, but St James's Palace was the only London palace left to her, the Whitehall Palace having been destroyed almost completely during the disastrous fire in 1698; and in St James's Palace the sounds of the May Fair, the shouts of the hucksters, the screaming and laughter and drunken brawling, could easily have reached her.

Throughout the country the reaction from the profligate days of the Restoration was becoming noticeable, and the voice of the Puritans, for so long drowned in the convivial roistering of the returned Cavaliers, was heard again. Queen Anne was herself a devoted member of the Anglican Church and, though no killjoy, preferred to see the pleasures of a tranquil prosperity to the excesses of dissolute licentiousness.

In the year of her accession, a royal proclamation was issued, to be

read in all the churches and Courts of Justice, urging the suppression
of vice and the encouragement of the virtues. It prompted the local
constables, who had long had their eye on the May Fair, to arrest
three alleged prostitutes, but the girls were stoutly defended by their
soldier friends and a scuffle broke out which developed into a large-
scale fight as more constables were brought in and more people
joined against them to defend the girls. In the end, one of the constables was killed, run through by a rapier, and three others seriously
injured.

The Justices of the Peace, indignant at the loss of their constable
and anxious to draw as much attention as possible to the disorderly
Fair, ordered a funeral sermon to be preached at St James's Church,
which was afterwards published 'at the Request of the Justices of the
Peace, High Constables, and other Officers and Gentlemen that
heard it'.

Thomas Cook, the alleged murderer, was a butcher and prize-
fighter, who managed to escape and make his way back to Dublin,
where he kept a public-house. Unfortunately for him, he bragged
once too often about his exploits at the May Fair and was appre-
hended, brought back to London, tried at the Old Bailey, convicted
and hanged at Tyburn. But this nearly provoked another riot, for
there were some who insisted that he was innocent and, as a token of
respect, brought his body back from the gallows to lie in state at
Clerkenwell before its burial.

The following year another arrest was made for Constable
Cooper's murder, William Wallis, a sergeant in the Guards, being
tried and also sentenced to death. But each year the May Fair continued merrily.

In November 1708 there was a 'Presentment' of the Grand Jury of
Westminster, complaining that the Fair was 'a publick nuisance and
Inconvenience'.

> In a place call'd Brookfield, in the Parish of St Martin in the
> Fields, in this County, call'd May Fair . . . many loose, idle and
> disorderly persons do rendezvous, and draw and allure young
> Persons and Servants, and others to meet them to Game, and
> commit lewd and disorderly Practices, to the great Corruption
> and Debauchery of their Virtue and Morals; and in which many
> and great Riots, Tumults, Breaches of the Peace, open and notori-
> ous Lewdness, and Murder itself, have been committed, and are
> likely to be committed if not prevented by some wise and prudent

Method. And for that the said Fair, being so near Her Majesty's Palaces, it is, and may be very dangerous to Her Royal Person and Government, by seditious and unreasonable Men, taking thereby an Occasion to execute their most wicked and traiterous Designs. Wherefore, and because the said Fair, as it is now used, both actually is, and hath, so fatal a Tendency to the Corruption of Her Majesty's Subjects, Violation of Her Peace, and Danger of Her Person, we humbly conceive it worthy the Care of those in Power and Authority to rectify the same.

The following month a similar Presentment was made by the Grand Jury for the County of Middlesex and early in the following year two more by the Westminster Grand Jury, in which they referred to the fact that Charles II had suppressed the St James's Fair for the same reason, 'which, however, has revived again by another Name, as also their old evil exorbitant Courses'.

In 1709, the year that Barbara, Duchess of Cleveland, died of dropsy, a tract was published lamenting the granting of the Fair:

In this time sad Experience hath demonstrated, that this Grant however well intended, hath been of very ill Consequence, tending to corrupt the *Minds* and *Manners* of very many people; insomuch that it is now one of the most pestilent Nurseries of *Impiety* and *Vice*; and one of the most Notorious Occasions of *Riot* and *Disorder*. Multitudes of the *Booths* erected in this Fair, are not for *Trade* and *Merchandise*, but for *Musick, Showes, Drinking, Gaming, Raffling, Lotteries, Stage-Plays,* and *Drolls*; which are constant and open scenes of *Impiety* and *Profaneness*, and very frequently the Stalls of *Vice*, and *Impurities* not to be mentioned.

This was followed by a royal proclamation, strictly enjoining the proprietors and owners of the Fair 'not to permit any booths or stalls to be erected while the Fair should be holden, for any plays, shows, gaming, music meetings, or other disorderly assemblies'.

Still the Fair went on and one of the most famous figures to be seen there during the first half of the eighteenth century was Tiddy-dol, the gingerbread man, an odd character whose real name was Ford and whose memory is perpetuated in Hogarth's picture of the Idle Apprentice being hanged at Tyburn, for Tiddy-dol, a good businessman, was on the spot, selling his gingerbread to the watching crowds. And later generations remember him in the restaurant standing today in Hertford Street, Shepherd Market, which has been named after him.

He was a tall, handsome man, and dressed himself with great care and style, affecting 'a white gold-laced suit of clothes, laced ruffled shirt, laced hat and feather, white silk stockings, with the addition of a fine white apron'.

When he was not at the May Fair, his usual stand was in the Haymarket, where he would harangue his customers with a ceaseless flow of patter: 'Here is your nice gingerbread, your spice gingerbread; it will melt in your mouth like a red-hot brick-bat, and rumble in your inside like Punch and his wheelbarrow.' And to fill in time he would rattle off a lot of jingling nonsense – 'I live, when at home, at the second house in Little Ball Street, two steps underground, with a wiscum, riscum and a why-not. Walk in, ladies and gentlemen; my shop is on the second floor backwards, with a brass knocker on the door.' Or, for a change, he would burst into song, chanting the tail end of some popular ballad, with the 'ti-tiddy, ti-ti, tiddy, tiddy dol' which gave him his nickname.

On one occasion he was missing from his Haymarket stand for a whole week, and so well known was he that an enterprising publisher of news-sheets, every bit as keen on business as Tiddy-dol, published a lurid account of his murder, which sold in thousands, until Tiddy-dol, who had been paying a visit to a country fair, turned up again and ruined the circulation figures.

But the May Fair was running down, for houses and streets on the ground surrounding it, already known as May Fair and later as Mayfair, were going up all the time now and the Fair was being squeezed out of existence.

The Old Greyhound, at the western end of Piccadilly, was pulled down and on the site Sir Henry Hunloke built a fine house which, in 1764, was bought by the Earl of Coventry.

Year after year there had been complaints from the new residents of Mayfair about the Fair, but now the Earl, whose house backed on to it, found the noise so distracting and distasteful that he made a final protest, so forceful and effective, that at last the Fair was brought to an end.

V

Mayfair in the Early Eighteenth Century

It was during the early years of the eighteenth century, as the Fair was running downhill, that the main building of Mayfair took place and the three squares, Hanover Square, Grosvenor Square and Berkeley Square, with the important streets adjoining them, became the residences of the rich, the famous and the titled.

By this time the residents were so numerous that a separate parish was carved out of St Martin-in-the-Fields and the church of St George, Hanover Square, was built. The new parish included the manor of Ebury, which had come into the possession of Sir Thomas Grosvenor when he married Mary Davies.

Ebury was part of the Manor of Eia, a stretch of land bounded on the north by the eastern end of the Bayswater Road, around Tyburn, and Oxford Street, as far east as Davies Street. It reached southwards to the Thames, from about Tachbrook Street to the Chelsea Hospital. Its western boundary was the Westbourne stream, from part of which the Serpentine was later to be constructed, and the eastern boundary was the Tyburn brook. This piece of land, over the northern part of which so much of eighteenth-century Mayfair was to be built, had been appropriated by the Crown from the Abbots of Westminster, at the time of the Dissolution, and by the seventeenth century had been bought by Hugh Audley.

Hugh Audley, born in 1577, was the son of a prosperous mercer of the City of London, and when he died, in 1662, he was described as 'infinitely rich', for after being called to the Bar, he had had the good fortune to be made a chief clerk to the Court of Wards, an appointment for which, in accordance with the practice of the times, he had paid £3,000.

The Court of Wards was a medieval survival from the days when a feudal knight had to pay a large fee to the King before inheriting his property. If, when he died, his heir was an infant, the King was regarded as the child's guardian and was entitled to a large proportion of the income from the estate, and also had the right to choose the child's marriage partner. This provided two types of royal reward for the hopeful and needy courtier, which cost the King nothing. He could assign to the courtier the wardship of an heir or heiress or, alternatively, he could bestow on him a rich bride. By the time of Henry VIII, the business of extracting these feudal dues was handed over to the hated Court of Wards, and here Hugh Audley worked from 1619 until 1643.

There had already been many complaints about the workings of the Court and a member protested in the House of Commons, as early as 1614, about the increasing numbers of clerks employed, saying what is still so apt three hundred and sixty years later, that 'where Clerks increase, the Grievance of the Subject groweth'.

The Court was abolished in 1646, but Hugh Audley had had nearly a quarter of a century in which to amass a great deal of money, which he increased by lending at interest and by investing in land, for he bought the Manor of Ebury for £9,400, small plots of which he leased, from time to time, for building land, thereby incurring endless future litigation. He has been accused of grasping meanness, but his work in the Court of Wards was accepted legal practice, nor was the interest he charged on his loans ever extortionate, so perhaps the fairest comment on him is that 'In the Court of Wards he gained money by doing good office, viz. in hindering some great persons to make a prey of young Heires, for some fees allowed him by the Heire's relations; and therefore he was the father of the fatherless.'

By the time of the Restoration, he was a childless old man in his eighties, enormously rich but with no home of his own and living with the Rector of St Clement Danes and his family, with whom he was distantly related.

There was endless manoeuvring on the part of his family and friends to be included in his will and, like many rich old people, he changed his mind very often, but in the end he left his Middlesex property to Thomas and Alexander Davies, his great-nephews.

Thomas was an eminent bookseller, who was knighted and became Lord Mayor of London. Alexander had been earning his living as a scrivener but at the age of twenty-six he found himself a landed proprietor, having inherited the Manor of Ebury. He straightaway planned to go in for speculative building. Much of his inheritance of Ebury was already let on lease, so he offered Thomas £2,000 for eighteen acres of his Millbank property to develop. He then proceeded to build a fine house for himself and his young wife, and to plan the riverside terrace of smaller houses which is now known as the Grosvenor Road.

On 17 January 1665 their daughter Mary was born, but in July of the same year Alexander died of the plague. Mary, his widow, was only twenty-one, and as Alexander died intestate the infant Mary inherited, by law, two-thirds of her father's property and the other third went to her mother for her lifetime. But Alexander's affairs were in considerable disarray, for neither his own house nor the speculative property was finished. He had not paid his brother the promised £2,000 and there were many bills and unpaid debts outstanding.

Less than nine months later, Mary Davies married a widower, John Tregonwell, mainly, it seems, to help her sort out the complications of the inheritance, and this he appears to have done very competently, despite law suits and family quarrels. Half of the Ebury property he found to be under a lease which had only another ten years to run, after which time its potential value, as he must have realised, would be enormous. The infant Mary was also an asset, for she was an heiress of valuable land on a rising market, and when offers came in for her hand in marriage, as they certainly would, they could exact a bride price which would maintain her in splendid style until she was old enough to marry.

The Tregonwells completed Alexander's large and stylish house, into which they moved, and also finished the building of 'the faire Streete towards the Thames side' he had planned. They then began to produce a family of their own and little Mary was cared for by her aunt, Mrs Mason, who acted as her governess. From the beginning, Mary's status as an heiress was well stage-managed, for in addition to her governess she had a nurse and two maid-servants, and when she was taken for an airing, she drove in a coach and six.

Her first offer of marriage came in 1672, when she was seven years old, and was made by Lord Berkeley of Stratton on behalf of his eldest son, Charles, who was now eleven. Apart from being a good leg-up socially for Mary, the marriage seemed highly suitable materially, for the northern part of Mary's inheritance of Ebury had a common boundary with Lord Berkeley's land. A contract was signed, therefore, subject to Mary's consent when she reached the age of twelve, and to Lord Berkeley's depositing £5,000 immediately with her guardians and settling £3,000 in land on his son when Mary was old enough to agree to the marriage.

Lord Berkeley duly paid over the £5,000, which the Tregonwells proceeded to spend, but when the time came to honour the second part of the agreement there was trouble. The money Lord Berkeley had been promised from King Charles for long years of service did not materialise and he was unable to produce the £3,000 in land. The contract collapsed and Lord Berkeley was entitled to have his £5,000 back.

To prevent Mary being stolen and held to ransom, the Tregonwells sent her to France for a time, closely guarded by Mrs Mason. They then set about finding, as quickly as possible, a new suitor who would produce the £5,000 owing to Lord Berkeley. According to Mrs Tregonwell, there was no lack of offers and the choice fell on Sir Thomas Grosvenor of Eaton who, at this time, before the Ebury estate was developed, was considerably richer than his young bride, for he owned large estates in Cheshire.

Lord Berkeley argued that since the marriage contract with his son had broken down through no fault of his, he should be paid interest on his £5,000 as well as the principal, and Sir Thomas duly handed over £6,500. He also had to pay Mrs Tregonwell an allowance of £500 for maintaining Mary until she was old enough to join him in full marriage and an annuity of £50 to Mrs Mason.

Thus Mary Davies was satisfactorily sold and in 1677, at the age of twelve, she was married at St Clement Danes and became Lady Grosvenor, Sir Thomas being at this time twenty-one. By the time she was fifteen she had joined him at his new Palladian mansion at Eaton, in Cheshire, while the great house at Millbank, which Mrs Tregonwell alleged was maintained mainly to support the splendour of young Mary's position as an heiress, was let to the 2nd Earl of Peterborough, and the Tregonwells moved into a smaller house near by.

The Grosvenor marriage seemed to go smoothly for the first few years. Sir Thomas was elected to Parliament as Member for Chester when he was still only twenty-four years old and three sons were born to them.

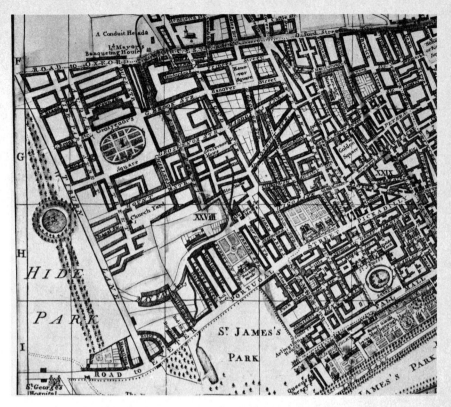

George Foster's map of 1728 showing Mayfair.

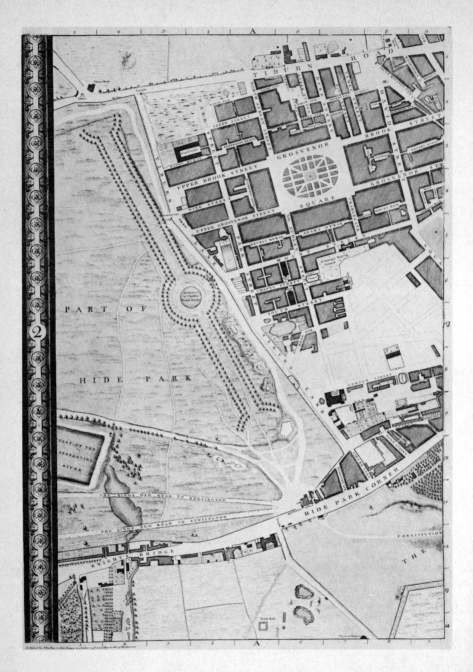

The Mayfair section of John Rocque's map of London, 1746.

The Lady's Ramble to May Fair.
A song.

Tiddy Dol.

Crewe House, Curzon Street, now the offices of Thomas Tilling Ltd.

The Earl of Chesterfield's House seen from Hyde Park, 1750.

Grosvenor House, Park Lane.

(*Bottom*) The house pictured by
Hanslip Fletcher shortly before being demolished in 1927.

Dorchester House.

The first difficulty appeared when Lady Mary was converted to Roman Catholicism and invited many Roman Catholics to Eaton, at a time when Roman Catholicism was politically unacceptable in England. The situation caused Sir Thomas both embarrassment and grief, and worse was in store for him since, by 1697, there were unmistakable signs that Lady Mary was going off her head. Only three years later, Sir Thomas died, while still in his early forties, leaving behind Sir Richard, eleven, Thomas, six, and Robert, five, with a baby daughter born three or four weeks after his death.

Sir Thomas had taken care in his will to entrust his children, until they were twenty-one, to the 'sole tuition and guardianship' of Sir Richard Myddelton of Chirk, Thomas Cholmondeley and Francis Cholmondeley, and the boys had a resident, Protestant tutor, the Reverend Dr Charles Madison, but even before Sir Thomas's funeral Lady Mary had introduced a Catholic chaplain, Father Fenwick, into her household.

She was thirty-five, immensely wealthy, very strong-willed, quite mad and growing madder every day. Already there was talk of putting her under restraint, but her family decided that it might prejudice the future of the boys if their mother were confirmed as a lunatic.

Father Fenwick seems to have induced her to make a journey to Rome. They set off first for London, where Lady Mary stayed at Millbank for a time, and while she was here she met Father Fenwick's sister, Mrs Turnour, and his elder brother, Edward Fenwick. Soon they were on their travels again, Mrs Turnour and her small daughter accompanying them, with a few servants. They left Millbank, crossing the river by the horse ferry and driving down to Dover. They took passage for Calais and drove first to Paris, where the exiled King James and a number of English Catholics and Jacobites had established themselves.

After her little girl had been touched by King James for the King's Evil, Mrs Turnour returned to England, but Lady Mary and Father Fenwick now undertook a circuitous journey to Rome, ostensibly to be able to take part in the celebrations of the Holy Year of Jubilee, though they did not arrive until they were all over. After a few months they made the long journey back to Paris, arriving late on a Sunday night at the Hotel Castile, where accommodation had been reserved for them.

Lady Mary, worn out by her weeks of difficult travelling, during part of which she had been carried in a litter, took at once to her bed and did not meet Edward Fenwick that night, who had come over to Paris to greet the returned travellers. The next day she was well enough to receive him and one or two other visitors but on the following Wednesday she was taken seriously ill. A doctor was called and prescribed the usual drastic and murderous-sounding remedies of the time – emetics, opium pills and bleeding – and by the end of the week it was small wonder that she was barely conscious. At this point, on the Saturday, the fourth day of her illness, Edward Fenwick announced that he and Lady Mary had become man and wife.

Crazy as she was, Lady Mary had enough wits left to deny that such a marriage had ever taken place. She rid herself of the Fenwicks as quickly as possible and returned to her mother at Millbank. And when Edward Fenwick began to claim the rents of her Ebury property, telling the tenants that they must in future pay their rents to him, a law suit began which was to last for four years.

Fenwick alleged that the marriage had taken place in June 1701, and that he had now become entitled to Lady Mary's fortune of at least £30,000, as well as to an interest in her property in Cheshire, Westminster and Chelsea. In the Queen's Bench, the jury found for Fenwick, and it seemed as though the Grosvenor fortune was in dire jeopardy. To add to the confusion, a lunatic called Colonel Colepeper suddenly announced that he had married Lady Mary before Fenwick's alleged marriage, and also put in his claim, but he did not get very far, and in 1705 the trustees of the Grosvenor children brought an appeal which was successful.

Lady Mary, incurably insane by now, was looked after by the trustees until her death in 1730. Her son, Sir Richard, died in 1732, in his early forties, and was succeeded by his brother Sir Thomas, who died the following year, so it was the youngest of the three, Sir Robert, who survived to continue the Grosvenor line, marrying Jane Warre, whose mother was a daughter of the first Mary Davies, by her second marriage with John Tregonwell.

It was these three brothers who developed the northern part of Ebury Manor, but it was Sir Richard who during his comparatively short life became known as the 'great builder', as 'great as the Duke of Bedford'.

Work was begun on Grosvenor Square, probably about 1716, when Sir Richard was twenty-seven years old. He wanted his square and the houses surrounding it to be the finest London had ever seen. The site was on relatively high ground and it was on the edge of the country. He planned first of all the central oval garden, six acres in extent, which was planted formally by William Kent, with flower-beds, shrubs and trees: and in the centre Sir Richard placed a gilded statue of George I, dressed as a Roman Emperor on horseback. This infuriated the Jacobites and soon after it appeared 'some villains dismembered it in the most shameful manner, and affixed a traiterous paper to the pedestal'. The King had to have a new sword and the horse a new leg, but the statue survived for another century or more.

Round the garden were built four-storey, red-brick terrace houses, larger than were to be found in any of the other London squares nearer the City, with small gardens and accommodation for the coachmen and upper servants in mews behind.

Building on the rest of the estate – Brook Street, Grosvenor Street, Duke Street, North and South Audley Street – went on at the same time, and the *Daily Journal* for 12 July 1725, announced that: 'The several new streets designed in Grosvenor Buildings, lying between New Bond Street and Hyde Park were lately particularly named; upon which occasion Sir Richard Grosvenor, Bt, gave a very splendid entertainment to his tenants and others concerned in these buildings . . . There is now building a Square called Grosvenor Square, which for its largeness and beauty will far exceed any yet made in and about London.'

By this time the extension to Old Bond Street, begun in 1686, had reached as far as Clifford Street, and was known as New Bond Street, while the further extension of New Bond Street to reach Oxford Street was under way by 1721.

To the north-east, the building of Hanover Square had also begun, around 1716, but Berkeley Square was not to take shape until the 1740s.

In the same year as Sir Richard's entertainment for his new tenants, the newly built parish church of St George, Hanover Square, was consecrated. It was built on land given by General William Stewart, one of the first residents of Hanover Square, and at the same time he also bequeathed £4,000 towards the building and maintenance of a charity school within the parish.

The architect of St George's was John James, a pupil of James Gibbs, who built St Mary-le-Strand and St Martin-in-the-Fields. It is a beautifully simple building, in the Palladian tradition of Wren, and the portico, with its six Corinthian columns, is outstanding in dignity and grace. It was one of the fifty new churches planned by Parliament, during the reign of Queen Anne, to replace the London churches destroyed during the Great Fire. The painting of the Last

Supper over the altar has been ascribed to James Thornhill and some of the carving to Grinling Gibbons, but there are no monuments and few tablets and memorials, for the church was not used for burials, the parish burying ground being farther west, between Mount Street and South Street, until it filled up, when it was moved to the north of Hyde Park, in the Uxbridge Road near Tyburn.

As you enter the church today, the impression is one of lightness and simplicity, the plain white walls and ceiling, picked out in gold, and the shining gilt of the great organ in the west gallery, contrasting with the dark oak of the pews, the gallery and the pulpit. The only colour is the stained-glass window over the altar, representing the Tree of Jesse, which is thought to be sixteenth-century work, brought over from a convent at Malines.*

Round the front of the gallery, in gilt letters, are the names of all the church-wardens, dating from 1724, with General Stewart's name appearing for 1725.

There were very soon complaints about the new building which crowded round the church, however. Sir Richard had hoped to make Grosvenor Street one of the finest in London, with the vista of St George's at its eastern end, and it was sited in the direct line of the church portico. Unfortunately his estate ended at the Tyburn, just west of Bond Street, and the adjacent land was part of the City of London's Conduit Mead Estate.

The planning of the two estates was not co-ordinated and when Maddox Street was built a few years later its curve entirely blocked the view of St George's from Grosvenor Street, so that, approaching from Grosvenor Square, one comes upon the church quite suddenly.

As early as 1736, Ralph in his *Critical Review of the Public Buildings of the Metropolis* said that 'though situated in the very centre of the vista that leads to Grosvenor Square' it is so closely surrounded by houses that it can only 'be seen in profile'. Nevertheless, from the south end of St George Street, looking up to Hanover Square, with the church on the right, the view is splendid.

The living of St George's was one of the richest in London and the church was soon to become the height of fashion for splendid weddings, but during the first half of the eighteenth century there was another establishment to rival it, so far as nuptial ceremonies were concerned. This was the Mayfair Chapel in Curzon Street, built in 1730, close to the market and the fair-ground, on the spot where Lombard House now stands.

* It was placed in the church in 1841.

It was a place where, without a licence, the publication of banns or the consent of parents, 'Fleet' marriages were solemnised. They were, of course, irregular, but provided the parson had taken Holy orders, these marriages were, at the time, considered perfectly valid and binding.

Fleet marriages first took place in the Fleet prison, which had a strange code of laws governing its prisoners, who were mainly in for debt. Some were allowed out on bail for days at a time, provided they kept within a mile and a half of the prison and paid a licence of eightpence a day, together with a shilling a day for the tipstaff, who was obliged to accompany them wherever they went.

People who wanted to be married quickly and secretly could always find a run-down clergyman among the prisoners who was willing to perform the ceremony in the prison chapel for a fee, from which the clerk of the prison extracted his due share, but in 1686 the incumbent of St James, Aldgate, having fallen foul of the Ecclesiastical Commissioners, opened a rival establishment. This spurred the Fleet parsons to establish themselves in rooms near the prison, usually let out by the pubs, and to advertise their services by means of touts. At one time there were at least forty of these 'marrying houses' in the vicinity of the Fleet, including that presided over by the renowned Bartholomew Basset, clerk of the Fleet chapel, who rented rooms in the Fleet cellars at £100 a year.

Some of these establishments were run by women, who had inherited the business along with a register, but most were kept by innkeepers, ready to supply copious drink to the happy couple, both before and after the event, so that any lingering doubts were drowned in the euphoria of excessive alcohol. And they proclaimed the extra amenities offered by their establishments with an addition to their inn sign, which was usually the Hand and Pen. The Cock near the Fleet bridge, the Rainbow Coffee House at the corner of the Fleet ditch, and a dozen more around Fleet Street and the Fleet market all provided chaplains and chapels or private rooms, where marriages took place on every day and night throughout the year.

It was a pretty grim neighbourhood for romance. As late as 1824, Miss Weeton, the governess, on her first trip to London described the Fleet market 'which stood in the middle of Fleet Street, the dirtiest heap of lumber I ever saw. There had been several heavy rain showers that morning, and the streets in some places were near ancle [sic] deep in mud. At the crossing places, there were such long strings of vehicles of every sort, that foot passengers had to wait a considerable time to catch an opening, and then it was run that run could.'

The chaplains were usually parsons who had fallen on hard times and ended up in the Fleet prison for debt – and they would marry anyone for a small fee or the price of a drink. They entered the marriage in a register, but if the next day the husband had second thoughts about his venture, there was many a parson who for a second fee or another drink was not above quietly removing the entry. And there were, of course, the men who pretended to be parsons and were not, like 'one . . . a watchmaker, who goes in a minister's dress, personating a clergyman, and taking upon him the name of "Doctor" to the scandal of the sacred function. He may be seen at any time at the "Bull and Garter" or the great "Hand and Pen", with these words written, "The Old and True Register" near the Rainbow Coffee House.'

Early in the eighteenth century, an attempt was made to stop this abuse by making the marriage shop parsons swear 'not to marry any without banns or licence unless it be such poor people as are recommended by the Justices in case of a big belly', but it made no difference. The marriage houses were too convenient a solution for runaway lovers and those who, for one reason or another, wanted a swift and secret marriage.

Henry Fox made a runaway marriage with Lady Caroline Lennox at the Fleet prison chapel in 1744, after her father, the Duke of Richmond, had refused to countenance the marriage, and at the Trinity Chapel at Knightsbridge, a place providing the same amenities, Sir Robert Walpole was married.

Alexander Keith, who had had plenty of experience in solemnising clandestine marriages in the environs of the Fleet, was appointed to the newly built Mayfair Chapel in 1730, and as soon as he began advertising in the daily papers his willingness to celebrate marriages without banns or licence he was never short of customers, from all walks of life. At a guinea a time, he prospered, constructing, said Horace Walpole, 'a very bishopric of revenue'.

During 1742, while at St George's forty marriages were solemnised, Alexander Keith performed nearly seven hundred ceremonies. Dr Trebeck, the rector of St George's, started a suit against him in Doctors Commons. Keith attended in person, declaring that he had been admitted to priest's orders by the Bishop of Norwich, but the Court found against him and he was excommunicated by the Bishop of London. Keith retaliated by holding a service in his chapel at which he cheerfully excommunicated not only the rector but also the bishop and the judge of the court. For this outrage he was arrested for contempt of the Holy and Mother Church and committed to the Fleet, but while he was in prison four of his assistants continued to celebrate Fleet marriages for a time, until they were turned out and the Mayfair Chapel became respectable again. However, they took the house on the opposite corner of what is now Trebeck Street, where it joins Curzon Street, and opened up business once more. On 20 July 1744 they were advertising in the *Daily Post*: 'To prevent mistakes, the little new chapel in Mayfair, near Hyde Park Corner, is the Corner House opposite to the City side of the Great Chapel, and within ten yards of it, and the Minister and Clerk live in the same Corner House where the little Chapel is; and the licence on a Crown Stamp, Minister and Clerk's fees, Together with the Certificate, amount to One Guinea as heretofore, at any Time till Four in the Afternoon. And that it may be better known, there is a porch at the door like a Country Church porch.'

Keith was frustrated but undaunted. He continued his business while in prison and aired his grievances as often and as publicly as possible.

On 12 January 1749 another advertisement for the chapel appeared in the *London Gazette*.

'The way to Mr. Keith's Chapel is through Piccadilly, by the end of St James's Street, and down Clarges Street, and turn on the Left-hand. The Marriages (together with a Licence on a Five Shilling Stamp and Certificate) are carried on for a Guinea, as usual, and Time till Four in the Afternoon, by another regular Clergyman, at Mr. Keith's Little Chapel in May-Fair, near Hyde-Park Corner, opposite the great Chapel and within Ten Yards of it. There is a Porch at the Door like a Country Church Porch.'

This was the year that his wife died and he ordered that her body should be embalmed and put on display at an apothecary's shop in South Audley Street, where it proved a Mecca for the morbid and a splendid advertisement for himself and his grievances for many months, until he was given permission to attend her funeral.

The *Daily Advertiser* for 23 January 1750 carried the notice: 'We are informed that Mrs. Keith's corpse was removed from Her Husband's House in May Fair the middle of October last to an Apothecary's in South Audley St. where she lies in a room hung with mourning, and is to continue there till Mr. Keith can attend the Funeral': and this highly personal touch was followed by a fresh advertisement for the chapel and its marriages, with directions for finding it.

Four of Keith's sons also died while he was in prison and the corpse of one of them he ordered to be carried on a bier from the Fleet prison to the churchyard of St Paul's, Covent Garden, with plenty of stops on the way so that the watching crowds had ample opportunities to read the inscription on the lid of the coffin, which gave a detailed account of the ill-usage of that public benefactor, Alexander Keith, father of the corpse.

Keith also published, in 1747, a pamphlet entitled OBSERVATIONS ON THE ACT FOR PREVENTING CLANDESTINE MARRIAGES, but the points he made could hardly be admitted as strong defence for his arguments. 'As I have married many thousand', he said, 'and have consequently, on these occasions seen the humour of the lower class of people, I have often asked the married pair how long they have been acquainted. They would reply, some more, some less, but the generality did not exceed the acquaintance of a week, some only of a day – half a day.

'. . . Another inconveniency which will arise from the Act will be, that the expense of being married will be so great, that few of the lower class of people can afford it; for I have often heard a Fleet parson say that many have come to be married when they have had but half-a-crown in their pockets and sixpence to buy a pot of beer, and for which they have pawned some of their clothes.'

For a man who publicly advertised his services for a guinea a time, that was no way to talk.

The Act to prevent the marriages was not passed for several years after this and the Mayfair marriage trade continued briskly. In 1752 Horace Walpole wrote about the marriage of one of the beautiful Gunning sisters, who had taken London Society by storm. 'The event which has made the most noise since my last is the extempore wedding of the youngest of the Miss Gunnings, who have made so vehement a noise of late,' he wrote to Sir Horace Mann on 27 February. 'About a fortnight since, at an immense assambly at my Lord Chesterfield's, made to show the house, which is truly magnificent, the Duke of Hamilton made violent love at one end of the room while he was playing faro at the other; that is, he saw neither the bank, nor his own cards, which were of three hundred pounds each; he soon lost a thousand . . . However, two nights afterwards, being left alone with her, whilst her mother and sister were at Bedford House, he found himself so impatient, he sent for a parson. The

Doctor refused to perform the ceremony without licence and ring. The Duke swore he would send for the Archbishop; at last they were married with a ring of the bed-curtain, at half an hour past twelve at night, at May Fair Chapel.'

But the following year came the end, with the passing of the 1753 Marriage Act, which made marriages not only religious contracts but also civil contracts for which banns and a licence were necessary. But the Act did not become law until Lady Day of 1754, and during the few months grace afforded to those who were suddenly assailed with love-sickness, business at the Mayfair Chapel boomed.

Horace Walpole wrote that 'The Duchess of Argyll harangues against the marriage bill not taking place immediately, and is persuaded that all the girls will go off before next Lady-day'. True enough on the last day of grace no less than sixty-one couples arrived in Mayfair to be married, bringing the number of marriages recorded there since Keith had arrived some twenty years earlier to around seven thousand.

The new houses in Grosvenor Square had quickly become the 'very focus of feudal grandeur, elegance, fashion, taste and hospitality', but to reach their parish Church of St George, Hanover Square, the residents had to make their way, or be carried in their sedans, through the Berkeley wood, which sloped down to the Tyburn brook. This was not only a troublesome journey in the dark days of winter but a highly dangerous one, for the wood was a notorious haunt of footpads.

In 1730, therefore, at the time that South Audley Street was built and Alexander Keith was advertising his clandestine marriage facilities in the Mayfair Chapel, Sir Richard Grosvenor leased a plot of land at £20 a year, for ninety-nine years, to Benjamin Timbrell, carpenter, Robert Scott, carpenter, William Barlow, bricklayer and Robert Andrews, gentleman, for the building of a proprietary chapel, first known as Audley Chapel and later as the Grosvenor Chapel.

It was carefully sited to face straight down the short length of what was then Chapel Street and is now Aldford Street, on to Tyburn Lane and Hyde Park, and that siting is still extraordinarily effective, for from Hyde Park today the sight of the elegant little brick chapel, with its tall windows, plain pillared portico and bright blue clock faces is arresting amid the aggressively towering blocks of Park Lane.

It was designed by a builder from Mount Street called Price, for a congregation of about twelve hundred people, and it was completed

early in 1731, when Sir Richard presented the organ. The Grosvenor
family was allotted the front pew in the gallery and Sir Richard
assigned the vault and the burial-ground behind for the use of St
George's, Hanover Square, the chapel receiving its income from pew
rents and fees for burial in the vaults. In 1831, when the lease had
expired, the chapel was bought by the Vestry of St George for
£2,000 and it is now a chapel of ease.

Among the famous people who lie buried in its vault are Lady
Mary Wortley Montagu, who died in 1762, John Wilkes, who died
in 1797 and Elizabeth Carter, who died in 1806.

During the 1850s, when many London cemeteries were closed,
including the churchyard of St Paul's, Covent Garden, described at
the time as a 'plague-spot of human flesh and human remains' the
burial-ground of St George's, behind the Grosvenor Chapel, was
closed: and at the same time the vaults of several churches were
permanently sealed, including those of St George's and the Grosvenor Chapel: and a few years later, when the Duke of Wellington
asked to see the coffins of his parents in the chapel vaults, no entrance
could be found.

During the Second World War the chapel suffered broken windows and a damaged roof and portico from air-raids, but it survived,
and the coffins in their hidden vault remained undisturbed. From
1943 until the end of the war the chapel, so reminiscent of many
eighteenth-century New England churches, was used by the Protestant chaplains of the American forces who had arrived in Grosvenor
Square the year before.

Today, after the war damage repairs, it is beautifully maintained,
still almost starkly simple, with its white walls and gallery, its dark
oak pews and doors, and the brilliant blue and gold of the domed
ceiling over the altar, while the garden behind, converted from the
old St George's burial-ground, is one of those surprising oases of
quiet lawns and trees which redeem the ceaseless spread of London's
rebuilding.

When the Grosvenor Chapel was built there was another chapel in
Mayfair, standing on the south side of Conduit Street, nearly facing
George Street. This was the Trinity Chapel, built on the spot where
James II's movable chapel on wheels had been brought to rest after
his flight. It had accompanied him on his royal progresses throughout
his short reign, and in the last days, when he visited Hounslow Heath
and the army which was to turn against him, the chapel was set up in
the camp.

On the abdication of James and the landing of King William, the chapel was brought back to London and placed in the fields of the Conduit Mead. Dr Tenison, then the rector of St Martin-in-the-Fields, asked permission from King William for it to be converted into a chapel of ease for his large and widely scattered congregation, and by July 1691 it was opened for services of the Established Church. One of the members of the first congregation was John Evelyn, who recorded that 'This church, being formerly built of timber on Hounslow Heath by King James for the mass priests, being begged by Dr. Tenison, was set up by that public-minded, charitable and pious man.'

In 1716 the chapel was converted into a brick building and towards the end of the eighteenth century the vicar and church-wardens of St Martin's decided to sell it as a proprietary chapel, the proceeds being distributed among the poor of the parish.

For many years it remained very fashionable, 'no pulpit being more frequently honoured by voluntary discourses from the most eminent dignitaries', according to the *Gentleman's Magazine*: and by the beginning of the nineteenth century, the preaching of the Reverend Dr Beamish made it so popular that galleries had to be built to accommodate the increasing numbers of the congregation. But with his passing, the popularity of the Trinity Chapel faded. It was an ugly building and in 1875 it was pulled down to make way for a new shop, and in recent years the Westbury Hotel has been built on the site.

By the middle years of the eighteenth century Mayfair was growing quickly and gaining prestige all the time. Hanover Square and Grosvenor Square were built, but in Berkeley Square the paint on the new houses was hardly dry yet. In John Rocque's map of Mayfair, published in 1747, Oxford Street is still Tiburn Road to the west of New Bond Street and Oxford Road to the east: and Park Lane is Tiburn Lane: and where the two roads met, near the gibbet, was the turnpike. The north-west corner of Mayfair, the part of the Grosvenor estate near the gallows, is blank, a murky, desolate region still, but Park Street was built, though not yet reaching as far north as Tiburn Road. It is shown running from Woods Mews, near which is marked a Guards Station, to South Street. Otherwise the existing plan of Mayfair is all there, Brook Street and Grosvenor Street running into Grosvenor Square from New Bond Street, Upper Brook Street and Upper Grosvenor Street leading from the west side, towards Tiburn Lane. South Audley Street and Charles Street (renamed Carlos

Place) ran from the south of the great square, North Audley Street and Duke Street from the north, towards Tiburn Road. This does not mean that these streets were already lined with houses from end to end. Building began from Grosvenor Square and proceeded outwards, and was not completed until after the gallows were removed in 1783 and Tyburn Road became Oxford Street and the lonely, rural Tyburn Lane was transformed into the elegant Park Lane.

The eastern boundary of Mayfair is shown on the map as Great Swallow Street, into which Conduit Street ran from New Bond Street and Hanover Street and Prince's Street from Hanover Square.

In the east, Swallow Street, which was eventually to be almost lost in the building of Regent Street, divided Mayfair from Soho. In the south-east corner of Mayfair, Air Street, according to the rate books of St Martin-in-the-Fields, was built at least as early as 1659. Sackville Street went up about 1680 and seems to have been named after Sackville, the Earl of Dorset, but nothing is known of the builders, and Vigo Street was built about 1720.

By 1718 the 3rd Earl of Burlington, who was very young when he succeeded to the title, had made his alterations to his great-grandfather's red-brick Burlington House, and he spent so much money on it, as well as in lavish hospitality and generous patronage of the arts, that he soon found himself heavily in debt. He had to develop his land to the north of the house in order to raise money and the houses he built here, though mostly comparatively small, were beautifully designed and for many years very fashionable. Burlington Gardens was built about 1729 – a quiet street lined with poplars, its houses all detached in their own small gardens. From Burlington Gardens, Cork Street, Burlington Street and Savile Row were planned running north-eastwards, Cork Street and Burlington Street ending in Clifford Street, and Savile Row later being extended beyond the eastern end of Clifford Street to New Burlington Street, which now runs into Regent Street, all these new streets being named after members of the Boyle family.

St George's, Hanover Square, the Grosvenor Chapel, the Mayfair Chapel, and the Trinity Chapel were at the height of their popularity and were filled every Sunday with distinguished congregations. The Fair was fast running down and the shops in the narrow, twisting streets which had grown up round Edward Shepherd's market, henceforth to be known as Shepherd Market, were busy supplying the needs of their rich customers. As early as 27 May 1721, the *London Journal* had announced that 'the ground upon which the

May Fair formerly was held is marked out for a large square, and several fine streets and houses are to be built upon it'. The square was never built but it was from about this time that Curzon Street and its tributaries were first planned. The rate books show only a few houses in the street in 1749 but by 1751 there were fifty-nine. Curzon Street was first known as Mayfair Row. George Augustus Curzon, the 3rd Viscount Howe, lived at Number 36 until his death in 1758 and the magnificent Curzon House, designed by Robert Adam, now Number 20, was built about this time for the Curzon family, on the site of an older house dated 1705.

Alexander Keith's days of prosperity were over and he died in prison in 1758. There is nothing now left in Mayfair by which to remember him, though the memory of the man who brought about his downfall lingers on in the street named after him, Trebeck Street, which runs by the site of Keith's chapel, from Curzon Street into the market.

VI

Hanover Square

Hanover Square, the oldest of the Mayfair squares, was built between the years 1716 and 1720, on land belonging to Harley, the son of the great Lord Harley, Earl of Oxford, who brought about the downfall of the Marlboroughs and whose kinswoman, Abigail Hill, supplanted the Duchess Sarah in the affections of Queen Anne.

Lord Harley, the son, had married Lady Henrietta Cavendish Holles, heiress of John, Duke of Newcastle, and thereby acquired the Marylebone estate, which extended beyond the Marylebone Road in the north, westwards to Marylebone Lane, as far south as St George Street,* taking in the upper part of New Bond Street in the west and Swallow Street in the east; and eastwards as far as the area where Portland Place, Langham Place and Regent Street were to be built during the early years of the nineteenth century.

When this land was bought by John Holles, the 1st Duke of Newcastle, early in the eighteenth century, it was lonely farmland crossed by the Tyburn stream, but fashionable London was moving westwards and about 1715 plans for the building of Cavendish Square and its surrounding streets were made. The square was laid out in 1717 and the central garden planted with trees and shrubs and surrounded by a low wall and railing. The building of the houses, however, was a slow business, for the scandal of the failure of the South Sea Company, in 1720, brought ruin to many investors who had planned to

* Formerly George Street.

take up leases of plots in London's new building projects. Harcourt House went up on the west side, being completed about 1722, and the Duke of Chandos made plans to build a vast mansion which would occupy the entire north side of the square. This was never completed, for on the death of his infant son and heir, shortly afterwards, he died of grief, but it was about this time that Hanover Square was laid out, a plot of four acres planned due south of Cavendish Square and linked to it by the straight line of St George Street to the south of the Oxford Road and Holles Street to the north, to make a direct approach to the grand courtyard of Chandos House, with its circular pool, partially enclosed by the curving east and west wings of the mansion.

The building of Hanover Square proceeded more rapidly than that of Cavendish Square and the *Weekly Medley* was reporting in 1717:

> Round about the new square which is building near Oxford Road, there are so many other edifices that a whole magnificent city seems to be risen out of the ground, and one would wonder how it should find a new set of inhabitants. It is said it will be called by the name of Hanover Square. The chief persons that we hear of who are to inhabit that place when it is finished, having bought houses, are the following: The Lord Cadogan, a general; also General Carpenter, General Wills, General Evans, General Pepper, the two General Stuarts, and several others whose names we have not been able to learn.

It became, in fact, in these early years, a fashionable place of residence for Whig army men who had served under Marlborough.

Applebee, in his journal for 4 September 1725, had much the same to say about the new square as the *Weekly Medley*:

> I went away towards Hyde Park, being told of a fine avenue made to the east side of the park, fine gates and a large *visa*, or opening, from the new square called Hanover Square ... In the tour I passed an amazing scene of new cities, no town nay, no place in the world, can show; nor is it possible to judge where or when they will make an end or stop building.

None of the comely red-brick terraced houses which once surrounded the square, with their three main floors, attics and basements, has survived, and today the square is usually so full of traffic that there is little opportunity to glance northwards to Cavendish Square and reflect on what might have been nor to appreciate the

delightful view from Harewood Place down the slope of the square
to St George's Church, but it is still there, much as it was when James
Ralph wrote his *Critical Review* in 1736 and was moved to rare
praise.

> I must own that the view down George Street, from the upper
> side of the Square is one of the most entertaining in the whole city:
> the sides of the Square, the area in the middle, the break of the
> buildings that form the entrance to the vista, the vista itself, but
> above all the beautiful projection of the portico of St George's
> Church, are all circumstances that unite its beauty and render the
> scene perfect.

Yet the Oxford Road, only a few yards away, which separated the
short approaches to Hanover Square and Cavendish Square, known
as Holles Street and Lady Holles Street, was still a lonely country
road, rough and deeply rutted, with only a few isolated and un-
important houses built along the northern side; and it had such an
evil reputation for footpads and cut-throats that few people ventured
there alone after dark.

When Hanover Square was first planned its position was so isolated and rural that the land sold at half a crown a foot, though, as the
houses went up and the right people moved into them, the price soon
rose to fifteen shillings a foot.

In 1736 the *General Evening Post* of 23 September reported on the
building development surrounding the square.

> Two rows of fine houses are building from the end of Great
> Marlborough Street, through the waste ground and his Grace the
> Duke of Argyll's garden into Oxford Road, from the middle of
> which new building a fine street is to be made through his Grace's
> house, King Street and Swallow Street, to the end of Hanover
> Square, Brook Street, and the north part of Grosvenor Square, the
> middle of his Grace's house being pulled down for that purpose;
> and the two wings lately added to his house are to be the corners of
> the street which is now building.

This new street was Princes Street and about the same time
Hanover Street was begun. Both now run into Regent Street, but at
this time, many years before Regent Street was built, they joined the
narrow, insignificant Swallow Street.

James Ralph was highly critical of the garden in the square, which,
in the early days, seems to have been left in as sorry a mess as St

James's Square had been. 'I do not know what to make of it,' he wrote. 'It is neither open nor enclosed. Every convenience is railed out, and every nuisance railed in. Carriages have a narrow, ill-paved street to turn round in, and the middle has the air of a cow-yard, where blackguards assemble in the winter to play hustle-cap, up to the ankles in dirt.'

However, matters were put right before very long, for in early engravings of about 1750 the garden is shown neatly laid out and crossed by paths. It was enclosed with posts and rails and there were entrances at each corner and in the middle of each side. Later in the century, according to a Pollard print of 1787, the grass plot had been made octagonal and lamp-posts were set at intervals in the railings.

Hanover Square maintained its tradition of high fashion through-out the eighteenth century, but Oxford Street was held back and remained undeveloped for years, because it was still the route for the Tyburn hangings.

As early as 1720, when John Strype published his revised edition of John Stow's *Survey of London*, he said that plans had been discussed for moving the Tyburn gallows to some other spot, possible Kings-land, to save the residents of Hanover Square and the surrounding new streets from the annoyance caused by the passing of the death-cart down Oxford Street, with the accompanying crowds of rowdy, morbid sightseers. The last port of call for the condemned prisoner was the Blue Boar in Holborn, where he and his friends and relations had their last drinks together, so by the time they reached Oxford Street they were probably all fairly drunk and noisy, while the rest of the crowd treated the whole business as an opportunity for junketing. They swarmed along the route in their hundreds, creating a paradise for itinerant vendors and also for pickpockets. Yet it was to be many years before the gallows were moved.

'Executions are frequent in London; they take place every six weeks, and five, ten or fifteen criminals are hanged on these occa-sions,' wrote M. de Saussure in 1725, while thirty-six years later, Count Kielmansegge, in his *Diary of a Journey to England*, wrote that 'Tyburn was formerly a village, which vanished when the city ex-tended in that direction, so that at present the name of Tyburn only applies to a site where the gallows and a turnpike stand'.

It was not until 1783 that the gallows, after standing for five hun-dred years near the site of the Marble Arch, were removed to New-gate prison, so that during most of the eighteenth century the aristo-cratic inhabitants of Hanover Square turned their backs on Oxford

Street. The entrance to the square by way of what is now Harewood Place, but which on Rocque's map of 1747 is marked Lady Holles Street, was a short, tree-lined neatly paved way, barred at its northern end by posts and rails.

By 1728 the *New Review of London* gave the names of three peers, six earls and two dukes living in the square, and with these great names were associated some odd stories. Prior, in his *Life of Malone*, quotes a conversation he had with Horace Walpole in 1789, in which Walpole described a copy in his possession of a 'very curious letter of Lady M. W. Montagu's, giving an account of a private society that used to meet about the year 1730 at Lord Hillsborough's in Hanover Square, where each gentleman came masked, and brought with him one lady – either his mistress or another man's wife, or perhaps a woman of the town – who was also masked. They were on oath not to divulge names, and continued masked the whole time. There were tables set out for supper, artificial arbours, couches, etc., to which parties retired when they pleased, and called for what refreshment they chose . . . This institution probably lasted but a short time. The late Captain O'Brien told me that his father, Sir Edward, was one of the members.'

This house was probably the one at the corner of Brook Street which came to be known as Downshire House, where the 2nd Marquis of Salisbury was later to live; and in 1835 Prince Talleyrand, the French Ambassador, by then a very old man, was living there.

One of his callers was Lord Sefton, who gave Raikes a cruel account of his visit, duly recorded by Raikes in his journal.

This morning he was ushered into the dressing-room of this celebrated octogenarian, who was under the hands of two *valets de chambre*, while a third, who was training for the mysteries of the toilette, stood looking on with attention to perfect himself in his future duties. The Prince was in a loose flannel gown: his long locks (for it is no wig), which are rather scanty, as may be supposed, were twisted and *crepus* with the curling iron, saturated with powder and pomatum, and then with great care arranged into those snowy ringlets which have been so much known and remarked upon all over Europe. His under attire was a flannel pantaloon, loose and undulating in those parts which were restrained by the bandages of the iron bar which supports the lame leg of this celebrated *cul-de-jatte*.

'He gave his audiences to his countrymen in his salon in Hanover

Square,' said a writer in the *Morning Post*, about the time that Queen Victoria came to the throne, 'with a round hat on his head, on the front of which was a tri-coloured cockade six inches square, whilst lying *tout au long* on the sofas were three young *sans-culottes* of July he had brought with him to give himself an air of Republicanism. Louis Philippe got settled on his throne, the tri-coloured cockade was torn off the round hat and thrown into the fire, and the new-born embryos of Republicanism were sent back to Paris.'

Sydney's Smith's description of Talleyrand talking was equally cruel. 'When he did speak he was so inarticulate I could never understand a word he said . . . he had no teeth, and I believe, no roof to his mouth – no uvula, no larynx, no trachea, no epiglottis, no anything. It was not talking; it was gurgling.' Yet Macaulay, who met Talleyrand for the first time at Holland House, in 1832, though sparing no detail in describing his odd appearance, including his hair 'thickly powdered and pomatumed', which hung down on each side of his face, as straight as a 'pound of tallow candles', declared that his conversation was so compelling that one soon forgot 'his ugliness and infirmities'.

An early eighteenth-century resident in Hanover Square was George Grenville, Lord Lansdowne, who was a patron of both Dryden and Pope, and a friend of Dean Swift, who often came to Hanover Square to visit him. At Number 18, on the site on which the Oriental Club was later built, lived that strange character Francis Dashwood, Lord Despenser, from 1771 to 1781. He was, of his own admission, the 'worst Chancellor of the Exchequer that ever appeared', knowing nothing of business or finance, and having, according to Horace Walpole, a 'coarse, blunt manner of speaking . . . with the familiarity and phrase of a fish-wife'.

In his early youth, said Walpole, 'accoutred like Charles the Twelfth, he had travelled to Russia in hopes of captivating the Czarina', but he is best remembered as the founder of the Hell Fire Club. He and some of his friends hired the ruins of Medmenham Abbey near Marlow and refurbished it as a monastery, complete with cells, a refectory and a chapel, and here, clad in monks' habits, they met to indulge in the rather childish orgies of black magic. 'Whatever their doctrines were', said Walpole, 'their practices were rigorously pagan; Bacchus and Venus were the deities to whom they almost publicly sacrificed; and the nymphs and the hogsheads that were laid in against the festivals of this new church, sufficiently informed the neighbourhood of the complexion of those hermits.'

Lord Despenser's house was rebuilt in 1827 by Wyatt for the Oriental Club, which had been founded a year or two earlier by Sir John Malcolm, living just off the square in Princes Street, and soon after it was opened it was unkindly described as 'looking like a hospital inside, in which a smell of curry powder pervaded the wards filled with venerable patients, dressed in nankeen shorts, yellow stockings and gaiters, and facings to match'. The Club lasted for many years but the building has disappeared during post-war reconstruction.

During the 1790s, Admiral Rodney was living in the square when his favourite daughter eloped to Gretna Green with the son of Sir William Chambers; but after recovering from his first anger, the Admiral amiably remarked:

'Well, well! What is done can't be undone; but it's odd that my own family is the only crew that I never could manage, and I only hope that Jessy will never mutiny under her new commander!'

At the same time, Lord and Lady Palmerston, parents of the future Prime Minister, were residents in the square and a few years later, in 1816, Mary Somerville was living at Number 12, with her parents, Sir William and Lady Fairfax, although by this time she had been widowed and remarried. Born in 1780, Mary Somerville became a mathematician and physicist of such distinction that she was elected to the Royal Society. This was an astonishing feat for a young woman of the eighteenth century and she confessed that at first she concealed her interest in such unwomanly matters and studied in secret. Yet she came to be considered one of the most remarkable women of her day. Nevertheless, she was no forbidding blue-stocking. Tom Moore said, after meeting her, that 'she gained on him exceedingly' and added that 'so much unpretending womanliness of manner, joined with such rare talent and knowledge, is indeed a combination that cannot be too much admired'. It sounds as though he had been distinctly nervous in the first place and enormously relieved when he found that her learning did not put him to shame.

This house, which once bore an L.C.C. plaque recording Mary Somerville's residence there, was the last of the old houses in the square to survive and was pulled down to make way for the new Harewood House office block.

On the east side of the square, at the south-east corner of Hanover Street, the Assembly Rooms of Sir John Gallini prospered during the last quarter of the eighteenth century. Gallini, coming to England from his native Switzerland during the early years of George III's reign, had been engaged to teach dancing to the young princes and princesses. He made a great deal of money, received a knighthood, married the daughter of Lord Abingdon, and in 1774 moved to Hanover Square, taking over Lord Dillon's house. Here, in partnership with John Christian Bach and Charles Abel, he converted the early Georgian house into his Hanover Square Rooms, where concerts were held, as well as balls and masquerades. It was another blow to Mrs Cornelys and her club at Carlisle House in Soho Square, which had been flourishing since about 1762 and had become the talk of the town for all that went on there.

It was a haunt of 'Old Q', the Duke of Queensberry, and his friends, and at one of the masked balls, when the notorious Elizabeth Chudleigh arrived as Iphigenia, she was wearing so little clothing that, according to Horace Walpole, she was 'in a state almost ready for the sacrifice'.

Sometimes there were as many as seven hundred people at these Carlisle House parties and on one occasion Mrs Cornelys was issuing a notice 'begging the chairmen and hackney-coach drivers not to quarrel, or to run their poles through each others windows'.

It was when she arranged a 'harmonic' meeting and engaged Italian singers that the Italian Opera House in the Haymarket protested at the infringement of their privilege and Sir John Fielding, the Bow Street magistrate, ordered the arrest of her principal singer, Guardini. After that nothing went right for her. The opening of the Pantheon in Oxford Street, in 1771, which offered concerts, balls, promenades and a supper room, seriously affected her business. She tried to open a new establishment in Bishopsgate but the City thoroughly disapproved of the goings-on at Carlisle House and refused permission. She struggled on in Soho Square for a few more years, but in 1775, by which time Gallini was successfully established in Hanover Square, she sold up. She tried her luck at Knightsbridge for a time, where the speciality of the house was asses' milk, but she was no business woman and ended up in the Fleet prison for debt.

Gallini's establishment was very different from Mrs Cornelys's house, for it was entirely decorous and his concerts were attended by many members of the Court, including the King and Queen. In fact George III was so interested in them that he is said to have had an additional room built on the side of the house for the use of the royal family, which was known as the Queen's tea-room.

In 1804, when Gallini had retired, the 'Concerts of Ancient Music' were held here, again under royal patronage, for the members of the royal family were often to be seen in the royal box. These concerts had first been arranged in 1776, organised by a committee of music-loving members of the aristocracy and held originally in a concert hall near the Tottenham Court Road and later at the King's Theatre in the Haymarket.

' "The Concert of Ancient Music", at present more generally known by the appellation of the "King's Concert" is a branch that seceded from the Academy of Ancient Music,' wrote Sir Richard Phillips in 1804. 'It generally commences in February and continues weekly on Wednesdays till the end of May. Six directors, chosen from among the nobility, select in turn the pieces for the night, and regulate all its principal concerns. The leading feature of its rules is the utter seclusion of all modern music. So rigid are its laws on this head, that no composition less than twenty-five years old can be performed, without the forfeiture of a considerable sum from the director of the night.'

As Sir Richard pointed out, this tended to make for a 'Want of variety in the performances' and also the 'discouragement of living genius'.

The Hanover Square Rooms played an important part in the cultural and social life of London for they were used for other kinds of concerts, for balls, lectures, innumerable public meetings and exhibitions.

From 1785 until 1834 the annual performance of the Messiah took place here, for the benefit of the Royal Society of Musicians. Miss Linley's famous needlework pictures were on show in 1798, before being moved to Leicester Square, where Miss Weeton mentions seeing them during her visit to London in 1824. From 1833 Cramer's Philharmonic Concerts were held here and from 1862 the Royal Academy of Music, which opened in Tenterden Street, leading off the north-west corner of the square, before moving to the Marylebone Road, gave their concerts.

The famous last encounter between the Prince Regent and Beau Brummell is said to have taken place in these rooms. They had already become estranged when Beau Brummell, with Alvanley, Henry Pierrepoint and the young Sir Harry Mildmay, planned the Dandies' Ball at the Hanover Rooms. The Prince Regent was not invited, but when he intimated that he would like to be present, they had no option but to send him an invitation.

The four hosts then planned how they would receive him. Jesse, in his *Life of Beau Brummell*, described what happened.

When the approach of the Prince was announced, each of the four gentlemen took in due form, a candle in his hand. Pierrepoint, as knowing the Prince, stood nearest the door with his wax-light, and Mildmay, as being young and void of offence, opposite. Alvanley, with Brummell opposite, stood immediately behind the other two. The Prince at length arrived and, as was expected, spoke civilly and with recognition to Pierrepoint, and then turned and spoke a few words to Mildmay; advancing, he addressed several sentences to Lord Alvanley, and then turning towards Brummell, looked at him, but as if he did not know who he was or why he was there, and without bestowing on him the slightest symptom of recognition. It was then, at the very instant he passed on, that Brummell, seizing with infinite fun and readiness the notion that they were unknown to each other, said aloud, for the purpose of being heard, 'Alvanley, who's your fat friend?' Those who were in front, and saw the Prince's face, say that he was cut to the quick by the aptness of the satire.

For Beau Brummell it was the end. Having gambled away all his money, he had to leave the country in a hurry and ended up at Caen, where he managed to subsist on the poorly paid job of British Consul, but when he died, in 1840, he was nearly penniless.

The last concert was held in the Hanover Square Rooms in 1874, after which the building was turned into the Hanover Square Club, with a membership similar to that of the Travellers' Club.

At the end of the eighteenth century the most important house in the square was the Adam mansion built for the Duke of Roxburgh. Having been crossed in love, he turned to collecting books, and it was here that he housed his famous library until, in 1795, he moved to St James's Square and sold Roxburgh House to the Earl of Harewood, when it became known as Harewood House.

It was a long, three-storeyed house, the roof being surmounted by a stone balustrade, and it faced on to the square, with its mews opening on to Oxford Street. There was a large bow window on the west side, overlooking Lady Holles Street (now Harewood Place), and also a side entrance and porch, so that carriages could set down and pick up passengers under cover. The rails and post barring the way to the square were replaced by a pair of iron gates, which were opened only when the Harewood family was in residence.

Lord Harewood had inherited from his elder brother, Beau Lascelles, his wonderful collection of porcelain, said to have been the

finest in the country, and it remained here until the family sold the
house in 1894 to the Royal Agricultural Society and the gates leading
to Hanover Square were removed.

Harewood House was built several years after the gallows had been
removed from Tyburn and the Oxford Road had emerged from its
grim, unkempt condition into the well-paved Oxford Street. Building began at once and soon spread the full mile of the street, but from
the outset it was a street of shop-keepers catering for the needs of the
prosperous residents surrounding it. It made the northern boundary
of exclusive Mayfair uncomfortably close to unaristocratic commerce and it is probably from this time that Hanover Square began
to decline as a place of high fashion, but it was after Swallow Street
was almost lost in the creation of Regent Street that the decline became marked and people began to move away to the southern and
western parts of Mayfair.

Plans for Nash's Regent Street were made in 1813 and when
he designed the Regent Circus, now known as Oxford Circus, he
said he had planned it to avoid 'the sensation of crossing Oxford
Street', for Oxford Street never attained the exclusiveness and
elegance of the new Regent Street. Yet when Sophie v. La Roche
visited London in 1786 she found Oxford Street enchanting, though
admittedly she always saw things through the rosiest of spectacles.
Thus, in the most glowing terms, she wrote home to her family in
Germany:

> We strolled down lovely Oxford Street this evening, for some
> goods look more attractive by artificial light. Just imagine, dear
> children, a street taking half an hour to cover from end to end,
> with double rows of brightly shining lamps, in the middle of
> which stands an equally long row of beautifully lacquered coaches,
> and on either side of these there is room for two coaches to pass one
> another; and the pavement, inlaid with flag-stones, can stand six
> people deep and allows one to gaze at the splendidly lit shops in
> comfort. First one passes a watchmaker's, then a silk or fan store,
> now a silversmith's, a china or glass shop. The spirit booths are
> particularly tempting, for the English are in any case fond of
> strong drink. Here crystal flasks of every shape and form are exhi-
> bited: each one has a light behind it which makes all the different
> coloured spirits sparkle. Just as alluring are the confectioners and
> fruiterers, where, behind the handsome glass windows, pyramids
> of pineapples, figs, grapes, oranges and all manner of fruits are on

show. We inquired the price of a fine pineapple, and did not think it too dear at 6s or 3 fl.

Sophie also had much to say about the astonishing variety of lamps for sale – large and small, of lacquer, silver and brass.

'Up till eleven o'clock at night there are as many people along this street as at Frankfort during the Fair, not to mention the eternal stream of coaches,' she wrote.

All shopkeepers lived on their premises at this time, and she described looking through to the living-rooms adjoining the shops, waxing sentimental about 'many a charming family scene – some are still at work, others drinking tea, a third party is entertaining a friendly visitor; in a fourth parents are joking and playing with their children . . .'

On 2 October, before she left for home, she took another look at Oxford Street.

> This afternoon I took a walk up and down that lovely Oxford Street, so as to take a good look at all the houses and the numerous shops . . . I found another shop like the one in Paris, containing every possible make of woman's shoe; there was a woman buying shoes in here for herself and her small daughter; the latter was searching amongst the dolls' shoes in one case for some to fit the doll she had with her. But the linen-shops are the loveliest; every kind of white wear, from swaddling clothes to shrouds, and any species of linen can be had. Nightcaps for ladies and children, trimmed with muslin or various kinds of Brussels lace, more exquisitely stitched than I ever saw before. I already wrote you about the petticoats for infants of six months to hoary age . . .

Among the shops Sophie would have passed in Oxford Street in 1786 was Hayward's Lace Warehouse, which had been established at 73 Oxford Street in 1770, and two furriers, Nicholay and Sneider, Sneider's opening at 92 Oxford Street in 1785.

In 1831 the massive bronze statue of William Pitt was erected in Hanover Square in the southern part of the garden, looking down St George Street towards the church. The sculptor was Sir Francis Chantrey, and the statue cost £7,000, for he charged a good deal for his work and amassed a fortune, but he left a handsome legacy to the Royal Academy and his Chantrey Bequest, for the buying of works of art, now amounts to some £3,000 a year.

An hour or two after the statue was put into position, and before the unveiling ceremony, a mob of agitators for the Reform Bill tried to pull it down by throwing a rope round the neck, but the figure stood firm. The clamps holding it together were leaded and no amount of pulling could shift it; and William Pitt stands to this day, nearly a hundred and fifty years later.

As trade and commerce pressed round the north-east corner of Mayfair and the residents moved away, their houses were taken over by learned societies and clubs. While Harewood House was by now the headquarters of the Royal Agricultural Society, Number 12 became the home of the Shire Horse Association. The Royal Orthopaedic Hospital moved to Number 15 in 1856. The Zoological Society and the Anthropological Society were at Number 3. At Number 17 the Arts Club was established in 1865. This was said to have been Mrs Jordan's home at one time, presumably after she and the Duke of Clarence, after living together for twenty years with their family of ten illegitimate Fitzclarences, had parted so that the Duke, who had come close to the throne after the death of Princess Charlotte, might marry and succeed to the throne as William IV, with the well-justified but unfulfilled hope of having some legitimate children. But the societies gradually moved away from Hanover Square to larger headquarters and one by one the old houses in the square disappeared, as office blocks and flats were built in their place.

By the end of the nineteenth century the dressmakers had moved in, the first being Lady Duff-Gordon who, as Madame Lucile, achieved international fame as a dress designer and was one of the first gentlewomen of late Victorian times to flout the conventions and earn her own living. She had married at seventeen, but divorced her husband five years later, and was faced with the prospect of supporting herself and a small daughter. She had always been a clever dressmaker and now began making clothes for her friends, and when her younger sister Elinor married Clayton Glyn at St George's, Hanover Square, and became Elinor Glyn, Lucy made the bridesmaids' dresses and the wedding gown, which were so much admired that it gave an impetus to her own business. By 1890 she had set up in Old Burlington Street as a dressmaker, calling herself Madame Lucile, and she was so successful that she soon had to move into larger premises in Hanover Square, first at Number 17, where she married one of the directors of the company she had formed, Sir Cosmo Duff-Gordon, and then at Number 23.

It was Lucile who first created the atmosphere of a drawing-room as a background for the discussion and choosing of clothes and she was the first to introduce mannequins as they are seen today and the mannequin parade. Mannequins had been used in Paris before this but the translation from the lay figure to the living model was a slow and cautious progress. To prevent the slightest suggestion of indecorum the girl was dressed from head to foot in a black satin garment like a pair of sombre, long-sleeved combinations and her feet were shod in stern, utilitarian laced boots; and the dress to be displayed was worn over all this. 'And as a guarantee of the respectability of the establishment the director could be relied upon to choose only the plainest of girls to show off his creation,' wrote Lucile in her memoirs. 'I shall never forget being taken to see the models of a famous house in Paris and the positive shock I felt when I saw lovely evening dresses in pale shades being worn by girls whose arms and necks, in dingy black satin, emerged from the low-cut décolletés. I decided that nothing on earth would induce me to show such atrocities.'★

In 1906 Reville and Rossiter opened in Hanover Square and in the late 1920s one of their young designers was Victor Stiebel. Now the dressmakers have all departed, but there are still signs of the business in the square, for a large part of the west side is occupied by Celanese House and the Courtauld building, and the Brook Street extension of Fenwick's in New Bond Street reaches almost to its south-west corner.

During the first winter of the last war a film company long since liquidated was occupying one of the flats in the Reville building, in the north-west corner of the square, and here I had my first experience of the film business, having been sent there to write scripts for propaganda films and allotted an office in a very sketchily converted kitchen. But during my probationary period my first job was to write a précis of *The Bing Boys*, a revue dating from the First World War. As I was handed a very ancient and tattered prompt copy, I was warned that several writers had been tried before on the job and failed, as no one could understand what it was all about. With my instinct for survival working overtime, I examined that prompt copy with great care and soon discovered that the second act had been bound in front of the first act. Having sorted it out, no problems were left. The story did not mean much either way, but, to be fair,

★ *Discretions and Indiscretions.* Lady Duff-Gordon (A. Stokes, New York, 1932). (Quoted in *Shops and Shopping*, Alison Adburgham.)

it was never intended to; and I gained a very easily earned good mark.

I soon found myself working with Austin Melford, one of the post-1914 war Co-optimists, who entertained me with an unending stream of amusing stories. When the Co-optimists were first formed, he told me, many of them were by no means in the first flush of youth, and during their dance routines the sound of the cracking of their ageing knee joints sounded from the wings like the rattle of machine-gun fire.

There was a very obliging housekeeper around in those days, always happy to bring us coffee and sandwiches when our creative abilities showed signs of flagging. We never knew her name, but she always answered cheerfully to the cry of Mrs Reville.

During the time I was there I was never once visited by a romantic ghost from the eighteenth century, for the last lingering vestiges of elegance had long since departed from the square; and after pouring out my heart and soul on to a typewriter in that ill-ventilated and ill-lit kitchen for two or three weeks, the report which launched me for a time on the uncertain and fluctuating fortunes of that particular film company read: 'Mucks in O.K.'

Today the square is given over to banks, air-lines and office blocks, all newly built and shining with a great deal of plate glass. The new Harewood House houses Radio London and William Pitt invariably spends most of the summer months above a string of parked coaches belonging to tourists from the Continent. Old Hanover Square has nearly gone. Building in Tenterden Street is changing the north-west corner and the demolition workers are at it again in St George Street.

Yet something remains. In the little garden, which is no more than an acre or so in extent, there are new paths, new seats, new rose-beds, but still the old plane trees, mature, tall and shady. The garden has been revived and the old trees give it a character that no new planting could have achieved.

The garden is delightful, with a little pool and a fountain, and it is beautifully tended, open to anyone who has the time and the inclination to visit and enjoy it, yet maintaining the air of a private garden rather than a public park.

VII

Grosvenor Square

Arthur Dasent, the historian of Grosvenor Square, compiled a list of all the residents of the fifty mansions of Grosvenor Square, from the time they appeared in the rate books, in 1725, and it reads like the pages of *Debrett*, for, as he said, 'the square was strewn with the strawberry leaves and blue ribbons of the Garter'.

It was, of course, very much larger than Hanover Square, covering about six acres, and the garden and the houses surrounding it were all on a grander scale. At first the garden was enclosed by a low brick wall, but this was soon replaced by railings.

Yet it was not to everyone's taste. James Ralph, in 1734, was writing in his *Critical Review*: 'Grosvenor Square is not only the last addition which has been made to the town, but the last in situation too; and 'tis generally understood to be the finest of all the squares. I am sorry I have the opportunity to say it has so few advantages to recommend it ... It was meant to be fine, but has miscarried very unfortunately in the execution. There is no harmony or agreement in the parts that compose it ...'

He liked the garden but deplored the brick wall surrounding it as being clumsy and a 'blemish to the view which it was intended to preserve and adorn'.

He prefers the east side and dislikes the triple house on the north side, which 'could have been built only with the view of taking in some young heir to buy it at a great rate'. The south and west sides he considers to be 'little better than a collection of whims and frolics in building, without anything like order or beauty, and therefore deserving no further consideration'.

Ralph was, of course, monstrously unfair on too many occasions, and early prints of the square show how delightful it must have been for the characteristic early Georgian, red-brick houses with their stone facings, pedimented doorways and intriguingly patterned fanlights, and the ironwork of the link extinguishers over their railings were each a little different from each other, but had an overall similarity in design which made for a pleasing harmony.

It is sad in many ways to have to speak of these houses in the past tense. As late as 1907 Beresford Chancellor, in his book on London Squares, declared that Grosvenor Square, which a century earlier had been described as 'the most magnificent square in the Metropolis' was still the 'fashionable centre' and went on to say:

> We cannot conceive the fate of such squares as Russell Square, Bedford Square, or Brunswick Square overtaking it any more than we can contemplate the turning of Berkeley Square into offices or business premises: but in the ever-tending migration westwards, who shall say but that it may not yet undergo a transformation as complete as that which has overcome Cavendish and Hanover Squares, and become so heterogeneous as to its inhabitants that it will, like them, almost defy logical classification.

What he feared has come to pass. Until the late 1960s two of the old houses survived but now there is not one left. Residents began to move away during the First World War. In 1935 Arthur Dasent was saying that several houses in the square were standing empty; and the Second World War almost completed the exodus.

Moreover, it is difficult to identify the exact site of the old houses by the numbers of such buildings – embassies, banks, hotels and blocks of flats – which are still displayed, for the square was renumbered in 1877 and the picture has been further obscured by houses in the past having been either divided or enlarged, by throwing two into one.

Nevertheless, if there are any ghosts still lingering in Grosvenor Square, they will have seen a great deal of English social and political history of the last two and a half centuries and have some good stories to tell – exciting, scandalous, amusing and sometimes violent.

The south side of the square was the first to be completed and one of the earliest residents here, at Number 43, which was formerly

Number 38, was the Duchess of Kendal, who arrived in 1728. As Ehrengard Melusina, Baroness von der Schulenburg, she had been a maid of honour to the Electress Sophia of Hanover. About the time that Sophia's son, who was to become George I, had divorced his wife, Sophia Dorothea of Celles, for her romantic love affair with Count Koenigsmark, and banished her for life to the lonely castle of Ahlden, he had taken the Baroness Schulenburg for his mistress and remained tolerably constant to her for many years, to the dismay of his mother, who deplored the tall scrawny Baroness for her lack of looks and intellect. 'Look at that mawkin and think of her being my son's passion,' lamented the old lady who, if she had lived but a few months longer, would have succeeded Queen Anne as Queen of England.

George had another close friend at this time, the Baroness von Kielmansegge, younger, but even plainer than Schulenburg, and by contrast enormously fat. Her parentage was doubtful but many thought she was George's half-sister, a daughter of his father by the Baroness von Platen.

Schulenburg did not accompany George to England immediately on his accession. She seems to have been highly nervous at the prospect of coming to live in a country where, only seventy years earlier, the people had executed their king.

The Baron and Baroness von Kielmansegge, however, were part of the royal entourage, for George had appointed the Baron his master of the horse. Here again, though, there was a slight hitch in the arrangements, for the Kielmansegges were great spenders, at their home near the Palace of Herrenhausen, and their creditors would not let the Baroness leave the country. But she overcame this problem by a midnight flit in disguise, bringing her children with her, and caught up with the rest of the royal party at The Hague.

When Schulenburg heard that the Baroness had arrived safely in England and was comfortably established at the new Court she changed her mind, packed quickly and followed, bringing with her two 'nieces', Petronella Melusina, who had been born in 1693, and Margaret, born in 1703, both of them her children by George I.

When Baron von Kielmansegge died in 1717, the Baroness remained at Court and was given a pension and the title of the Countess of Darlington, while Schulenburg was created the Duchess of Kendal.

The position of the Countess of Darlington was equivocal and there is no doubt that the Duchess of Kendal was soon in the ascendancy.

There was a strong belief that the King 'married her with the left hand' shortly after she arrived in England, and she was, in effect, as Sir Robert Walpole said, 'as much Queen of England as ever any was, that he (the King) did everything by her'.

They were devoted, and night after night, he was contented to spend the evening playing cards with her.

'In private life he would have been called an honest blockhead,' wrote Lady Mary Wortley Montagu, 'and Fortune that made him a king, added nothing to his happiness, only prejudiced his honesty, and shortened his days . . . The mistress that followed him hither was so much of his own temper, that I do not wonder at the engagement between them. She was duller than himself, and consequently did not find out that he was so . . .'

Horace Walpole, as a child of ten, was taken to meet the King on the eve of his departure for the visit to Hanover during which he died, and in later years, when he described the meeting, and his recollection of the King, he said:

> So entirely was he my object that I do not believe I once looked at the Duchess, but as I could not avoid seeing her on entering the room, I remember that just beyond his Majesty stood a very tall, lean, ill-favoured old lady; but I did not retain the least idea of her features, nor know of what colour her dress was.

Of the Countess of Darlington he was able to give a sharper picture. 'Two large and fierce black eyes rolling beneath two lofty arched eyebrows, two acres of cheek spread with crimson, an ocean of neck that overflowed and was not distinguished from the lower part of her body, and no part restrained by stays.'

These two women came to be hated in England for their rapacity and corruption and were viciously lampooned, the fat one dubbed the Elephant and Castle and the thin one the Lamp-post.

Soon after their arrival, they came upon Queen Anne's jewels at St James's Palace, which they appropriated and divided between themselves. They were involved in the selling of honours and places of profit under the Crown. Sir Henry St John, for example, paid the Duchess of Kendal £5,000 for his baronetcy. Walpole declared that she would have sold the King's honour for a shilling advance to the best bidder and a pamphleteer burst forth with the allegation that 'we are being ruined by Trulls, nay, by ugly old Trulls such as could not find entertainment in the most hospitable hundred of Old Drury'.

But the worst of the scandals associated with them was the money they made from the South Sea Bubble, when thousands were ruined.

The company had been formed at the end of Queen Anne's reign, when the Tory Government ran into financial difficulties and the Whig financiers showed a disinclination to lend them money. The company took over the Government's floating debt of nearly £10,000,000, Robert Harley promising six per cent interest. This money was to be raised by assured revenue from permanent duties on wines, silks, tobacco and similar luxury imports, and a monopoly of trade with the South Seas, which was incorporated by Act of Parliament. To investors in the company, many of whom were very naïve, it seemed that they were now to tap unlimited supplies of the fabulous gold of Mexico and the silver of Peru. Negotiations with Philip V of Spain very soon disillusioned the officials of the company and all they obtained was the privilege of supplying the Spanish colonies with Negro slaves for the next thirty years and the right to send one ship a year for trade, but the shareholders knew nothing of this. By 1720 the National Debt had risen to over £30,000,000 and the company offered to take it over at five per cent for seven years and afterwards at four per cent, for which, outbidding the Bank of England, they were to pay £7,500,000.

There was a frenzy of investment in the company. The new Bill went through Parliament, Sir Robert Walpole alone opposing it, denouncing 'the dangerous practice of stock jobbing, and the general infatuation, which must end in general ruin'.

Few took any notice of him. People poured in their money. The stock rose from 30 to 300 in a single day. By the end of May 1721 it was 530. When the price tended to fall a little it was revived by rumours of free trade with Spain and vast, untapped sources of wealth which would eventually yield shareholders fifty per cent. Another story was circulated that Gibraltar and Port Mahon were to be exchanged for Peruvian sea-ports, so that the company would be able to send out a whole fleet of trading ships.

Everyone who could raise any money took to investment. Scores of smaller companies were launched at the same time, as, for example, companies 'For importing walnut trees from Virginia' and 'For buying and fitting out ships to suppress pirates'. Then there was Puckle's Machine Company for discharging round and square cannon-balls and bullets, and making a total revolution in the art of war. The gullible public believed it all and had been so persuaded that the joint-stock company was the way to undreamed of riches that some even fell for the outrageous 'Company for carrying on an undertaking of great advantage, but nobody to know what it is'. The promoter asked for £500,000 capital in 5,000 shares of £100 each, with a deposit of £2 on each share. He opened his office in Cornhill one morning at nine o'clock and by the time he closed his doors that afternoon at three o'clock he had sold a thousand shares and collected £2,000 in deposits.

But it was in the South Sea Company that most people poured their money.

'During the infatuation,' wrote Smollett, 'luxury, vice and profligacy increased to a shocking degree; the adventurers, intoxicated by their imaginary wealth, pampered themselves with the rarest dainties and the most costly wines. They purchased the most sumptuous furniture, equipage, and apparel, though with no taste or discernment . . . and their discourse evinced the most disgusting pride, insolence and ostentation.'

By 2 June the stock had risen to 890. Many people now thought it wiser to sell, and it was soon rumoured that among them were several members of the Court, about to leave for a visit to Hanover with the King. The next day the stock slipped to 640. To restore confidence, the directors ordered their agents to buy and by August the figure was up to 1,000. Then it was rumoured that Sir John Blount, author of the scheme and chairman of the company, had sold out, along with several directors. Within days the stock had tumbled to 400. Then it sank steadily lower. Shocked and bewildered shareholders came to realise that their money had been lost in a vast swindle. Only one ship had ever been sent to the Spanish colonies. Thousands lost everything and there were several suicides. Aislabie, the Chancellor of the Exchequer, resigned. The treasurer of the company fled with all his records, and five directors were arrested.

The investigating committee which was quickly appointed discovered that in the accounts false entries had been made, records had been altered or destroyed and fictitious stock sold. This stock had been distributed among certain members of the Government and favoured people in society, to give the impressive appearance to the finances of the company which enabled the Bill authorising its activities to pass through Parliament. It was issued on the 'heads I win, tails you lose' principle. No money was paid over, so if the stock fell nothing was lost. But if the stock rose, as it did, the company promised these 'shareholders' the amount they would have gained if they had paid for it in the first place.

Among those who benefited, while stock was rising, each to the tune of £10,000, were the Duchess of Kendal and the Countess of Darlington, who salted their profits away in Germany, but Aislabie, who made £800,000, was sent to the Tower and forced to pay back his fortune to help those who had suffered.

When only six years later, in 1727, the King made his last journey to Hanover, the Duchess of Kendal accompanied him, although by this time he had taken a new mistress, Anne Brett, who had been left behind at St James's Palace with the promise of being made a Duchess on the King's return.

Shortly after his death in Hanover, the Duchess of Kendal returned to London. There was no place at Court for her, when George II and Queen Caroline succeeded, for George I and George II had disliked each other as much as George II disliked his own son, 'poor Fred', the Prince of Wales. The Duchess of Kendal had no financial worries, for apart from the personal fortune she had amassed during her years at the English Court, George I left her £40,000. After a short stay in a house in Old Bond Street, where Atkinson's perfumery shop was later established, she took the lease of Number 43 Grosvenor Square, for her London home, and here she lived from 1728 until she died in 1743.

Her younger daughter had married Count von Lippe but the elder, Petronella Melusina, who in 1722 had been created the Countess of Walsingham, was still unmarried and already in her middle thirties. She was her mother's heiress and lived with her in Grosvenor Square.

We have little idea what the inside of the house was like, but in 1960, when the house next door, Number 44, was occupied by Lady Illingworth, panelling was removed from the upstairs drawing-room to reveal a mural similar to that which William Kent had painted for George I on the grand staircase of Kensington Palace, and which at the time was said to have been the King's idea. As in the palace, the murals in Grosvenor Square depicted groups of people leaning over a balcony. There were eight people, divided between three panels, a courtier in full-bottomed wig talking to two Polish noblemen, a flower girl disporting with a youth, and a strawberry girl spurning the approach of a wild-looking customer. The house had been considerably altered by the Illingworths and these murals had formerly decorated the staircase, part of which had been thrown into the drawing-room.

According to the rate books, Philip Stanhope, the 4th Earl of

Chesterfield, arrived in 1734 from St James's Square to live at Number 45, which was formerly Number 40, but contemporary accounts say that he came to live in the house adjoining that of the Duchess of Kendal, so it may well be that Numbers 43 and 44 (formerly 38 and 39) at one time adjoined. The Duchess was rich enough to have maintained an establishment of this size and who more likely than she to have commissioned William Kent to paint the murals which would have reminded her of her former days of power and glory at the palace with the King? Old and ugly and avaricious as she was, she must have had a heart not far below the surface and they had been together for many years. Yet Number 44 according to the rate books was occupied by Oliver St George from 1728 until 1731 and then by his widow until 1746.

For purely political and financial reasons, Lord Chesterfield married Petronella, the Countess of Walsingham, in the year that he moved to Grosvenor Square, but he continued to live in his own house at Number 45, while she remained with her mother, which would appear to be one of the odder arrangements in a society which was admittedly given to idiosyncrasies. She was forty by now and Lord Chesterfield a year younger. He had already, during his long love affair with Mademoiselle de Bouchet, had the illegitimate son to whom he addressed his famous letters, and he seems to have celebrated his marriage with Petronella by taking a new mistress, Fanny Shirley, reputed to be 'a great beauty'.

Yet he often visited his wife and mother-in-law next door, enjoying an evening at cards and 'playing away all his credit'.

His treatment of Petronella was quite indefensible but she seems to have taken it philosophically. All she asked was that in public he treat her with respect and this he always did, for his public manners and deportment were impeccable.

He had already deeply offended George II by his friendship with Lady Suffolk, one of the King's mistresses, and his marriage with Petronella, who was the King's half-sister, widened the breach for he had hated both her parents, yet Petronella was an amiable, inoffensive soul and was said to have made Chesterfield 'a most exemplary wife, and he rewarded her very ungratefully'.

He did once accompany her to Bath, but mostly they lived entirely separate lives, for in regard to women he had no moral conscience, as his letters to his son show all too clearly.

He wrote to young Philip Stanhope in English, as well as French and Latin, from the time he was five years old until his death at the age of thirty-six, giving him much sound if cynical advice on the proper behaviour of a gentleman, and urging him always to avoid the coarser forms of vice. But when the boy was only eighteen, he was telling him that, in regard to women 'a man of sense only trifles with them, plays with them', and later he was to advocate the advantages of adultery over wedlock.

Not that the boy took much notice of this paternal advice, for after his death it was revealed that he had secretly married a very ordinary and lowly young woman and had two children.

Dr Johnson declared that the Chesterfield letters 'taught the morals of a whore and the manners of a dancing master', but Johnson, ever inclined to carping criticism, had a grudge against Lord Chesterfield.

He had been commissioned by a group of important London booksellers to prepare his dictionary and, in the manner of the day, had sent a copy of the prospectus to Lord Chesterfield. Chesterfield at this time was Secretary of State and had been 'the butt of dedications', and not knowing Johnson personally, he contributed ten guineas to the work and left it at that. Johnson called on Chesterfield at his house in Grosvenor Square, presumably to thank him, but he was kept waiting overlong in an antechamber, the servant telling him that Lord Chesterfield 'had company with him'. So Johnson continued to wait, but when at last the door opened, out walked no distinguished and important company but Colley Cibber, the actor and playwright from Drury Lane. According to the story as told by Boswell, Dr Johnson 'was so violently provoked when he found for whom he had been so long excluded, that he went away in a passion and vowed he never would return'.

Johnson himself denied that there was ever any quarrel between himself and Lord Chesterfield and assured Boswell that 'his Lordship's continued neglect was the reason why he resolved to have no connexion with him'.

Seven years later, on the eve of the publication of the dictionary, Lord Chesterfield wrote high praise of Johnson's work in the weekly paper *The World* but the Doctor, over-sensitive and difficult, was convinced that the praise was given only in the hope that the dictionary would be dedicated to Chesterfield, and this prompted his famous letter:

Seven years, my lord, have now passed since I waited in your outward rooms, or was repulsed from your door; during which time I have been pushing on my work through difficulties of which it is useless to complain, and have brought it at last to the verge of publication, without one act of assistance, one word of encouragement, or one smile of favour. Such treatment I did not expect, for I never had a patron before. The notice which you have been pleased to take of my labours, had it been early, had been kind; but it has been delayed till I am indifferent, and cannot enjoy it; till I am solitary, and cannot impart it; till I am known and do not want it.

Johnson's admirers applauded him for thus rejecting what they regarded as Lord Chesterfield's condescension, for he had many enemies. Among them was Horace Walpole, for Chesterfield had contributed to his father's political eclipse, and also Lord Hervey, the friend of Queen Charlotte, who described him as 'very short, disproportioned, thick and clumsily made; with a broad, rough-featured, ugly face, with black teeth and a head big enough for a Polyphemus', yet Johnson was generous enough to grant that his manner was 'exquisitely elegant'.

Lady Chesterfield, judging from the looks of her parents, would seem to have been no more comely than her husband, but her cousin, Madame d'Elitz, who joined her in Grosvenor Square in 1736 was, according to Lord Hervey, 'a very handsome lady, though now a little in her decline, with a great deal of wit, who had had a thousand lovers, and had been catched in bed with a man twenty years ago and been divorced from her husband upon it. She was said to have been mistress to three generations of the Hanover family; the late King, the present, and the Prince of Wales before he came to England, which was one generation more than the Duchess of Valentinos, who had been mistress to Henry II, could boast of in France.'

'The present King had quitted Madame d'Elitz for Madame Walmoden,' continued Hervey, 'upon which a quarrel ensued between the two ladies, and the King thereupon had turned Madame d'Elitz out of the palace (Herrenhausen) the year before.'

The quarrel had broken out when a ladder was discovered at Madame Walmoden's bedroom window. A gardener gave the alarm, thinking it was left by a burglar, but after a search of the grounds the only trespasser they could find was a member of the Schulenburg family, whom the Captain of the Guard, thinking to be acting with discretion, ordered to be released, but Madame

Walmoden declared that it was all part of a plot to compromise her, cooked up by Madame d'Elitz and her Schulenburg relations.

The King was extremely angry when he heard this version of the story and ordered the re-arrest of Monsieur Schulenburg. Madame d'Elitz obviously thought it wiser to make herself scarce and it therefore happened that 'just when the King set out for Hanover this year, Madame d'Elitz set out for England, where she now was with her aunt and sister, the Duchess of Kendal and Lady Chesterfield'.

The apparent confusion in relationships here is because Lady Chesterfield was always described as the Duchess of Kendal's 'niece' and was not officially recognised as her daughter by George I.

The year 1736 in which Madame d'Elitz arrived in Grosvenor Square, was a decisive one for Miss Fane, living round the corner in Grosvenor Street. She had been a mistress of Lord Hervey, but Frederick, Prince of Wales, had filched her from him and bought her a house at Wimbledon, where she spent much of her time, leaving only a maid and man-servant in the Grosvenor Street house.

Here she used to return secretly once or twice a week to meet Lord Hervey, who would arrive after dark and leave before dawn, but they found it difficult to provide themselves with a proper supper and fresh fruit, so while Lady Hervey was abroad for a few weeks, they changed the rendezvous to Hervey's lodgings in St James's. This arrangement worked splendidly until Miss Fane had a fit one night and Hervey, to his intense embarrassment, thought she had died on him. However, after an hour or two, with the help of strong cordials and hot towels, he revived her, dressed her, got her into the street, found a roving chair-man and returned her to Grosvenor Street. But it was at this juncture that Prince Frederick's marriage with Princess Augusta of Saxe-Gotha was arranged. His other mistress, Lady Archibald Hamilton, being already in the ascendancy over Miss Vane and confident that her position would remain unassailed for a time, seized the opportunity to discomfort Miss Fane by insisting that the Prince send her out of the country. He therefore sent her, through Lord Baltimore, one of those chilly notes of dismissal, telling her to go to Holland for two or three years or he would stop her allowance of £1,600 a year. Her son, whom he acknowledged to be his – though his mother, Queen Caroline, who disliked him and cast doubts on his virility at this time, always ascribed the child to Lord Hervey – he undertook to educate in England.

Miss Fane turned to Lord Hervey for help, and as he was anxious in the first place for her not to go abroad, and secondly to embarrass

Prince Frederick, he composed a letter for her to send in reply which was so reproachful and conciliatory that the Prince, well aware that it was none of her own writing, was shamed into allowing her to keep her allowance and the house in Grosvenor Street for life, to live where she pleased and retain the care of her son.

However, less than two months afterwards the baby died of convulsions, and a week later Miss Fane herself was dead, dying in Bath, where she had gone for the waters.

Lord Chesterfield lived on at his house in Grosvenor Square until about the time he resigned office in 1748. His magnificent Chesterfield House in South Audley Street was almost ready by this time and the following year he moved in, although the famous house-warming party did not take place until two or three years later.

His relationship with Lady Chesterfield was by now only formal and she does not seem to have joined him at Chesterfield House. Her mother died in Grosvenor Square in 1743 and the following year the house was occupied by Lord Maynard, but Petronella lived on until 1778, surviving her husband for five years. She disappears from the story, in the self-effacing way in which she seems to have spent her entire life, appearing again only at the very end, when her husband lay dying. She took to evangelism, which was all the rage in Mayfair during the late 1740s.

Selina Hastings, the Countess of Huntingdon, had turned Methodist and become intimate with the Wesleys and George Whitefield, and after the death of two of her sons from smallpox in 1743, followed by that of her husband in 1745, she turned even more to religion. She appointed George Whitefield her chaplain and moved to London, to her house in Park Street, in order that he and the Wesleys could preach to the aristocracy of Mayfair and undertake the formidable task of bringing them into the 'new light'.

Lady Jane Coke, writing in 1748 to her friend Mrs Eyre, said, 'All the news I have heard from London, at least the most extraordinary, is Lady Townshend's being much with Lady Huntingdon. Wesley preaches at her house every Thursday and Sunday, and as Lady Huntingdon gives leave to everybody to come who send to desire it, it is now the fashion to go, and Lady Townshend never misses.'

Walpole, writing the following year, said, 'Methodism is more fashionable than anything but bragg, half the women in the town play very deep at both,' and again: 'My Lady Huntingdon, the

Queen of the Methodists, has got her daughter named Lady of the Bedchamber to the Princesses, but it is all off, as she will not let her play cards on Sundays.'

Whitefield and the Wesleys were later to disagree over a question of doctrine, and Lady Huntingdon tried, though in vain, to reconcile them.

At one time, congregations of some fifty members of Mayfair's aristocracy would arrive at Lady Huntingdon's to hear the Methodists preach, including on occasion Lord Chesterfield, though Lady Huntingdon despaired of his redemption because of his association with Lady Suffolk.

One Sunday evening, Whitefield, not knowing that Lady Suffolk was in the congregation, preached a sermon which described her state so exactly that she took it to be a deliberate attack on her moral character. She just managed to sit it out and then flew into a violent rage, attacking Lady Huntingdon and accusing her of having contrived the whole affair. Her sister-in-law, Lady Betty Germaine, tried to appease her, as well as two more of her relatives, Lady Eleanor Bertie and the Dowager Duchess of Ancaster. She insisted that she had been insulted, but in the end they made her apologise.

During the middle years of the eighteenth century there was a splendid crop of earls and dukes, countesses and duchesses living in Grosvenor Square, but along with the picturesque elegancies of powdered wigs and hooped skirts, sedans and carriages, link men and running footmen, there were mortal dangers in this remote corner of London after dark and there are many tales of attack by highwaymen and cut-throats in the shadowy square and its surrounding streets, for the wealthy inhabitants were usually well worth attacking for the jewellery and money they carried.

Things were particularly bad after the Treaty of Aix-la-Chapelle, in 1748, at the end of the War of the Austrian Succession, when numbers of returned soldiers, unemployed and penniless, were roaming the streets, and in 1749 Lady Jane Coke was writing, 'Everybody writes me there is such robbery in the streets that it is quite frightful.' And it continued for many years.

On 10 June 1777, the Annual Register reported that His Excellency the Neapolitan Ambassador 'was attacked in his carriage in Grosvenor Square by four footpads, one of whom presented a pistol to his coachman, two more one to each of the footmen, while the fourth robbed his Excellency of a gold watch and money'.

The Prince of Wales and the Duke of York, when they were very young men, were riding in a hackney coach down Hay Hill when they were stopped and robbed by a group of highwaymen.

Then there was the highwayman who got away by escaping from Piccadilly down the narrow, unpaved Berkeley Street, through the Lansdowne Passage which ran between the gardens of Lansdowne House and Devonshire House, put his horse to the steps at the Curzon Street end and galloped back into Piccadilly, past the astonished eyes of Thomas Greville, who was living close by in Bolton Street.

After that, a bar was placed at the Curzon Street steps to stop such a thing happening again.

But the thieves did not always escape. J. T. Smith, in his *Book for a Rainy Day* says that he once saw Dr Johnson 'follow a sturdy thief, who had stolen his handkerchief in Grosvenor Square, seize him by the collar with both hands, and shake him violently, after which he quickly let him loose; and then with his open hand, give him so powerful a smack on the face, that sent him off the pavement, staggering'.

Lord Cathcart, writing to his son in 1774, tells him that as his sisters and Mr Graham (afterwards Lord Lynedoch) were going in a coach to Lady Brown's, they were attacked by footpads on Hay Hill. One opened the door and demanded their money, but Graham jumped out and captured him, while his companion ran off.

At Lord Chesterfield's old house in Grosvenor Square, after two short tenancies, first by a duchess and then by an earl, Sir Richard Grosvenor, the ground landlord, moved in on his marriage, in 1755, with Henrietta Vernon, a member of the Strafford family, and here their son, who was to become the 1st Marquis of Westminster, was born in 1767.

But the marriage was disastrous and Lady Mary Coke, Lady Grosvenor's aunt, recorded each step of the débâcle with gleeful satisfaction, for she disliked her niece most heartily.

In 1769 the young Lady Henrietta began a liaison with none other than the Duke of Cumberland, a 'weak and debauched boy', youngest brother of George III. 'Strange things are said of Lady Grosvenor,' wrote Aunt Mary in her journal on 15 September 1769. 'I was told she came every day to Kensington Gardens for a very bad purpose.'

On 6 January 1770 she was writing with even more satisfaction, for Sir Richard had already begun divorce proceedings.

So Lady Grosvenor is at last catched . . . As to herself, I think I am generous when I say I don't rejoice at her present distress, for though I am persuaded a person who is gone never considered her but in the light of a woman of the town, yet it gave her an opportunity of behaving with great impertinence to me, which, however, I kept to myself.

The 'person who is gone' was the Duke of York, with whom Lady Grosvenor had had an earlier affair. By June 1770, Lady Mary Coke was giving more details of the affair with the Duke of Cumberland.

When Lady Grosvenor went into Cheshire last year she made four days' journey, and the Duke of Cumberland met her at every inn upon the road, was there some hours before her, and marked two bedchambers with chalk, which, her ladyship understanding, made choice of one of them, where she lay; the other was always engaged for the Duke, who pretended to be a Welsh gentleman, and always left the inn at six o'clock in the morning.

Lady Grosvenor, said Horace Walpole, was 'a vain young woman, of a good person, moderate beauty, and no understanding'. The indiscretion with the Duke of York had been a scandal, but being 'still more indiscreet with the Duke of Cumberland, their letters were intercepted by the husband; and never was the public regaled with a collection of greater folly'.

Somehow – probably through the theft by a servant – the letters came into the hands of the editor of a gossiping paper – the *Middlesex Journal* – which published them all. While disapproving in theory of such unwarrantable intrusion into a purely personal and private matter, in practice people read them avidly and Lady Mary Coke, raising her hands in delighted horror, declared that 'though I never had any great idea of her delicacy, I own the indecency of her style quite shocked me'.

Sir Richard won £10,000 damages from the Duke, who thereupon deserted Lady Grosvenor, 'adding perfidy to ridicule and abandoned the lady to her shame'. He took up with a Mrs Bailey, the wife of a timber merchant, and 'it was uncertain', said Walpole, 'which was most proud of the honour, the husband or the wife', but the affair was short-lived and before long the Duke met his match with Mrs Horton, a widow, 'who had for many months been dallying with his passion, till she had fixed him to more serious views than he had intended'. They were married and then fled to Calais until the anger of the King and his mother, the Dowager Princess of Wales, should have abated a little.

Sir Richard Grosvenor continued to maintain Number 45 for his town house until his death in 1802, after which it was occupied by a long succession of distinguished men and women, including Edward Harcourt, Archbishop of York, who have now faded into blameless obscurity.

Sir Richard's son, the 1st Marquess of Westminster, lived at a double house in the square, Numbers 15 and 16, from 1825 to 1845, and his grandson was created the 1st Duke of Westminster in 1874.

At Number 1 there arrived, in 1740, the Dowager Duchess of Leeds with a beautiful daughter who had been betrothed to Lord Granville. 'There are not above two or three and forty years difference in their ages and not above three bottles difference in their drinking in a day,' observed Horace Walpole, 'so it is a very suitable match!' However, the match did not materialise and she eventually married Lord Portmore, the son of James II and the plain but amusing Catherine Sedley.

By 1743 the house was occupied by the 2nd Duke of Buccleugh, grandson of the Duke of Monmouth, who until the end maintained that the marriage of his mother, Lucy Walters, to Charles II was valid and that he was the rightful heir to the throne. He had secured the restoration of the honours his grandfather had forfeited at the time of the rebellion and his execution, but they did him no good, for after the death of his first wife, Lady Jane Douglas, in 1729, he had slipped downhill very rapidly, preferring the most disreputable and lowly company to that of his aristocratic neighbours in the square; in 1744 he married a washerwoman, and when he died a few years later, in 1751, he was buried 'very meanly' in Eton College Chapel, and no one bothered to erect a memorial to him.

Charles Poulett, the 3rd Duke of Bolton, was the next tenant, living here from 1752 until his death two years later, but he was no great improvement on the Duke of Buccleugh, for he was notorious for the large amount of money he made corruptly, in the provision of uniforms for the Army.

> Now Bolton comes with beat of drums
> Though fighting be his loathing
> He much dislikes both guns and pikes,
> But relishes the *clothing*.

He had married Lord Carberry's daughter, Lady Anne Vaughan. Lord Carberry had made his fortune in the slave trade, while Governor of Jamaica, and when Anthony Ashley Cooper fell in love with Lady Anne, her father would not countenance the match, considering his fortune and style of living too modest. So a marriage was arranged for her with Charles Poulett, who deserted the poor girl at the church door and returned to live with his mistress, Lavinia Fenton, who had made her name as Polly Peachum in the *Beggar's Opera*. And when Lady Anne died in 1751, the Duke straightaway made an honest woman of Lavinia, who had been his mistress for twenty-three years. She became a Duchess and he brought her to Grosvenor Square.

Number 4, in the centre of the east side, was one of the largest houses in the square. It was built about 1728–9, but ten years later, as it was still unoccupied, the builder raffled it, and it was won by two men, Hunt and Braithwaite. They valued the house at £10,000 but sold it for £7,000 to the Duke of Norfolk, who was looking for a new town house, having lent Norfolk House in St James's Square to Frederick, Prince of Wales, after he and his family had been turned out of St James's Palace by his irate father; and ultimately this vast house in Grosvenor Square, the new Norfolk House, became the Italian Embassy.

At Number 9, in the north-east corner, there lived for a short time the beautiful Duchess of Gordon, wife of the 4th Duke. She married off three of her five daughters to dukes. A fourth, Louisa, was married to the Marquess Cornwallis, but before the engagement was made, he expressed some doubts about the match because of the taint of insanity in the Gordon family. He was reassured, however, if a little surprised, when the Duchess, who had been separated from the Duke for many years, was able to promise him that 'there was not one drop of Gordon blood in Louisa's veins'.

A later occupant of this house was John Adams, the first minister from the United States, who lived here from 1786 to 1788, at a time when Lord North was living at Number 30 in the opposite corner. It could have provoked some awkward encounters but both men were likeable, although John Adams always felt ill at ease in London because he was not given a sufficiently large allowance from the United States to maintain the splendid style of living of his fellow ministers.

As for Lord North, Horace Walpole had much to say about him. Writing in 1770, a few years before he incurred such great calumny for the mishandling of American affairs and the loss of the colonies, Walpole said of him:

Nothing could be more coarse or clumsy or ungracious than his outside. Two large prominent eyes that rolled about to no purpose (for he was utterly short-sighted), a wide mouth, thick lips and inflated visage, gave him the air of a blind trumpeter. A deep, untuneable voice, which, instead of modulating, he enforced with unnecessary pomp, a total neglect of his person, and ignorance of every civil attention, disgusted all who judge by appearance, or withhold their approbation till it is courted. But within that rude casket were enclosed many useful talents. He had much wit, good humour, strong natural sense, assurance and promptness, both of conception and elocution.

Number 9 still stands, the only Georgian house remaining in the square, although it is tucked away in the far corner and really belongs to Brook Street. Its brick work has been blackened with the years and it has obviously been very much altered, but it has a lived-in, vital air about it, although today it is no longer a private house but a department of the Japanese Embassy.

The 1st Marquess of Abercorn, who lived at Number 25 on the west side of the square, from 1764 to 1804, was one of those endearing members of the aristocracy, all good breeding, impeccable manners and eccentricities, who has disappeared entirely from English life. When his second wife was planning her elopement with Sir Joseph Copley he sent her a message begging her 'to take the family coach, as it should never be said that a Lady Abercorn left her husband in a hack chaise'; and he insisted that when the maidservants made his bed, they should wear white kid gloves.

The 6th Duke of Hamilton and the beautiful Miss Gunning, whom the Duke married so hurriedly at Alexander Keith's chapel, come into the story again now, for their daughter, Lady Elizabeth Douglas-Hamilton, married the 12th Lord Derby in 1774, when he was twenty-one and she was nineteen; and in 1777 they came to live at Number 26. She bore him three children but was never in love with him, and is said to have been 'a reluctant beauty sacrificed to her husband's arms by the vanity of her mother'. Very soon she had left him for the 3rd Duke of Dorset, who lived handily close by at Number 18, having arrived in the square at the same time as the Derbys.

Lord Derby refused to divorce Elizabeth, but within a few weeks of her death had married the beautiful actress, Elizabeth Farren, who was living not far away in Green Street. The marriage took place at the Duke's house in Berkeley Square but the entry appears in the register at St George's, Hanover Square, for 1 May 1797. Thomas Creevey was a friend and frequent visitor of the Derbys and thoroughly approved of the new Lady Derby. 'We dined at Lord Derby's, nobody but us,' he wrote on 11 November 1809. 'Lord Derby excellent in every respect as he always is, and my Lady still out of spirits for the loss of her child, but surpassing even in her depressed state all your hereditary nobility I have ever seen, though she came from the stage to her title.'

Number 35 was occupied for a short time in 1753 by the 1st Duke of Leinster, whose wife was a great granddaughter of Charles II, but it attracted more attention in 1790 when John Wilkes came to live here with his daughter Mary; and until his death in 1797 Wilkes walked from here to his City office every day.

In his *Reminiscences*, Angelo says:

> Mr Wilkes removed to the corner of South Audley Street, with one front leading into Grosvenor Square, and the last time I had the honour to meet him was immediately after the Mount Street rioters broke the glass of his parlour windows, which perhaps were the most valuable of any in the world, for the whole of the lower sashes, composed of very large panes, were of plate glass, engraved with eastern subjects in the most beautiful taste. These were naturally the more valued by Mr. Wilkes as they were the ingenious labour of his daughter.

The fire had gone out of Wilkes by now for he was in his sixties and had led an exhausting life, profligate in many ways, yet full of solid achievement. He treated his wife abominably, but it was a marriage arranged by his father when Wilkes was under age and the bride ten years older than he. She was the daughter of a wealthy London grocer and a strict Dissenter, who disapproved of the gay, witty Wilkes from the outset. So he squeezed all the money he could from her, which included an estate at Aylesbury, and they soon parted, with Wilkes having the custody of his only legitimate child, Mary, to whom he was devoted.

Wilkes fell in with Sir Frances Dashwood and his circle and became involved in the Medmenham Abbey orgies for a time, but he was too intelligent to regard them as anything but rather puerile. His real work lay in his writing for the *North Briton*, in which he proclaimed himself a free-thinker and urged the need for Parliamentary Reform, yet his free-thinking was more of a mental exercise than a sincere conviction, for he once confessed that he himself was never a

'Wilkite'. He was by inclination a man of fashion, with a taste for the arts, particularly French and Italian music, poetry and literature; and Walpole was probably near the mark when he said that 'wantonness, rather than ambition or vengeance, guided his hand; and, though he became the martyr of the best cause, there was nothing in his principles or morals that led him to care under what government he lived. To laugh and riot and scatter firebrands with him was liberty – Despotism will for ever reproach Freedom with the profligacy of such a saint!'

Wilkes was by no means handsome and had a diabolical squint, but his manners were polished, his conversation witty, and even those who did not trust him found him unfailingly amusing. He also had great courage, for he led the struggle to end the secrecy with which Parliamentary proceedings were conducted and he established the right of the Press to discuss national figures and public affairs.

It was his attack on Lord Bute which induced the minister to resign. When he wrote an article in the *North Briton* criticising the speech from the throne, on the opening of Parliament, he was arrested and committed to the Tower for seditious libel, and although he was very soon set free again, since his arrest and detention were not legal, he was expelled again from Parliament, threatened with further prosecution and forced to take refuge in France for a time.

In 1768 he returned to England and once more stood for Parliament, but on his election George III demanded his expulsion. He was charged once more with libel, and when he did not appear in Court he was outlawed and committed to prison for a time. The following year he was again standing for Parliament. Three times he was elected and three times expelled.

Then he began publishing the Letters of Junius, and when the action against the anonymous journalist failed, the Government had to concede the right of the Press to criticise not only Parliament and its ministers but also the Crown; and it is from this time that public agitation first began to influence English politics.

Wilkes died at his house in Grosvenor Square in 1797, and although Leigh Hunt had sneered at the 'Defender of Liberty' who had managed to make so much money out of the cause that he could afford three houses – in the Isle of Wight, Kensington Gore and Grosvenor Square – far from amassing a fortune from his writing and his work, he died insolvent, and was buried very quietly in the

Grosvenor Chapel, with a simple memorial tablet bearing the inscription: 'A Friend of Liberty'.

In 1763 Mrs Eliza Bowes, the widow of George Bowes, came to live at Number 40, and four years later her only daughter Eleanor married John Lyon, the 9th Earl of Strathmore; but in 1776, after they had had a family of nine children in as many years, John died and within twelve months Eleanor had married an ill-favoured but plausible Irishman called Andrew Stoney. The house in Grosvenor Square was made over to him and here the family continued to live for a time, Eleanor having two more children by Stoney. He turned out to be a bankrupt lieutenant on half pay, and when he discovered that his wife's estates were secured to herself and that he had no legal claim on them, he bullied her into a deed of renunciation in his favour.

Thereafter, through the influence of Eleanor's family connexions and property, he prospered for a time, becoming High Sheriff of Durham and Member of Parliament for Newcastle upon Tyne. But they entertained so lavishly in Grosvenor Square that by 1781 they had overspent and had to depart for a smaller establishment in Chelsea for a time. However, five years later, by devious means, Stoney had recouped his finances and they were back in the square, this time at Number 48, which he took furnished. That year his wife left him and retired to Bloomsbury Square, but a few months later Stoney had her abducted and carried off to her father's ancestral home in County Durham.

That was his big mistake. Lady Strathmore managed to escape and Stoney was arrested and sentenced to three years' imprisonment. She obtained a divorce and the deed which had made over her estates and her fortune to Stoney was invalidated, since it was proved that it had been made under duress.

Stoney now had no money and in 1790 was committed to the King's Bench prison and until his death in 1810 he remained under its rules, which meant that although he had a certain amount of liberty he was still virtually a prisoner. Nevertheless, soon after his committal he took a fancy to a girl of fifteen, whose father was also in for debt, married her and had five more children. He died in obscurity and poverty but Lady Strathmore, who died at Christchurch in 1800, was given a splendid funeral at Westminster Abbey, clad, at her request, in the wedding dress she had worn for her marriage to the Earl of Strathmore.

Mr and Mrs Thrale came to live in the square for a time, a few months before Mr Thrale's death, moving to Number 37 in 1781. Mrs Thrale said the move from Streatham Place was on doctor's orders, as Grosvenor Square was considered to be a healthier spot for her ailing husband. Her critics said she wanted a better house, in which to entertain on a more lavish scale.

As at Streatham, a room was placed at the disposal of Dr Johnson, where he would spend the middle days of the week, returning to his house in Bolt Court for the week-end.

'Think of Johnson's having apartments in Grosvenor Square!' wrote Hannah More, 'but he says it is not half so convenient as Bolt Court.'

But Mr Thrale lasted for only another three months. He ate and drank too heavily, and on 2 April 1781, he died.

'I felt almost the last flutter of his pulse, and looked for the last time upon the face that for fifteen years had never been turned upon me but with respect and benignity,' wrote Johnson, deeply grieved at the loss of his old friend.

In 1797 that strange character William Beckford, whose daughter married the Duke of Hamilton, took a lease of Number 2. At twenty-one, he had inherited a million pounds and an income of over £100,000 a year, and he lived in a style to match, making long tours of the Continent with a retinue of thirty servants. He was a bibliophile on the grand scale and had a magnificent library, which passed to the Hamilton family.

As a writer, his most famous work was *The History of the Caliph Vathek*, which he first wrote in French. As a builder he was less successful, being greatly addicted to tall towers. He pulled down the old house at Fonthill where he was born and in its place built Fonthill Abbey, with a tower 278 feet high, which collapsed after a few years. In 1823 he sold the abbey and went to live at Bath, where he built Lansdowne House, with a tower only a hundred feet high this time, but crowned with a model of the temple of Lysistrates at Athens, made in cast iron.

In 1800 Sir William and Emma Hamilton were staying at William Beckford's house in Grosvenor Square and here, after the surrender of Malta to the English Fleet, they were joined by Lord Nelson for a time, just before his final separation from his wife.

It was during the Napoleonic Wars that Dudley Ryder, the 1st Earl of Harrowby, moved into Number 44, the house between the Duchess of Kendal's old home and that of her son-in-law Lord

Chesterfield. He was a descendant of the Dudley Ryder of the early eighteenth century, whose diary from 1715 to 1716 gives such a vividly honest picture of himself as a young man and his life in Hackney, where the family was then living.

Lord Harrowby was Secretary of State for Foreign Affairs and Lord President of the Council. He had bought Number 44 in 1804 and here he was regularly visited by all the leading statesmen of the time, for it was the custom for the members of the Cabinet to dine at each other's houses in regular rotation.

On Wednesday evening, 21 June 1815, the Cabinet, with the Prime Minister, Lord Liverpool, were dining at Lord Harrowby's house. Rumour was rife. Wellington and Napoleon had met – but what was the outcome of the battle? In the clubs of St James's the odds were heavily on the side of Napoleon – but there were rumours afloat that Nathan Rothschild had different news. He had a courier service sending him information from all over Europe, so that he could play the stock market ahead of his rivals, and there was talk of a resounding victory for Wellington at the village of Waterloo, outside Brussels.

As the members of the Cabinet sat late round the dinner table in Grosvenor Square on that midsummer evening, anxiously discussing the prospects, they heard a sudden burst of cheering outside in the square. The Duke of Wellington's aide-de-camp, Major the Honourable Henry Percy, was driving post-haste through the square in a chaise and four, embellished with captured French flags and trophies, and the excited crowd had guessed the good news. The Major hurried into the dining-room with the story of the victory of Waterloo and bringing Wellington's despatch to Lord Bathurst, the Secretary of State for War, which can be seen to this day in the museum of the Record Office.

Only five years later, the house was the focus of yet another national event, which could have ended in grim tragedy. This was the Cato Street conspiracy of 1820.

The freedom of speech for which Wilkes had fought was largely lost during the French Revolution and the Napoleonic Wars, through the Tory dread of Jacobinism, and this suppression was maintained for the first years of the peace. The ruling class held firmly to the reins of government and three-quarters of the Cabinet were peers of the realm, determined to ignore and repress the fermenting seeds of social revolution, which were nurtured by Robert Owen, preaching his ideas of an industrial democracy, and Cobbett, who was riding through the English countryside, maintaining the rights of the poor to free assembly and speech.

Of fifteen hundred men who had marched in protest at the price of bread, twenty-four had been condemned to death. At St Peter's Fields, the battlefield of Peterloo, fifty thousand unarmed cotton operatives were fired on by the yeomanry. Repressive measures grew sterner. Men were imprisoned, fined, transported and even hanged, for protesting against conditions of life and work and low wages. The time was ripe for social revolution, but the first attempt to overthrow the Government by force was made by a callous, brutal character called Thistlewood, a renegade gentleman who had gambled away all his money and already spent twelve months in prison for abusing and annoying Lord Sidmouth, the Home Secretary.

Thistlewood's plan now was to take advantage of the fact that the Cabinet would be all together, dining at Lord Harrowby's house on 23 February 1820. With his small band of malcontents, he proposed to break in and murder them all, in cold blood. He gathered about twenty-four men into the plot and they met in a stable loft in Cato Street, just off the Edgware Road. They decided that one of their number should call at Lord Harrowby's house while the dinner was in progress, posing as a messenger with a special despatch, and while he was talking to the footman, the rest of the conspirators, hidden in small groups in the darkness of the square, would rush in and murder not only the entire Cabinet but any of the servants who chose to resist them. Ings, the butcher, was particularly anxious to secure the heads of Lord Castlereagh and Lord Sidmouth, for which he provided two bags, and also the right hand of Lord Castlereagh, which he felt would become a valuable souvenir.

When this part of the scheme was completed successfully, they planned to fire a rocket from the house as a signal to their friends that all had gone well, and a nearby oil shop was to be set on fire to gather the crowds. They naïvely believed that, with a large mob collected, who would become mad with excitement at the sight of the mangled remains of the Cabinet, they would be able to capture the barracks in Hyde Park, sack the Bank of England, occupy the Tower of London, throw open the gates of Newgate Prison, and establish a provisional government, which would be proclaimed on the steps of the Mansion House, the Lord Mayor having presumably surrendered to them or been murdered during the rebellion.

In the Cato Street loft, which was approached by a single ladder, they collected pikes and guns and made hand-grenades, not knowing that one of their number, Edwards, was a government spy. He warned Lord Harrowby on the morning of the dinner party. The Duke of Wellington advised Lord Liverpool to hold the dinner and not alter the arrangements, but other members were not anxious to meet their would-be assassins, even with ample forewarning, so the dinner was cancelled, although the members of Lord Harrowby's staff, including the French chef, were not told at the time.

One of Thistlewood's spies, lurking in the shadows of the plane trees on that dark February night, saw guests arriving for a dinner party at the house of the Archbishop of York, two doors away, and mistook them for members of the Cabinet arriving at Lord Harrowby's house. He reported back to Cato Street that all was going according to plan and the conspirators made their final arrangements. But just as they were ready to set out, a party of Bow Street officers appeared at the foot of the loft ladder. Thistlewood ran their leader, Smithers, through with a sword and killed him on the spot. Someone snuffed the candles, and in the sudden darkness a terrible fight took place, during which Thistlewood escaped. In the middle of it all, young Captain Fitzclarence, a son of the Duke of Clarence and Mrs Jordan, arrived with a party of Coldstream Guards.

The Fitzclarence boys were never very effectual, and the Captain was late for the simple reason that he had lost his way in the dark, but he and his men were in time to arrest nine of the conspirators, including the Negro, Davidson, Ings, the butcher, a bootmaker, and a cabinet-maker, while Thistlewood was caught the next day, at a house in Moorfields.

All ten were lodged in the Tower of London, a place which one writer, at least, considered too good for them, declaring that its tradition of prisoners was too dignified for such common rogues, and the cells that held them could 'never be perfumed sufficiently to hold noble traitors or villains of medieval magnitude', which seems, even allowing for righteous indignation, to be stretching snobbery to its utmost limit. So on that fateful evening, when the Cato Street plot collapsed, the only violence done in Lord Harrowby's house was that the chef, not told until eight o'clock that his dinner had been cancelled, was so furiously angry that he pitched all his lovingly created dishes on to the fire of the vast basement kitchen.

Five of the conspirators, including Thistlewood, Ings and Davidson, were condemned to death and the rest to transportation for life to Australia. Here two at least became respectable and prosperous citizens, and can be said to have lived happily ever after.

Thousands came to watch the hanging of the five condemned men outside Newgate Prison and Thomas Raikes, another resident of Grosvenor Square at this time – at Number 10 – although he later moved to 13 Hill Street, recorded that 'all the surrounding rooftops were covered with spectators' and 'when they first looked out of the Sheriff's room, there was nothing to be seen but the scaffolds, surrounded by an immense ocean of human heads'.

During their trial and after their execution, there were many arguments for and against the Government's policy of suppressing any expression of grievances. One side argued that the conspirators had been inflamed by cheap agitation through the Press, which proved how harmful a free Press could be. The opposition claimed that it was utterly wrong to suppress or even interfere with such publications, as they were a useful safety-valve, affording a relatively harmless opportunity for airing grievances, and that if this were removed far more dangerous methods might be used, a point of view which gradually won the day.

The Harrowby family stayed in their house in Grosvenor Square throughout the next two generations, until the 3rd Earl died in 1900, but before describing the changes which overcame the square during the nineteenth century, it is time to consider her younger sister, Berkeley Square.

VIII

The Planning of Berkeley Square

Ornithologists declare that the nightingale never did sing in Berkeley Square, and looking at the square today one can't blame it, for there is very little to sing about. The plane trees in the garden are still beautiful, and the grass is green, but the people who sit there during their lunch-time break, to enjoy such sunshine as there may be, usually look exhausted after braving the constant stream of traffic which whips round it like a whirligig gone beserk, even if triumphant that they have reached this small oasis in one piece.

During the second half of the eighteenth century, Berkeley Square was perhaps the most fashionable and elegant of all the Mayfair squares, and a few houses which have survived on the west side, though no longer private residences, show how delightful it must once have been. Yet its planning and development were even slower than its run-down and ruination during the twentieth century.

It is a long and complicated story, which begins at the end of the seventeenth century, when Hinde and his syndicate were planning the development of Albemarle Buildings.

The young Lord Berkeley, for whom his father had made the plans which did not materialise for the purchase of little Mary Davies in wedlock, was never, after all, married, for when he was only twenty he died of smallpox. At the time, he was in command of the frigate *Tiger*, which was engaged in the hazardous task of attempting to root out the North African pirates from their strongholds along the coasts of Morocco and Algiers, a useful job, for these were the years when they were attacking any European trading vessels they sighted in the Mediterranean, seizing the cargoes and holding the passengers to ransom or selling them into slavery, for they had found the sale of white slaves to Africans and African slaves to Europeans equally profitable.

As a commander the young Lord Berkeley was no great loss to the Navy, however, and Pepys recalled the time when he 'ran his ship aground in the River'. His important office, at so early an age, was, in fact, no mark of good seamanship but one of the rewards it was customary to give to young men of high social standing.

His younger brother John succeeded to the title, as the 3rd Lord Berkeley, but in 1696 he also died, still in his early thirties, although he was already an admiral and Commander-in-Chief of the Channel Fleet. However, this was the Lord Berkeley who helped his mother sell some of the Berkeley land for building. It included not only the land on which the house and garden stood but a large area to the north called Brick Close, later to be known as Hay Hill Farm, on which Berkeley Square was later to be built, with Bruton Place and Bruton Street to the east and Farm Street, Hill Street, Hay's Mews and Charles Street to the west.

John Hinde's syndicate was already heavily involved in the laying out of Albemarle Buildings – Dover Street, Albemarle Street, Stafford Street and Old Bond Street, and in 1683 they agreed to begin developments on Hay Hill Farm as well as the laying out of the west and east side of the Berkeley House garden as Berkeley Street and Stratton Street.

Both on these lands and at Albemarle Buildings they sold off building plots, some of which were freehold and others leasehold.

By June 1683 the syndicate ran into its first trouble – a complaint to the Commissioner of Sewers for Westminster from residents south of Piccadilly about the drainage from the new buildings of Albemarle Ground into the Tyburn. If something were not done to prevent new sewers being connected with the Tyburn, they protested, they would 'be drownded in their Houses upon any great Rain', for the channel under the stone bridge which crossed Piccadilly was not large enough to carry away the rain and waste waters which ran into it.

The commissioners saw the reasonableness of this complaint and forbade any more sewers to be connected with the stream, but three months later Frith, for the Hinde syndicate, was complaining to the commissioners that their work on Albemarle Ground was held up. They had laid the foundations of several houses but could not continue until they could provide some means of drainage.

They were given permission to enlarge a sewer near the garden of Arlington House, into which their own sewage could run, but the syndicate seemed to think they had a better idea and built a new sewer near the top of St James's Street, which they connected with an existing sewer far too small to take it. The residents of the houses on the west side of St James's Street protested that they were in danger of being flooded and their foundations undermined.

The syndicate were thereupon ordered to change the course of their sewer and pay the cost of repair to any pavement broken up during the work.

By April 1686, there were more complaints. They were accused of again connecting their drains with the Tyburn, which was still an open stream, so that 'great quantities of soil and filth flowed into the fresh water'.

Apart from these problems, the syndicate was running into money problems. Hinde owed money to the Government for Hearth Tax. He had borrowed heavily and his returns were not enough to meet his debts, while the unsold parts of the land he had bought were heavily mortgaged.

In September 1685, six months before the last complaint about the sewers, Hinde was imprisoned in the Fleet for debt and was made bankrupt, owing many thousands of pounds, perhaps as much as £200,000. In prison he fell ill and less than eighteen months later he died miserably, his plans unfulfilled through no particular fault of his own. He was a victim of the vague methods of finance and raising of loans, of unfulfilled promises and unpaid debts, which ruined so many businessmen of the late seventeenth century, an attitude of mind so sharply at variance with the precision and artistic triumphs of the craftsmen, the sparkle and penetrating wit of the diarists and letter-writers, the meticulous writing and impeccable manners of so many members of society. The goldsmith from whom Hinde had borrowed heavily was also ruined and Frith and Thomas became involved in litigation with brickmakers and iron-workers, whom they accused of fraudulence and over-charging. Both died within the next few years, near penniless and pursued by debtors, Thomas in 1690 and Frith in 1695.

When Sir Thomas Bond died, a few months before Hinde, only one of the houses on his building plots had found an occupier. The rest were heavily mortgaged and his son created fresh mortgages.

Complicated litigation now followed in an attempt to establish the real ownership of the Albemarle properties and the Berkeley lands which had been offered for building. It was a tangle which was to take years to unravel and it was further confused by the fact that boundaries were often not clearly defined.

Twenty years later, Hinde's affairs were still under arbitration and in the meantime many of the houses, some half built, others completed, were falling into neglect and ruin. In the first years of the eighteenth century, when Strype was editing Stow's *Survey of London* and bringing it up to date, he said:

> Albemarle Buildings, so called, as being the Seat of the Duke of Albemarle, who bought it of the Earl of Clarendon, and before called by his Name: Which said House and Gardens being sold by the said Duke, was by the Undertakers, laid out into Streets, who not being in a Condition to finish so great a Work, made Mortgages, and so intengled the Title, that it is not to this Day finished, and God knows when it will. So that it lyeth like the Ruins of Troy, some having only the Foundations begun, others carry'd up to the Roofs, and others covered, but none of the Inside Work done: Yet those Houses that are finished, which are towards Piccadilly meet with Tenants.

Although Strype's edition of Stow's *Survey* was not published until 1720 this passage must have been written several years earlier and it applied only to the northern part of Albemarle Buildings. Dover Street, Old Bond Street and the southern part of New Bond Street, Albemarle Street and Stafford Street were all established and the houses occupied by members of the gentry and aristocracy. By 1708 Edward Hatton, in *A New View of London*, described Dover Street 'as a street of very good buildings, mostly inhabited by Gentry'. Albemarle Street was 'a street of excellent new Building, inhabited by Persons of Quality between the Fields and Portugal Street'; and Bond Street was 'a fine new street, mainly inhabited by Nobility and Gentry'.

Nevertheless, the development as originally planned was far from complete, the ownership of many of the leasehold properties was still in doubt and there remained the waste land to the north, as well as several half-built houses, rapidly falling into decay.

By 1705 the Court decided that the parts of Albemarle Ground not yet built on and the parts where houses had been half built or fallen into ruin should be let or sold and the proceeds put to the paying of mortgage debts to the creditors who were still claiming on the estates of deceased promoters who had borrowed from them. The property sold included nine occupied houses, one being the *Duke of Albemarle*, the little pub at the corner of Dover Street and Stafford Street, which is still in business and on one of the walls still bears the original Stafford Street sign:

$$\text{This is Stafford S} \frac{\text{ET}}{\text{TR}} \text{ 1686.}$$

Other occupied houses were in Dover Street and Albemarle Street, one of the Dover Street houses, identified as Number 11, being where John Evelyn died on 27 February 1705-6.

He had taken over the house in 1699, when his son died. 'Finding my occasions call'd me so often to London, I took the remainder of the lease my Son had in a house in Dover Street, to wch I now remov'd, not taking my goods from Wotton', he recorded in his diary.

Of the houses which were ruined or destroyed, one was on the site of Number 23, Dover Street, where in 1837 James Brown first opened Brown's Hotel.

The waste land to the north, which Hinde's syndicate had planned as the noble piazza to be called Albemarle Square, was bought by the Duke of Grafton and other residents who were living at the northern end of the streets and wanted to preserve what was left of a fast disappearing rural aspect, but ultimately the existing streets were continued northwards and Grafton Street was built.

Benjamin Jackson, a master builder, had acquired four vacant building plots on the west side of Albemarle Street in 1707, for which he paid £174. These plots he divided into three and built Numbers 48, 49 and 50. At Number 50, first occupied by Robert Mansfield, Francis Scott, later the Duke of Buccleugh, was living in 1721. After Jackson's death the three houses came into the possession of the Bladen family and from 1794 to 1799 Number 50 was occupied by Earl Cathcart, Commander-in-Chief of the Forces in Ireland and Scotland and Ambassador to Russia. About 1803 William Miller, the publisher, moved in, and in 1812 he was succeeded by John Murray, whose publishing house, still as distinguished today as it ever was, became one of the most important meeting-places in London of men of letters of the early years of the nineteenth century.

It was John Hinde's failure in the Albemarle Ground building scheme which caused the long delay in the building of Berkeley Square. Lady Berkeley died in 1698 and for nearly forty years after this the litigation dragged on. It was alleged that as John Hinde had not fulfilled his obligation to build on the Hay Hill Farm when he bought the land, the Berkeley family were entitled to cancel the sale and in the end the land reverted to them.

It was before the first house had been built in Berkeley Square that the disastrous fire destroyed Berkeley House, which the 1st Duke of Devonshire had bought in 1697 and where his grandson, the 3rd Duke, was living. It was reported in the *Daily Journal* of 17 October 1733.

> Yesterday morning a Fire broke out in Berkeley House, belonging to his Grace the Duke of Devonshire, in Piccadilly, the Occasion of which, we hear was by the Workmen leaving a Glue-Pot amongst the Shavings in the upper Part of the House, which boiled over whilst they were at Breakfast, and set Fire to the House, which entirely consumed the inside thereof, but the Library, and great part of His Grace's admirable Collection of Pictures, Medals and other Curiosities, were saved, together with great Part of the Furniture, notwithstanding which the Loss is computed to be upwards of £30,000. We hear one Person perished in the Flames, who was assisting in taking out the Books in the Study, the Fire breaking in upon them, two of whom jump'd out of Window to save their Lives. His Royal Highness the Prince of Wales was there, with several other Persons of Distinction; and his Royal Highness was pleased to order thirty Guineas to be given to those who assisted. The Right. Hon. the Earl of Albemarle attended in person, with a party of the Guards, to secure what Goods were saved, from being plunder'd by the Mob; and all Persons unknown were search'd as they went out. Centinels were placed at each Door.

This happened only a few months after the Duke of Devonshire had held a magnificent ball at the house, during which, recorded Lady Wentworth, the guests enjoyed 'a very handsome supper, viz. at the upper end cold chicken, next to that a dish of cake, parch'd almonds, sapp biskets, next to that, a dish of tarts and cheesecakes, next to that a great custard, and next to that another dish of biskets, parch'd almonds, and preserved apricots, and next a quarter of lamb'.

It sounds an odd mixture and she does not record in which order these delicacies were consumed.

Within a few weeks of the fire William Kent was drawing up plans for the new Devonshire House and by 1736 the first building began on the rural plot of land to the north which was to become Berkeley Square. Surrounding these fields were Hanover Square and New Bond Street to the north-east, on the City of London's Conduit Mead estate, the Grosvenor estate to the north, and to the west the Curzon family's development on Great Brookfield, which they had acquired as a mortgage repayment about 1715.

IX

Berkeley Square

The 4th Lord Berkeley and his son John entered into an agreement with two carpenters, Edward Cook and Francis Hilliard, for a building lease of about six and a half acres of the Berkeley fields for the development of their estate, and the architect for many of the houses was Isaac Ware, who a few years later was to design Chesterfield House for Lord Chesterfield.

The bricks for the new building estate were made on the spot, from brick-earth dug from the Berkeley fields. This at once provoked bitter complaints and litigation from near-by residents, who protested that the smoke would spoil their furniture and more particularly their paintings. They also said that the brickmakers had brought quantities of dirt and rakings from the streets to mix with the brick clay, which made the smell from the kilns even more unpleasant.

The builders replied that they planned to make their bricks only during the months of July and August, when the plaintiffs would have moved to their country seats; and they argued that they were merely following the usual building practice, which had been employed on the Grosvenor estate and in other parts of Mayfair.

So despite the fact that one of the kilns was only two hundred and fifty yards from the Duke of Grafton's house in Old Bond Street they won the day and the brick-making continued, though what happened to the furniture and paintings in the near-by houses history does not relate.

The first houses to go up were in Bruton Street and on the east side of the square, and they were finished about 1738, those on the east side of the square being known for a time as Berkeley Row. The houses on the west side were then begun and completed about 1745. These were described as being on the west side of 'a new intended square designed to be called Berkeley Square'.

A few of these houses still survive, the most beautiful of them all being Number 44, the small Palladian house designed by William Kent for Lady Isabella Finch. Bell Finch was one of the 'black funereal Finches', whose ancestor, Sir Heneage Finch, a gloomy, melancholy man, had bought the house in Kensington which was to become Kensington Palace, and whose son and grandson, the 1st and 2nd Earls of Nottingham, were said to have been even gloomier and blacker in temperament, as well as exceptionally swarthy in complexion. Bell, who had inherited the family's dark skin, was the seventh daughter of the 7th Earl of Winchilsea and connected by marriage with the Cokes and the Burlingtons.

Kent had already rebuilt Devonshire House for the 3rd Duke of Devonshire, and at the time of his engagement by Lady Finch he was also working on Holkham Hall in Norfolk for Sir Thomas Coke who, in 1744, became the Earl of Leicester. Into Number 44 Berkeley Square, he put all his art and experience and today the house, beautifully preserved and unspoilt by the extensions which later tenants have built at the back, over the small garden, is considered one of the six most architecturally important town houses in London. Kent began work on the house in 1741 and Lady Isabella, a spinster of forty who was Lady of the Bedchamber to Princess Amelia, a sister of George II, moved in during 1744, the rate book recording that 'She comed in since Mich'.

The exterior of the house is little different from others in the square – brick with stone facings, austere, dignified and beautifully proportioned, with its round-headed doorway approached by three shallow steps, its three pedimented first-floor windows with stone balustrades, the three small windows above, which in fact are dummies, the elegant iron-link extinguishers, lamp support and railings protecting the basement. The small square entrance hall is equally plain and simple, but passing through into the inner staircase hall one is confronted with a scene of breathtaking palatial beauty, for to the right rises the magnificent grand staircase. It is of Portland stone, the lower steps gently curved, and the balustrade is of delicate iron-work. At the half landing the staircase divides into two sweeping arcs, reaching the first floor past a screen of Ionic columns, and then continuing upwards to the minstrels' gallery and a coffered dome of gilded plaster and glass.

Like Kent's staircase at Holkham, which it closely resembles, the design was derived from the basilicas of ancient Rome and gives an impression of immense, soaring height and grandeur. Horace Walpole wrote that it was 'as beautiful a piece of scenery and, considering the space, of art as can be imagined'.

As Bell Finch was unmarried there are surprisingly few main rooms. On the ground floor, at the back, beyond the staircase, is the dining-room, with a carved marble fireplace at either end, one of which was installed by Kent, the other being a later replica, and three tall, sash-windows which overlook what was once the small, square garden; but the pride of the house is the grand salon on the first floor, a double cube which stretches the entire width of the house and rises above the small dummy windows, which from the outside appear to belong to a second storey. The ceiling is coffered and painted in squares with scenes from the lives of the gods and goddesses, Jupiter in the centre presiding over them all. The pictures are in grey monochrome on alternating red and dark blue backgrounds and each is surrounded with a gilded plaster frame, the ceiling rising above a richly sculptured cornice and frieze.

The window and door frames are similarly carved and gilded and the two chimney-pieces are of inlaid white and Siena marbles, with a winged cherub in the centre of each.

The painting of the ceiling has been ascribed to Zucchi, but this is by no means certain and the basic design was undoubtedly Kent's own work.

The pale grey and gold boudoir and adjoining bedroom at the back of the house, the walls of which were once, like the salon, hung with damask, are reached by a passage behind the staircase screen and above them, not visible from the square, are two smaller bedrooms and a number of minor rooms and attics, approached from doors off the landings by narrow, twisting stairs.

The house even has a ghost, but a very amiable one, in the person of the original major-domo, who in his green livery and grey-powdered periwig is said to watch carefully over the house still, and from time to time walk with a slight limp down the staircase, sleeping at night in one of the top bedrooms. And the passage behind the Ionic screen is still known as 'Lady Bett's hiding place' for it was from here that Bell Finch's friend, Lady Betty Germaine, daughter of

Frances Stuart, Duchess of Richmond.

Grosvenor Square in 1751.

Grosvenor Square, 1789.
A Pollard print.

Hogarth's The Idle 'Prentice Executed at Tyburn, published 1747.
On the extreme right stands Tiddy Dol, the gingerbread seller.

Rowlandson cartoon of the Tyburn Turnpike, 1813.

Oxford Street from Stratford Place.

Harewood House, Hanover Square in 1798.

Hanover Square in the eighteenth century.

A view of St George's Church, Hanover Square, from Conduit Street.

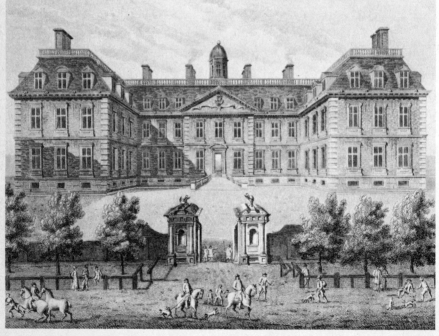

High Change in Bond Street ou La Politesse du Grande Monde.
A Gillray cartoon, 1796.

Clarendon House, erected by Edward Hyde during the reign of Charles II.

The hall and staircase
at 7 Albemarle Street, now the National Book League.

The staircase of the Clermont Club, 44 Berkeley Square.

Lansdowne House, Berkeley Square, 1808.

The company going to and returning from
His Majesty's drawing-room at Buckingham Palace, 1822.

Charles, the second Earl of Berkeley, used to peep through and report to Bell which visitors were mounting that glorious staircase, a fitting backcloth for their wide hoops and powdered periwigs, their flowered silks and damasks and delicate lace.

The tradesmen's bills for the building of the house have been preserved and amount to £6,435.17.0, but the plumber's bill, alas, was only £2.16.0.

While Lady Isabella was settling into her miniature palace, Hill Street and Charles Street were coming into existence. Hill Street was built about 1745 and Charles Street is mentioned in the rate books for the first time in 1750. The lease of the ground forming the centre of the square was granted to Cook and Hilliard in 1747 and comprised about three and a half acres, enclosed from the streets on the south and west side by 'Dwarf Walls and Wooden Rails and Pallisadoes set thereon'.

Although Berkeley Square became the height of fashion for a town residence, from the beginning various shops and business houses were established there, mainly on the north side, on land which was part of the Grosvenor estate, and at the southern end of the east side of the square.

On the north side was Hemley's coffee-house, which by 1744 was run by a vintner called Morgan Gwynn and became known as Gwynn's tavern. Francis Hilliard, the carpenter, had a house and business here and also William Bedcutt, a wax chandler, and John Madders, a woollen draper, while in the south-east corner lived Alexander Atkins, an undertaker, William Staddon, a distiller, Richard Jones, a hosier and William Lockwood, a tailor. The square also had its apothecary, Samuel Despaignol, who was, in addition, a surgeon and medical practitioner. He was one of the founders of St George's Hospital and in 1723 had undertaken, for a payment of £50 a year from the Vestry of the Parish, to 'take care of and administer Physick to the poor of the parish and act as parish apothecary'.

Kent's new Devonshire House, on the south side of the square, was plain and austere behind its high brick wall. 'It is spacious, and so are the East India Company's Warehouses, and both are equally deserving of praise', sneered Ralph. He particularly disliked the brick wall, but all the great mansions of London were protected by high walls at this time, for safety from midnight prowlers and the occasional rebellious mobs. Hardly any of these walls has survived in Mayfair but a few are still to be seen in the old parts of Hampstead.

Notwithstanding its plain exterior, the inside of Devonshire House was beautiful and, with its Tintorettos, Titians, Rembrandts and Van Dycks, housed one of the finest private collections of pictures in the country.

The 3rd Duke of Devonshire, who was responsible for the building of the house, died in 1755 and his son, the 4th Duke, who was an ardent Whig, did not long survive him, dying in 1764. He had married Lady Charlotte Boyle, the daughter and heiress of the 3rd Earl of Burlington – the architect Earl – and had already made Devonshire House a centre of the Whig party, but it was his son, the 5th Duke, and his beautiful first wife, Georgina, who made Devonshire House so famous.

Georgiana and her sister Lady Bessborough were both fervent Whigs and threw themselves whole-heartedly into the elections, which were full-blooded, riotous affairs, when the polling lasted for several weeks. In the election of May 1784, Sir Cecil Wray and his Tory supporters were making a desperate effort against Charles James Fox. The eastern portico of St Paul's Church, Covent Garden, was used for the hustings and as the days passed and the voting kept almost even, the partisans threw themselves with frenzied energy into the business of seeking out the more reluctant electors and persuading them to come to the polls. The Duchess and her sister took lodgings in Henrietta Street, to be near the scene of operations.

'These ladies being furnished with lists of outlying voters, drove in their carriages to their respective dwellings, sparing neither entreaties nor promises. In some instances even personal caresses were said to have been permitted in order to prevail on the sulky and inflexible; and there can be no doubt of common mechanics having been conveyed to the hustings by the Duchess in her own coach', wrote Sir Nathaniel Wraxall.

Fox drew ahead. The Countess of Salisbury began counter-operations on behalf of Wray, but she was too late. Fox, returned with a majority of 235, was chaired triumphantly through London to Devonshire House, where the Prince of Wales was waiting to congratulate him.

'All minor interests were swallowed up in this struggle,' wrote another observer, 'which held not only the capital, but also the nation, in suspense, while it rendered Covent Garden and its neighbourhood, during three successive weeks, a scene of outrage and even of blood.' Others wrote that 'the vulgar abuse of the candidates from the vilest rabble is not rendered endurable by either wit or good temper'. The tireless Duchess, at work by eight o'clock in the morning, canvassed in 'the most blackguard houses in Long Acre', and the story that she extracted a vote from a butcher with a kiss produced the verse:

> Condemn not, prudes, fair Devon's plan
> In giving Steel a kiss,
> In such a cause, for such a man,
> She could not do amiss.

Georgiana was the daughter of the first Earl Spencer and her marriage to the Duke of Devonshire had been arranged when she was only seventeen, but, young as she was, she soon became the centre of the powerful Whig circle which included the Prince of Wales, Fox and Sheridan. She was devoted to her sister Henrietta, Lady Bessborough, whose daughter, born in 1785, was to become the unhappy Lady Caroline Lamb. When Caroline was a child, she lived for a time at Devonshire House, but in that vast, luxurious palace she was left very much to her own devices, learning almost nothing until she was fifteen, except the intrigues of Whig politics.

It was in the early 1760s, towards the end of the Seven Years' War, that Lord Bute bought the land for Bute House from the 5th Lord Berkeley. This house with its garden occupied the whole of the south side of Berkeley Square, but as in the original sale of Berkeley House to the Devonshires it had been stipulated that no building should impair the Devonshire House view to the north, Robert Adam, whom Lord Bute chose for his architect, built Bute House facing not on to the square but eastwards, on to Hay Hill, so that the back windows of Devonshire House looked only on to its garden.

The house was magnificent and Lord Bute lavished as much care on it as Lord Clarendon had expended on Clarendon House a century earlier – and incurred the same criticism from the public. There was even a story that he planned to incarcerate twenty-seven fiddlers in a basement room, from which pipes would convey the music to other rooms in the house, where it could be turned on and off at will. The pipes were actually found, but it was an organ Lord Bute planned to install in the underground room and not a company of fiddlers.

The year 1763 was a fatal one for Lord Bute, the friend of the young George III and the Queen Dowager. It marked the end of the Seven Years' War with France and the signing of the unpopular Peace of Paris. Bute House, 'his magnificent residence', said Wraxall, 'exposed him to very malignant comments respecting the means by which he had reared so expensive a pile', for he was by no means a rich man when he began his political career. He was accused of corruption in negotiating the peace and accepting money from France. Junius attacked him bitterly and less than a year after becoming Prime Minister he resigned office. He sold Bute House, still not completed and in which he never lived, to Lord Shelbourne for £22,000, which was £3,000 less than he had already spent on it.

Lord Bute remained at his home in South Audley Street, where he lived until his death in 1793. A writer in the *Whitehall Evening Post* for 20 May 1763, referring to the famous May Day festival of the London sweeps, said:

> I happened to be going along South Audley Street about a fort-night ago while some chimney sweeps were dancing before Lord Bute's door and beating time as usual with their shovels and brushes. The motley band was decked with all their May-day finery; heads covered with enormous periwigs, clothes laced with paper, and faces marked with chalk. After the dance they asked for a contribution; this was refused, the sweeps were very angry, and so it was said, joined the opposition.

Lord Bute was an unhappy man. He had married the wealthy daughter of Lady Mary Wortley Montagu and it was to her that Lady Mary wrote many of her famous letters, in particular the one on the education of girls. However, Lady Bute took no more heed of her mother's advice than Philip Stanhope did of the advice of Lord Chesterfield, and when her youngest daughter showed signs of inheriting her grandmother's love of learning, she was sharply discouraged and accused of self-conceit and affectation.

Horace Walpole said of Lord Bute that his wealth contributed only to his unhappiness, and his domestic griefs were as poignant as his unpopularity.

> His eldest daughter, an amiable woman, was wedded to a capital brute, Sir James Lowther. His third daughter, whom the Northumberlands had obtained for their son, was discontent with her husband, and was confined by his family to the country under pretence of a gallant disposition, though the world suspected that the fall of her father had made the Duke and Duchess wish to get rid of the daughter. Lord Bute's second son, the heir of his mother's vast riches, had married ill, grew to hate his wife for having drawn him into marriage, and would not live with her ...

It was perhaps not the least of the Earl's sorrows, that though, by the interest of the Princess, Lord Bute and his Cabal retained their chief power in the secret councils, the King was not sorry to be delivered from the thraldom in which the Earl held him.

Lord Shelbourne moved into Lord Bute's great house and in 1784, when he was created the Marquess of Lansdowne, it became known as Lansdowne House. He, too, was to be accused of duplicity and in-sincerity in the years to come, but he was a highly intelligent man, with cultivated tastes, and during the 1760s created a cultured circle of friends and was the patron of several men of letters and science, including Dr Joseph Priestley, who as a young man lived under his roof for a time, while engaged in some of his philosophical and chemical researches and writing his political pamphlets.

More shops appeared in the square. In 1757 Dominicus Negri, an Italian pastrycook, had opened his shop at the sign of The Pot and Pineapple in the south-east corner, and on his trade-card he an-nounced that he made and sold 'all sorts of English, French and Italian wet and dry sweet meats, Cedrati and Bergamet Chips, and Naples divolini'. Whatever these may have been, they were highly successful and he prospered. Twenty years later he took Gunter into partnership and by 1799 Gunter was in business on his own.

Gunter had a splendid house in West Kensington, set in thirty acres of ground, close to the more modest villa which John Hunter had built for himself in 1764. Gunter Grove is the only reminder to-day of Gunter's magnificent kitchen gardens, the orchards and the famous hothouses in which he grew his pineapples and other exotic fruit for the Berkeley Square business. The delicious food he pro-vided for dinner parties and weddings, ball suppers and all manner of festivities, the turtle soup made from 'turtles killed in Honduras', the mammoth wedding-cakes and the wonderful ice-creams brought him fame throughout not only Mayfair, but the whole of London and far beyond.

In 1822 he places a notice in *The Times* which ran:

Messrs Gunter respectfully beg to inform the Nobility and those who honour them with their command that, having this day received one of their cargoes of ice by the Pistoff from Greenland seas, they are enabled to supply Ice Cream and Fruit Ices at their former prices. 7 Berkeley Square.

The success of the ices lay in the simplicity but impeccable quality of the ingredients – fresh cream, fresh fruit and sugar; and in the summer time the people of Mayfair would drive up to Gunter's and the waiters would bring the ices out to them, for them to eat in their barouches, under the shade of the plane trees.

All through the nineteenth and the early part of the present century, Gunter's were catering for Mayfair dinner parties, sometimes supplying as many as eight attendants as well as the cook, and giving almost unlimited credit to regular customers, some of whom were very slow payers. Between 1819 and 1828, despite several polite reminders to the steward at Kensington Palace, the Duke of Sussex ran up a bill for just on £700.

In the famous tea-shop were displayed the giant wedding cakes, under glass domes so vast that a small boy had to be inserted from time to time to clean them; but Queen Victoria's Jubilee cake topped them all, for it was ten feet six inches high, nine feet six inches in circumference and weighed more than a quarter of a ton.

For years tea at Gunter's was a holiday treat for hundreds of school-children. When the east side of the square was pulled down, in 1936 and 1937, the firm moved to Curzon Street, but with the gloomy fifties the cost of the sumptuous teas it provided became too high to be profitable, and sooner than lower its standards Gunter's closed the tea-shop, the catering side of the business moving to offices in Bryan-ston Street, still maintaining its standards and bemoaning the sad state of contemporary taste, which condones chips with everything, even – the ultimate degradation – with caviare.

Returning to the more discerning days of the eighteenth century, by 1767 there was a fishmonger's shop in the square and in 1773 a bookseller, Caesar Piguenit, set up business.

As late as 1753 the Tyburn stream, referred to in the Vestry Minutes as 'the Common Sewer', still ran open at the south end of the square, and in that year there was a petition to the Commissioner of Sewers, complaining that it had become a dangerous nuisance and asking for it to be covered in. This presumably was done, for two years later, when the wall and rails of the lower end of the square were in need of repair, the Vestry agreed to pay the scavenging con-tractors of the parish one penny a load 'for shooting Rubbish over the Sewer and against the Fence Wall the South end of Berkeley Square, in order to secure and support the same'.

The pavements of the square were not properly maintained, for although it was the duty of each householder to keep the pavement in front of his own house in proper repair, as often as not he did not do so, and about this time, when part of the pavement in the north-west corner of the square was 'much broken and greatly out of repair and dangerous for carriages and passengers', and the responsibility for mending it could not be pinned on to any one in particular, the Vestry, somewhat unwillingly, decided to repair it at their own cost.

The square had its full share of crimes of violence, although watchmen were appointed for duty as soon as it was built and occupied. They carried lanterns and were supplied with clappers and quarter-staves, but they were mostly old men, unfit for any other job, and all too often they were found to be asleep in their boxes when they were most needed, or else they discreetly retired at the first sign of any trouble. In November 1755 several watchmen, including one on duty in Berkeley Street, were sacked for neglecting their duty, and at the same time the Duke of Devonshire, on behalf of himself and several of the residents of the square, complained of the frequent robberies that had been committed, and asked that the public lamps, already provided, should be regularly lit.

That year, as John Goodyer of Charles Street was returning in a sedan-chair from the Cocoa Tree Club in Pall Mall, he was stopped by two footpads and one of his chair-men was shot dead. Coaches were stopped and robbed and houses were entered; and one Sunday night in 1766, Lord Shelbourne's caretaker was murdered when thieves tried to break into the house.

As with the other squares of Mayfair, it was a long time before anyone took the responsibility of laying out the garden or keeping it tidy. Berkeley Square had from the beginning been enclosed to prevent the general public entering it, but by the 1760s the wall and railings had broken down again and the enclosure itself was unkempt. By an Act of 1766, the inhabitants of the square agreed to share the cost of laying out the square properly and rebuilding the wall and railings. A body of trustees was appointed and a notice duly appeared in the *Gazetteer* and *New Daily Advertiser*, stating that 'By order of the nobility and gentry in Berkeley-Square, the workmen are to begin on Monday next, according to the plan approved of at Gwynn's tavern in Berkeley Square. There is to be a grass plot in the middle, a gravel walk round, and iron pallisadoes; but there is no statue or bason in the middle. The undertaker of the work has engaged to finish it completely for £7000.'

The plan went ahead very slowly. By the summer of 1767 it was reported that 'the grand plan for improving Berkeley-square is entirely laid aside as they could have no bason of water, the Square being ten feet lower at the South end than the north; it is now finishing with a handsome green walk next the railing, then a terras walk, and the rest laid out in a grass plot.'

However, it had already been decided that a statue of King George III would look well in the square. It was commissioned by Princess Amelia, and designed by the French sculptor, Beaupré, who worked under the direction of Joseph Wilton, the King's sculptor. It was made of lead, and it represented the King as Marcus Aurelius. It was not set up until 1772 and although the first reports on it were mildly polite, suggesting that it made a 'fine appearance' it was a dismal failure, and the following year was damned by the description which appeared in Noorthouck's *New History of London*.

> In the centre is an equestrian statue of his present majesty, erected there by the princess Amelia. This statue has a heavy look with it, owing to the stile it is dressed in; and this is armour, with something fastened over the shoulders, by a knot at the breast; from under which two naked arms appear: and however it may be dignified by the name of mantle, it is as clumsy as a piece of rug tied over the shoulders of a gypsy woman with a child in it behind. If there is no danger of the statue catching cold, it would be a kindness to take away this ill judged piece of drapery, which only obscures the proportions of the figure it covers.

Yet it was for practical reasons, rather than artistic ones, that in 1827 the statue had to be removed, for the rider was proving too heavy for his mount, and the lead being greatly affected by changes in the weather, 'the legs of the horse were soon bending in a sort of wrinkle frequently repeated'. With the poor beast sagging ominously at the knees the statue was removed, and in later years the 3rd Marquess of Lansdowne presented to the square the charming little marble statue of the girl pouring water from a vase which stands there today, while late in the 1780s Edward Bouverie, who was living at Number 13 in the square, had planted the beautiful plane trees which still flourish, nearly two hundred years later.

In 1779 Horace Walpole came to live on the east side of the square, at Number 11, only a few doors away from Gunter's, which, when the houses were numbered, became Number 7. Number 11 had been built in 1741 for Sir Cecil Bishop, and on his death Walpole, who had wanted a house in the square for some time, bought it. He was already in his sixties and suffering from gout. The villa at Strawberry Hill he found too damp during the winter and the lease of his father's house in Arlington Street, where he had been living, had expired. So in 1779 he was writing to the Countess of Ossory:

> I came to town this morning to take possession of (my house) in Berkeley Square, and am as well pleased with my new habitation as I can be with anything at present. Lady Shelbourne's being Queen of the palace over against me (Lansdowne House) has improved the view since I bought the house, and I trust will make your ladyship not so shy as you were in Arlington Street.

Eighteen years later, not long before his death in his eightieth year, he was writing in a sadly different tone:

> I scarce go out of my own house, and then only to two or three very private places, where I see nobody that really knows anything, and what I learn comes from newspapers that collect intelligence from coffee-houses; consequently what I neither believe nor report. At home I see only a few charitable elders, except about four-score nephews and nieces of various ages, who are each brought to me about once a year, to stare at me as the Methusalem of the family, and they can only speak of their own contemporaries, which interest me no more than if they talked of their dolls or bats and balls.

The house remained in the Walpole family for just on half a century, passing to his niece, Lady Waldegrave, on his death, not long after he had succeeded to the Earldom of Orford. But the 4th Lord Orford lost it one night in 1827, while playing cards with Henry Baring. He made the house his last stake, and Henry Baring won it. So with deep regret, Lord and Lady Orford had to move out and Henry Baring moved in.

At Number 12, Walpole's neighbours were the Keppel family. The house had originally been built in 1740 for 'Foul Weather Jack', Admiral Sir John Norris, but by 1767 the 3rd Earl of Albemarle moved in, and his brother, Admiral Keppel, also lived there when he was in London. In 1779 he was court-martialled for his share in the expedition to Havana, and when he was acquitted he was acclaimed a hero and showered with civic honours, while the enthusiastic crowds broke any windows which had not been illuminated in his honour.

Three years later there were similar demonstrations for Lord Romney, whom the crowds considered had not been sufficiently appreciated by the Government for his victories over the French.

'He paraded through the whole town to his own house at this end (in Hill Street) with a rabble at his heels breaking windows for not being illuminated, for which no soul was prepared', wrote Horace Walpole to Horace Mann. 'My servants went out and begged these Romans to give them time to light up candles, but to no purpose and were near having their brains dashed out.' So poor Walpole could do nothing but sit in an upstairs room, listening to his windows being broken by a volley of stones.

From 1765 to 1785 Number 13 was the home of Edward Bouverie, who planted the plane trees, and at Number 16 lived Anne Egerton, second cousin of the last Lord Berkeley of Stratton, to whom he had left for life the Berkeley estate in Mayfair – Berkeley Square, Charles Street, Hill Street, Bruton Street, John Street, Berkeley Street and Stratton Street, producing between them an income of £15,000 a year, which made her one of the richest women in England. She and her widowed mother had lived with Lord Berkeley and run his household when his marriage broke up, and when the mother died, Anne, by then thirty-one, continued to live with Lord Berkeley, who was then sixty-eight and childless. She was thirty-nine when he died and for the next thirty years she lived alone in Berkeley Square, never marrying but enjoying the security of her wealth and the house in the square which she loved.

At Number 20, on the corner of the north side of Bruton Street, Colley Cibber, one of the earliest residents of the square, was living from 1741 until his death in 1757, producing a child and a play each year, with remarkable regularity.

'It may be observed that my muse and my spouse were equally prolific, that the one was seldom a mother of a child but in the same year the other made me the father of a play,' he wrote. 'I think we had a dozen of each between us, of both of which kinds some died in infancy, and near an equal number of each were alive when I quitted the theatre.'

Next door to him, at Number 21, lived Lady Anne Barnard, the author of the words of Auld Robin Gray, and her husband, but early in the nineteenth century these two houses were rebuilt and made into one.

Number 25, in the north-east corner of the square, was for a long time the site of Thomas's Hotel, which opened around 1798. The hotel was often mentioned in the Mayfair annals of this time. When the Duke of Wellington called on Mrs Porter of Berkeley Street, to ask her to arrange a meeting for him with Harriette Wilson, the courtesan who was born in Carrington Street in 1786, he said: 'If you have anything like good news to communicate, address a line to Thomas's Hotel, Berkeley Square.' The rest of the houses along the north side, until well into the nineteenth century, were small shops and business premises. These were then replaced by four large houses, the most important of which was the London home of the 7th Duke of Marlborough for a time, but they have all now disappeared.

It was the west side of the square which was considered the most exclusive. As late as 1920 there were houses here which had been inhabited by only two, and occasionally only one family, since they were built in the eighteenth century.

Number 34 was the last of Lady Mary Coke's houses and was in her possession when she died in 1811. Earlier she had rented Number 43 and she also lived at one time in a small house in Hill Street.

Her name crops up over and over again in the records of Mayfair. She was born in 1727 but lived on until 1811 and spent many of these years in and around Berkeley Square. She was a Campbell, the fifth daughter of the Duke of Argyll, and was married against her will to Viscount Coke, the only son of the Earl of Leicester, in 1747. He was an extravagant, dissipated young man, who spent most of the night gambling and seldom arrived home before eight o'clock in the morning. From the outset the marriage was unhappy and Lady Mary was herself extremely vain and demanding. She was always quarrelling with her husband, and also with her father-in-law, who did his best to patch things up and was for ever paying his son's debts.

Despite the efforts of the Earl to keep them together, they separated after two years. 'Lady Mary', said Walpole, made her husband 'a declaration in form that she hated him; that she always did and that she always will.' Three years later Lord Coke died and Lady Mary, at the age of twenty-six, found herself free and independent, with an income of £2,500 a year. She never married again, though she fancied herself in love with the Duke of York for a time.

Unlike her neighbour, Bell Finch, Lady Mary had an exceptionally white skin, and in Lady Louisa Stuart's introduction to Lady Mary's *Letters and Journals*, she says that her beauty was by 'some allowed, some denied it; the dissenters declaring her neither more nor less than a white cat – a creature to which her dead whiteness of skin, unshaded by eyebrows, and the fierceness of her eyes, did give her a great resemblance ... She had the reputation of cleverness when young, and, in spite of all her absurdity, could not be called a silly woman; but she was so invincibly wrong-headed – her understanding lay smothered under so much pride, self-conceit, prejudice, obstinacy, and violence of temper, that you knew not where to look for it, and seldom indeed did you catch such a distinct view of it as certified its existence.'

Number 36, which from 1744 to 1761 was occupied by Lady Frances Williams, ultimately became for a few years the home of Alfred Harmsworth. Number 37, which in the early years of the nineteenth century was to be incorporated with Number 38 by Lord Jersey, was for a few months, in 1754–5, the home of the 2nd Duke of Chandos. Mrs Delaney described him and his first wife as the ugliest couple in England, and when the Duchess died he married his mistress at Keith's Chapel. She was Anne Jefferies, once the wife of an ostler at the Pelican Inn at Newbury, a famous and expensive posting-house on the way to Bath. The ostler either became tired of her or was in dire need of some ready cash, so he put a halter round her neck and sold her in the open market to the highest bidder, which seems the most unorthodox way imaginable of becoming a duchess.

The first owner of Number 38 was the 3rd Duke of Manchester, but in 1768 it came into the possession of Robert Child, the banker. Fourteen years later, when his daughter was only seventeen, she eloped one May morning with the young Lord Westmorland, of whom her father apparently did not approve, since he had not openly declared himself. According to all the rules of romantic elopement, her maid had a hackney coach all ready for her, hidden round the nearest corner, which took her to the spot where Lord Westmorland was waiting for her in a post-chaise. When her father discovered her escape he guessed where she had gone and immediately set off in hot pursuit in a second post-chaise, with a mounted servant riding ahead. The man caught up with them near Rokeby, in Yorkshire, but the young woman was no faint-hearted miss. As she saw him gaining on her she cried to her lover: 'Shoot, my Lord. Shoot!', whereupon young Lord Westmorland shot the servant's horse from under him and pressed on to Gretna Green.

Her father, seeing his servant's horse fall dead on the road, gave up the chase after that. The marriage took place, but he vowed that no Westmorland should ever be his heir. He left his fortune to the first daughter of the marriage, provided she took the name of Child, with the Christian name of Sarah. Three months later, when he was only forty-three, he died from the shock of the elopement, and his head-strong daughter did not survive him for long, for she died in Dublin, where her husband was Lord Lieutenant, when she was only twenty-eight.

Her daughter Sarah married Lord Villiers, who became the Earl of Jersey. Some records say that, like her mother, she eloped to Gretna Green one fine May morning, and others that she was married decorously at Number 38 Berkeley Square. She certainly spent the rest of her life according to the conventions of her class, for she became one of the six patronesses of Almack's, 'the Ladies' Club of both sexes', as Walpole described it.

During the Regency there was no royal lady presiding over the Court and Almack's, with its magnificent ballroom, became almost a substitute. It was so exclusive that the prestige of being admitted was as socially acceptable as presentation at Court; and it was here that the Duke of Wellington, arriving in black trousers, was refused admission because he was not wearing the knee-breeches which the management of Lady patronesses had decreed was the correct dress for gentlemen.

Lady Jersey died at Number 38 Berkeley Square, in 1867, when she was eighty-one, and four years later, when her last surviving son died, the house was taken by the Earl of Londesborough, and then, in 1888, by Lord Rosebery, who rebuilt the front of the house in red sandstone and made many alterations inside, including the enlargement of Lady Jersey's ballroom.

Number 39 was built for the 3rd Duke of Ancaster, and his second wife, Mary Panton, until she died in 1793, was mistress of the robes to Queen Charlotte, from the time of the Queen's marriage in 1761.

Number 40 had been the residence of the Duke of Newcastle during the Napoleonic Wars and afterwards was rebuilt by William Salting.

Number 41, at the corner of Hill Street, was the London home of the unfortunate Admiral Byng from 1744 until he was court-martialled and shot in 1756, for his retreat from the French, during the French capture of Port Mahon in Minorca. Yet there were many witnesses to assert that he had acted wisely at the time and the sentence deeply shocked his friends and sympathisers, Horace Walpole warmly declaring that he was 'most unjustly and wickedly put to death', a man who was 'marked for sacrifice by a set of Ministers, who meant to divert on him the vengeance of a betrayed and enraged nation'.

Soon after this appalling incident the house was let to Lady Raymond, and in February 1762, Horace Walpole was writing to George Montagu:

'We had a tempest of wind and snow for two hours beyond

anything I remember. Lady Raymond's house in Berkeley Square is totally unroofed; and Lord Robert Bertie, who is going to marry her, may descend into it like a Jupiter Pluvius.' Lord Robert had served in the *Ramillies* with Admiral Byng and was one of the defence witnesses at his trial.

Number 42, on the opposite corner of Hill Street, was built for Margaret, Countess of Coningsby and had a succession of titled and noble tenants, while at Number 43 Lady Blandford was living from 1741 to 1779. One of her frequent visitors was Lady Mary Coke who, despite her protestations to the contrary, could be very awkward at times. In June 1767 Lady Mary wrote, after dining with Lady Blandford:

> I never saw her have a worse dinner; a great round of boiled beef, little mutton pyes, beans and bacon, mackerel without fennel sauce. The second course, a neck of lamb, a gooseberry pye, and two other little things, not meat. You know I am not difficult, and yet I was at a loss to make my dinner. Boiled beef is a good thing, but a dish I seldom eat, and little mutton pyes are too savory for me; beans I hate, and mackerel without fennel sauce I can't eat . . .

In 1764 Walpole was describing a 'funeral loo' party he attended at Lady Isabella Finch's house, the beautiful Number 44.

By the end of the party, William Pulteney, Earl of Bath, who had been a widower for six years, owed her half a crown. He sent it the following morning, with the gallant sally that he wished he could give her a crown, whereupon Isabella, who would dearly have liked to marry him, promptly replied that though he could not give her a crown, she was perfectly willing to accept a coronet. But he did not rise to the bait, nor the even more direct one offered by Anne Pitt, the sister of Lord Chatham who, more than a little mad, besought her friends, though all in vain, to help her bring about the match.

Anne Pitt grew quite desperate about the Earl.

'My Lord Bath is here, very lively, but I have not seen him, which I am very sorry for, because I want to offer myself to him,' she wrote to Lady Suffolk. 'I am quite in earnest and have set my heart upon it, so I beg seriously you will carry it in your mind, and think if you could find any way to help me. Do not you think Lady Betty (Germaine) and Lord and Lady Vere would be ready to help me if they knew how willing I am? But I leave all this to your discretion, and repeat seriously that I am quite in earnest.'

In 1773, after the death of Lady Isabella Finch, Lord Clermont

bought Number 44. Lady Clermont was a friend of Marie Antoinette and also of Queen Charlotte, and both she and Lord Clermont,
a handsome, sporting Irishman, were aristocrats of the old school,
having great dignity and impeccable manners. They were renowned
for their exquisite dinners and were said to have the most skilled chef
in London and to serve the finest wines. They entertained here many
members of the French aristocracy and paid frequent visits to the
French Court at Versailles. Both the Prince of Wales and Mrs Fitzherbert often dined with them, sometimes together, sometimes
singly, and, according to Wraxall, the Prince 'enjoyed the privilege
of sending at his pleasure to Lord Clermont, of commanding a dinner
and naming the persons to be invited of both sexes – a permission of
which his royal highness often availed himself'.

Lady Clermont engaged Henry Holland to redecorate Bell Finch's
bedroom in the French manner, in white and gold, and it was in this
house that Georgiana, the Duchess of Devonshire, took refuge
during the Gordon riots of 1780, when the mob rampaged through
London, burning and looting and opening up the prisons. Devonshire House seemed a likely target and was not easy to defend, despite its protecting wall, so for several nights she slept on a couch in
Lady Clermont's salon.

There were several owners of Number 44 after the death of the
Clermonts, including the 4th Marquis of Bath, and the last family to
occupy it were the Clarks, who were here for three generations,
the last to use it as a private residence being Charles Damer Clark.

In 1959 it was bought by John Aspinall and became the Clermont
Club. John Fowler and Philip Jebb restored the old house, and the
extensions at the back, including the Gothic dining-room, have
changed nothing of the atmosphere of the original house.

Members play roulette and backgammon, blackjack and craps, in
the room where Lady Isabella entertained the Mayfair nobility of the
eighteenth century, and their bar is the alcove opposite the foot of
the grand staircase where her footmen sat to await her summons.

Next door, at Number 45, Lord Clive had been living when the
Clermonts first moved into Number 44. He took the house in 1760,
having been forced to cut short his third visit to India through ill-
health. Though he had laid the foundation of the British Empire in
India, he was later accused of corruption for accepting prize-money
and rewards from some of the Indian princes, without the consent of
the British Government. Few would now consider him guilty, for he
was only following the custom of the time, and during the enquiry,

which took place in 1773, he exclaimed angrily: 'By God, Mr Chairman at this moment I stand astounded at my own moderation,' for except perhaps in his early, inexperienced days in India, Clive had consistently taken a firm stand against the corruption of which he stood accused.

He was censured for abusing his powers and setting an evil example, but his 'great and meritorious services to the state' were fully recognised.

Clive was a sick man, often suffering agony from an internal complaint and taking laudanum to ease the pain. In November 1774, while still only forty-eight years old, his physical condition deteriorated and he had continuing paroxysms of pain, for which he took increasingly large doses of laudanum, and on the 22nd came the news of his death.

'The nation had another great loss last night,' wrote Walpole. 'Lord Clive went off suddenly. He had been sent for to town by some of his Indian friends – and died. Lord H. has just been here, and told me *the manner* of Lord Clive's death. Whatever had happened it had flung him into convulsions, to which he was very subject. Dr Fotherhill gave him, as he had done on like occasions, a dose of laudanum, but the pain was so violent that he asked for a second dose. Dr Fothergill said "if he took another, he would be dead in an hour". The moment Fothergill was gone, he swallowed another, for another, it seems, stood by him, and he is dead.'

Dr Johnson said sententiously that Clive was a man who had 'acquired his fortune by such crimes that his consciousness of this impelled him to cut his own throat, because he was weary of still life, little things being not sufficient to move his great mind', but a more realistic interpretation of the tragedy is that he was driven to suicide 'by the ingratitude and persecution of his country', and Macaulay wrote of his 'great mind, ruined by the weariness of satiety, by the pangs of wounded honour, by fatal diseases, and more fatal remedies'.

The Earls of Powis, the descendants of Lord Clive, lived on at Number 45 Berkeley Square, until the 4th Earl sold the house in 1937, and up till this time the family maintained the old custom of affixing the name of the occupier of the house to the front door, engraved on a small brass plate. Until the custom of numbering houses was introduced in 1762 this was the usual way of identifying them, but the brass plate on Number 45 was thought to have been one of the last in use on a London private house.

It is a beautiful Palladian house, designed in all probability by Henry Flitcroft for the first occupier, William Kerr, Earl of Ancrum, who took up residence there in 1750.

By the time Clive moved in he was extremely wealthy and writing to his wife from India in 1764 he said:

'I would have the Grand Flight of Rooms furnished in the richest and most elegant manner, a man of taste and judgement should be consulted and if any additional rooms can be built without spoiling or darkening the others you have my consent for erecting them. I do empower you to make the house at Berkeley Square as fine and convenient as you please immediately.'

Throughout the years it has been beautifully preserved and much remains as Clive knew it, including the wrought-iron lantern arch and link extinguishers before the entrance, the black and white tiled hall, the splendid staircase with its lyre-shaped wrought-iron balusters, the balustraded galleries on the second and third floors, the first-floor salon, with its high ceiling decorated with panels of flowers picked out in gold leaf and its marble mantelpiece, the Adam room, its walls lined with green damask, which leads from it, and Lady Clive's boudoir behind – the 'India paper drawing room'.

For many years the house has been the headquarters of Moral Re-Armament but at the moment of writing, in the spring of 1975, it is on the market for sale.

At Number 46 between 1745 and 1835 lived four successive Earls of Darnley and for the next four or five generations it belonged to the Mildmay family, while at Number 47 the young William Pitt, in December 1783, was staying with his brother John, the 2nd Earl of Chatham, when at the age of twenty-four he was asked to form his ministry. So it was here in Berkeley Square that he spent that Christmas, planning his first Cabinet.

From 1745 Number 48 had been the home of Lord Rochford, but in 1825 the 2nd Earl Grey was living there. In 1831 he let the house to Lord Brougham for three years, and when he wanted to return his agent found that the house was in a deplorable condition. The agent told Haydon, who reported it all in his *Table Talk*, that he had never seen a house left in a dirtier state.

'The bedrooms were simply unendurable; and hidden in the handsome satin curtains in the drawing-room he found a kitchen candlestick, and black-lead for the grates. The furniture was nearly all ruined by ill-usage and neglect, and although Lord Grey gave Brougham two months in excess of his term to move out, it was next to impossible to get him out, and when he went, instead of paying up the arbitrated sum – for he had insisted on "arbitration" as to damages – he sent a cheque short of £15. The cheque was returned, and in three days the full amount was sent.'

Brougham, remarked Haydon, 'was certainly wanting in delicate feeling in all the common transactions of life'.

After Lord Grey's death his widow sold the house and in 1867 it became the London home of the Thynne family of Longleat, Marquesses of Bath.

While Lord Rochford was living at Number 48 his brother Richard Nassau and his wife, the widowed Elizabeth, Duchess of Hamilton and Brandon, came to live next door at Number 49. This is a particularly fine example of an eighteenth-century terrace house, built, like all the others in the square, according to the accepted standards of good taste, from which it would have been considered vulgar to diverge. It became the home of Dean Duncombe, the Dean of York, and in 1902 William Salting moved here from Number 40. Throughout the years it was preserved with discriminating care and in the summer of 1974 the Bowater Corporation announced that it had sub-let the whole 14,600 square feet of its leasehold property at Number 49 Berkeley Square 'to an unnamed banking group. The rent has not been disclosed but earlier this year a figure of around £230,000 was being asked. Refurbished by Compass Securities some eighteen months ago, the property has been redecorated in the style of the 18th century.'

Once upon a time the house next door, Number 50, was the square's haunted house. Its first occupier, from 1745 to 1749, was General Frampton. In 1807 George Canning was living there and from 1841 to 1859 the house was taken by the Honourable Miss Elizabeth Curzon. It was then empty for a time and like many an empty house, developed an air of gloom and mystery.

There are many versions of what happened next, but Ralph Nevill, in his book *Romantic London*, tells what must surely be the true story, for he was a relative of one of the families concerned in the mystery.

Lady Mary Nevill, daughter of the 2nd Earl of Abergavenny, married a Mr Myers of whom her family did not approve, and for years the two families did not speak to each other. Their son, when he was about to be married, acquired Number 50 at a bargain price, as there were already rumours that it was haunted. Strange noises had been heard coming from it. Was it rats running among the bell-ropes? The wind rustling through the empty rooms and moaning down the chimneys? Or the lamentations of an uneasy ghost? The house had been empty for some time and the stories lost nothing in the telling. A young maidservant had seen something terrible in one of the bedrooms and gone mad. A young man who had decided to try and probe the mystery was found dead in a locked room.

All this the young Mr Myers ignored and set about preparing the house for his bride, ordering furniture, carpets and china and installing two maidservants. But a few days before the wedding the young woman jilted him and married someone else.

He was so shocked and heartbroken that he never left the house again and gradually went mad. For twenty years everything was left as it had been on the day he received the news – china and glass still in their crates, the carpets in rolls, as they had left the warehouse, the furniture unpacked.

Coal and provisions were regularly delivered to the house, but the servants seemed to have been infected with their master's gloom and reticence and would tell nothing. As the unfortunate young man never went outside the door, people refused to believe he was there at all. By day the house was silent but at night time he would sometimes wander through the cheerless rooms which each year grew shabbier and dirtier, and the fitful light of his candle, which could sometimes be seen from outside in the square, gave rise to the story that the house was inhabited by a gang of counterfeit coiners who had broken in through an underground passage from the mews at the back and established themselves in the basement.

The only contact he had with the outside world was an occasional visit from his sister, his only friend. When he died he left her everything but the house remained empty, squalid and decaying, until her death. Then in 1880 the Earl of Selkirk, undaunted by its grim story, took it. It was completely restored and redecorated and the ghosts retreated. Today the house is occupied by Maggs Bros, the booksellers, but the legend that it is still haunted dies very hard.

X

Round and About

In the streets surrounding Berkeley Square, which were built about the same time as the houses in the square, as part of the Berkeley estate development, the first residents were for the most part as aristocratic and wealthy as the highly privileged residents of the square.

In Bruton Street, leading from Bond Street to the north-east side of the square, one of the earliest residents was the 2nd Duke of Argyll, the 'Great' duke, who had been William III's ambassador to Spain and had taken part in the suppression of the first Jacobite rebellion in 1715.

> Yes! on the great Argyll I often wait
> At charming Sudbrooke or in Bruton Street

wrote Sir Charles Hanbury Williams.

In 1786 the brilliant but erratic Richard Sheridan was living there. Thirteen years earlier, when he was only twenty-two, he had married Elizabeth Linley, and the young couple came from Bath to settle in London. In 1775 his first comedy, *The Rivals*, was produced at Covent Garden, and the following year, with the help of his father-in-law, he had bought the patent of Drury Lane from David Garrick, who was growing old and tired, but the money was largely raised on mortgage, and Sheridan was for ever in debt, for he always lived far above his means.

The Rivals and *The School for Scandal* were both outstanding successes, but Sheridan had no head for business, and the financial affairs of the theatre were hopelessly mismanaged. Garrick came back from time to time, to help as much as he could, but only three years later he died. Sheridan struggled on. He introduced the little clown, Jo Grimaldi, at his Christmas pantomimes. Robert Baddeley was one of his star actors, and then, in 1782, came the great Sarah Siddons. She had not been a success when she had appeared at the Lane a few years earlier, but after gaining experience in the provinces she now returned to her years of triumph. By this time Sheridan had been elected to Parliament for Stafford and had become Under-Secretary for Foreign Affairs under Rockingham; and in 1783 he became Secretary to the Treasury in the Coalition.

At the Lane, Sarah Siddons' brother, John Kemble, arrived. Although he had not the outstanding talent of his sister, he was a dignified, intelligent actor and soon became Sheridan's leading man and manager. While Sheridan was stirring the House with his powerful speeches and exuberant oratory, particularly during the long-drawn-out trial of Warren Hastings, which lasted from 1787 to 1794, John Kemble was attempting to restore a certain amount of order from the financial chaos of Drury Lane.

With the cheerful carelessness of the Irish, Sheridan's financial troubles did not seem to affect his zest for either the theatre or his partisanship in the political problems of the day – the war with America, the Irish union and the liberty of the Press; and in an age of corruption, he was always regarded as incorruptible – a man of absolute integrity and honour, courageous, independent and essentially fair-minded. He was generous and, unlike so many politicians, free from malice, although brilliant in sharp repartee. 'The right honourable gentleman is indebted to his memory for his jests and to his imagination for his facts', he retorted to an opponent one day in the House of Commons.

While he was living in Bruton Street he was desperately short of money, and Wraxall tells the story of the important political dinner party he gave there, at a time when the duns were pressing him so hard that he dare not allow the front door to be opened. All his plate was in pawn as well as his books, but on the day of the party the pawnbroker promised to lend him back his plate and Becket, the bookseller in Pall Mall, agreed to fill his empty bookcases with rare and precious volumes, provided two of his men were present to remove them immediately after the party. He went even farther, and agreed that these two henchmen should dress themselves in livery and wait at table.

The food and drink were smuggled past the duns by being let down through the area railings. Preparations went ahead and the distinguished Whigs arrived for the party. They were first shown into the library, to admire the magnificent display of books. The dinner was almost ready to serve. The table in the dining-room was prepared – complete except for some vital pieces of equipment. The pawnbroker had not sent back the spoons and forks. A messenger was hastily sent round to plead with him. Sheridan improvised, drawing the guests into an extended literary discussion on the borrowed books. The cook fumed and fretted. When all seemed lost, the pawnbroker's heart was at last melted and he sent round the spoons and forks. There was no time to clean them. They were thrown on to the table, dinner was announced and the party turned out a huge success.

Lord Brougham also lived in Bruton Street for a time, when he was Lord Chancellor, but whether or not the house was as dirty as his home in Berkeley Square no one has ever recorded.

Probably the largest house in the street was Number 17, with its impressive Palladian front, vaulted entrance-hall and rococo ceilings. It was one of the houses designed by Isaac Ware, and it became the town mansion of the Earl and Countess of Strathmore, the London home of the Queen Mother and the birthplace of Queen Elizabeth; and it was demolished only in 1937, when most of the east side of Berkeley Square was pulled down, to make way for the large block of flats – Berkeley Square House.

Bruton Place, to the north of Bruton Street and parallel with it, was originally Bruton Mews, occupied by coach-houses and stables.

To the west of the square, Hill Street was first rated in 1745 and Charles Street in 1750, while Hays Mews, like Bruton Mews, was used for the accommodation of coaches, horses, and the servants who looked after them. Farm Street, to the north of Hill Street, and John Street – now Chesterfield Hill – running from north to south and crossing all four streets to the west, were built about 1753.

There were never any shops in Hill Street or Charles Street, and from the beginning the large, elegant houses were occupied by people of wealth and high social standing.

The little pub on the corner of Hays Mews and Charles Street, The Running Footman, is a relic of these eighteenth-century days, when it was frequented by the servants who attended the sedan-chairs and private coaches. Many of the streets of Mayfair, as else-where in London, were in total darkness after nightfall and even where they were lighted, the glimmer of the oil and cotton lamps was very dim. Lamps had to be trimmed two or three times during the night, and there were many dark and dangerous corners left, where footpads lurked.

Sedan-chairs had been introduced to London from France quite early in the seventeenth century, but at first they were not popular. There was a 'loathing that men should be brought to as servile a condition as Horses'; but by Queen Anne's time this commendable objection had been satisfactorily overcome, for the prospect of personal comfort can suppress the stirrings of many a qualm of social conscience, and throughout a greater part of the eighteenth century sedan-chairs were fashionable.

The chair-men had their stands throughout the West End and people who possessed their own private chairs employed 'running footmen' who ran ahead through the dark streets, bearing aloft flaring flambeaux to light the way. The iron cones in which they extinguished them at their journey's end are still to be seen over a few London Georgian doorways, for the danger of fire was ever a hazard, particularly in terraced town houses, and it was essential that the torches should be properly controlled.

The sign of The Running Footman, in Charles Street, bearing the declaration 'I Am The Only Running Footman' shows a liveried young man running, a feather in his cap and carrying a long cane surmounted by a silver ball. He was on daytime duty, for these men were also employed to run in front of a carriage, sometimes for considerable distances, to add prestige to the traveller; and they were also used to carry messages.

A good running footman would achieve about seven miles an hour, or even more if he were put on his mettle, and during the eighteenth century, when wagers were laid on anything that could move, running footmen were often run against a horse and carriage. Ralph Nevill, in his *Romantic London*, records that some time before 1770 the Duke of Marlborough wagered a running footman against his own phaeton and four, from London to Windsor. The Duke won by a short head but the footman died of exhaustion.

For long distances they held a supply of hard-boiled eggs and white wine in the silver ball at the top of their cane, to keep them going, which sounds an odd mixture but was no doubt welcome from time to time.

Sometimes they disencumbered themselves of their breeches and wore nothing but a short tunic held down by a heavy gold fringe, worn under a short jockey jacket.

In London Old Q, the 4th Duke of Queensberry, who lived in his mansion in Piccadilly from 1768 until his death in 1811, was the last of the aristocrats to use a running footman, and he would time an applicant for the job from his balcony, as the young man showed his paces running up and down Piccadilly.

One of the most famous residents of Charles Street during the eighteenth century was Beau Brummell, during his palmier days. He lived at Number 44, where he entertained generously and gave exquisite dinner parties. And it was in Hill Street that Mrs Elizabeth Montagu entertained the distinguished circle of friends who came to be known as the Blue Stockings.

Born in Yorkshire in 1720, Elizabeth had been given a far better education than most wealthy girls of her time. Her mother had attended Mrs Makin's famous school and encouraged her large family in their pursuit of learning. The children lived in a cultured and enlightened household and Elizabeth also spent many months of her childhood at her learned grandfather's home at Cambridge, where she met scholars, philosophers, men of letters and travellers, and was encouraged to listen to their conversation and discussions, understanding what she could and helped by her kindly grandfather to study further such matters as especially interested her. She had a good brain, a lively, critical mind and a retentive memory. She was a voracious reader but as a girl she was also happy to follow the usual social round of balls, parties and theatre-going.

When she was twenty-two she married Edward Montagu, who was some years older. They were fortunate, for unlike so many marriages of the time, this was a love-match and a union of intellectual interests. Edward Montagu had great wealth from the coal-mines he owned in the north of England, but he was also a scholar and an eminent mathematician.

The eighteenth century is full of quite bewildering paradoxes and the bridal pair, after a few days in London, set off for their honeymoon tour of the Montagu estates in Yorkshire accompanied, according to the best traditions of polite society, by Elizabeth's sister, for it would have been considered quite unseemly for the bride, not after all so very young, to have spent her honeymoon alone with her husband, unchaperoned.

The early years of Elizabeth Montagu's married life were saddened by the death of her infant son, and she never had any more children, but otherwise her marriage remained singularly happy, and although Edward was always of a quiet and more retiring disposition than his wife, they took their place in the exclusive circle of Mayfair society and its social round. These gaieties were interrupted for a time, during the '45 rebellion, and Edward Montagu was one of the Hanoverian loyalists who went north to raise and equip an army in Yorkshire for George II.

'I have not heard of any assemblies since I came to town', wrote Mrs Montagu that autumn, 'and indeed, I think people frighten each other so much when they meet, that there is little pleasure arising from society.' But by the following year, life was back to normal in Mayfair.

The Montagus had several homes and at one time lived in Dover Street, but in 1748 they moved into their town house in Hill Street, dividing their time mostly between Hill Street and their Berkshire home at Sandleford near Newbury, with trips to their Yorkshire estates and to Bath and Tunbridge Wells in between times. Elizabeth was to keep Hill Street for her London home for the next thirty years, staying on there after her husband's death in 1775 until in 1781 she moved to her vast mansion in Portman Square, where she remained until her death in 1800.

It is difficult to identify the house in Hill Street, as the houses were not numbered until after she moved, and during the nineteenth century they were re-numbered. In the rate book for 1780 she paid £100 rent and £11.5.0 for the poor and highways rate, about the same as her neighbours, who included Lady Leicester, Lord Willoughby de Broke, the Bishop of Oxford, Lord Galway, the Earl of Sefton, Lord Mountstuart and Lord Poulett.

When they moved into Hill Street in 1748 it was not paved and the roadway was rutted and muddy. The London crowds still came each month to watch the Tyburn hangings and often enough they must have swarmed down Tyburn Lane to visit the fair and the market in May Fair. This was the year that Lord Chesterfield was preparing to move from Grosvenor Square to his new Chesterfield House close by and he was well aware of the potential dangers in this outlying corner of London.

'As my new house is situated among a parcel of thieves and murderers, I shall have occasion for a house-dog', he wrote to Mr Dayrolles in June 1748.

Despite its dangerous approach, the inside of Mrs Montagu's

house was elegant, if surprising, for she favoured the growing taste for Chinese decoration.

'Sick of Grecian elegance and symmetry, or Gothic grandeur and magnificence,' she wrote, 'we must all seek the barbarous gaudy *goût* of the Chinese; and fat-headed pagods and shaking mandarins bear the prize from the finest works of antiquity; and Apollo and Venus must give way to a fat idol with a sconce on his head! You will wonder I should condemn the taste I have complied with, but in trifles I shall always conform to the fashion.'

On Christmas Eve, 1752, she was writing from Hill Street:

'I proposed answering my dear Mrs Boscawen's letter yesterday, but the Chinese room was filled by a succession of people from eleven in the morning till eleven at night.'

A few weeks later, already wearying of many aspects of Mayfair's social life, she described running 'from house to house, getting the cold scraps of visting conversation, served up with the indelicacy and indifference of an ordinary, at which no power of the mind does honours; the particular taste of each guest is not consulted, the solid part of the entertainment is too gross for a delicate taste, and the lighter fare insipid. Indeed, I do not love fine ladies . . .'

Yet she did not relax her social duties and her letters describing it all give a fascinating picture of the life of the close-knit Mayfair circle. In November 1754, the day after her arrival in Hill Street from the country, she wrote:

'In my town character, I made fifteen visits last night. I should not so suddenly have assumed my great hoop, if I had not desired to pay the earliest respects to Lady Hester Pitt, who is something far beyond a merely fine lady.'

By the following year, however, she decided that she could no longer bear the superficiality and emptiness of the monotonous social round, the malicious gossip, the mindless conversation, and in particular the endless card parties, while party politics she disliked, considering that they were 'pursued for the benefit of individuals, not for the good of the country'.

The moment of decision came, she said, one evening in 1755, when she was about to dress for Lady Townshend's ball. A new 'pink silver negligée' lay ready for her to put on, but she suddenly felt that nothing would induce her to bother to go. Instead she spent a peaceful evening by herself, reading.

She and her husband did not, by any means, stop entertaining, but she became more selective in the people she invited to Hill Street and in the people whose friendship she cultivated. She decided to give parties at which the guests could make a real contribution to the enjoyment, by their conversation, wit and knowledge.

She met Benjamin Stillingfleet, the philosopher and brilliant conversationalist, who became one of the earliest visitors to her literary parties in Hill Street. His dress was sober but he had been noticed to wear blue stockings, and at one party, when he was not present, somebody remarked that 'we can do nothing without the blue stockings'. The remark amused them and after that the little group who formed the nucleus of the parties became known as the Blue Stockings.

In 1758 she met Elizabeth Carter, the spinster daughter of a Kentish clergyman. She was three years older than Mrs Montagu and was to be acclaimed as possibly the most erudite woman in the country. She had just published her most famous work, the translation from the Greek of *Epictetus*, which had won high acclaim from all the critics, including the captious Dr Johnson.

Mrs Montagu was still busy with the social round of Mayfair, 'going wherever two or three fools were gathered together, to assemblies, visiting days, etc. Twenty-four idle hours, without a leisure one among them!', but she met an increasing number of men of letters, including Dr Johnson, and herself tried her hand at writing by publishing anonymously three of the *Dialogues of the Dead*. They appeared in 1760, the majority under the name of her close friend, the poet and generous patron of many young authors, the 1st Lord Lyttelton, while hers were advertised as written 'by another hand'. Her identity was for long kept a secret and the *Dialogues* achieved a modest success.

At first Mrs Montagu held breakfast parties, and she was giving these before the Blue Stockings were fully established, for Madame du Bocage described one in her *Letters on England, Holland and Italy*.

In the morning, breakfasts, which enchant as much by the exquisite viands as by the richness of the plate on which they are served up, agreeably bring together the people of the country and strangers. We breakfasted in this manner to-day, April 8, 1750, at Lady [*sic*] Montagu's, in a closet lined with painted paper of *Pekin*, and furnished with the choicest movables of *China*. A long table, covered with the finest linen, presented to the view a thousand glittering cups, which contained coffee, chocolate, biscuits, cream, butter, toasts and exquisite tea. You must understand that there is no good tea to be had anywhere but in London. The mistress of the house, who deserved to be served at the table of the gods, poured it out herself. This is the custom, and, in order to conform to it, the dress of the English ladies, which suits exactly to their stature, the white apron and the pretty straw hat, become them with the greatest propriety, not only in their own apartments, but at noon, in St James's Park, where they walk with the stately and majestic gait of nymphs.

Mrs Montagu was not the only one to give these literary breakfasts, but within a year or two she changed them to evening parties, when lemonade, tea and biscuits were served, and eventually to elaborate dinner parties.

The group who first met at Mrs Montagu's in Hill Street included Mrs Vesey, Mrs Boscawen, Elizabeth Carter, Lord Lyttelton, William Pulteney, the Earl of Bath, Mr Stillingfleet and Horace Walpole, but Mrs Vesey gave similar parties. She was the wife of the Rt Hon Agmondsham Vesey, whom she disliked, but she was happy with her friends, particularly Mrs Montagu.

She lived in Bolton Row and later in Clarges Street and Sir William Forbes, writing of her entertainments in his *Life of Beattie*, said that without attempting to shine herself, she had 'the happy secret of bringing forward talents of every kind, and for diffusing over the society the gentleness of her own character'.

Wraxall had the same impression, saying that among the circle of Blue Stockings Mrs Montagu was in the first place and Mrs Vesey came second, aspiring only 'to follow at a humble distance the brilliant track of Mrs Montagu'. Mrs Vesey seemed to aspire to assemble persons of celebrity and talents, under her roof or at her table, than assumed or pretended to form one of the number. Not so handsomely lodged in such magnificence yet she entertained with less form, as well as less ostentation. Mrs Vesey's repasts were at once more select, and more delicate!

She was older than Mrs Montagu, a simple soul who in later years became so absent-minded that she seemed entirely oblivious to a great deal that was going on around her. Horace Walpole made fun of the parties but nevertheless enjoyed them. 'Mrs Montagu is one of my principal entertainments at Mrs Vesey's', he said. She 'collects all the graduates and candidates for fame, where they vie with one another till they are as unintelligible as the good folks at Babel'.

Elizabeth Carter was a very different proposition, so intellectual that even Dr Johnson respected her, and not only for her mind but because she was a good cook and needlewoman as well. She had been an untiring student from her earliest childhood and was said to have developed headaches from which she suffered all her life, by drinking green tea and snuff in order to keep awake.

Mrs Boscawen, the widow of the admiral, was a close friend of Mrs Delaney, a cultured woman of intelligence and wit, who was always welcome, while Lord Lyttelton and William Pulteney had been close friends of Mrs Montagu for many years.

The parties developed gradually and it was not until 1767 that Mrs Montagu completed the Chinese room at Hill Street. 'Mr Adam has made me a ceiling, and chimney-piece, and doors which are pretty enough to make me a thousand enemies,' she wrote to Lord Kames. 'Envy turns livid at the first glimpse of them.'

Mrs Chapone was also to be found at these parties from time to time, another intellectual who, like Elizabeth Carter, wrote for Dr Johnson's *Rambler* and who, according to Wraxall, 'under one of the most repulsive exteriors that any woman ever possessed, concealed very superior attainments, and extensive knowledge'. Even earlier than Mrs Montagu she had fulminated at the senseless, eternal card-playing of society.

Dr Johnson, Sir Joshua Reynolds, David Garrick and Horace Walpole were the four most famous names to be found at the parties and later came Hannah More, Dr Burney and Fanny, and after her success at Drury Lane in 1782, Mrs Siddons, but by this time Mrs Montagu and her parties were established in Portman Square.

It was in the winter of 1776-7 that Wraxall, on the strength of his *History of France* and other historical works, was admitted to the Blue Stocking circle at Hill Street and he said that Mrs Montagu's 'very elegant house in Hill Street constituted the central point of union for all those persons who already were known, or who emulated to become known, by their talents and productions. She opened her house to them and frequently entertained at dinner, where her plate and a table plentifully covered, disposed her guests to admire the splendour of her Fortune, not less than the lustre of her Talents'.

Mrs Montagu, he said, was approaching her sixtieth year, but being thin, spare and in good preservation, she looked younger. 'All the lines of her Countenance bespoke intelligence, and her Eyes were accommodated to her cast of features, which had in them something satirical and severe, rather than amiable or inviting.'

He was obviously frightened of her but conceded that 'she possessed great natural cheerfulness, and a flow of animal spirits; loved
to talk, and talked well on almost every subject; led the Conversation, and was qualified to preside in her Circle whatever subject of
discourse was started' but qualified it by saying that her manner 'was
more dictatorial and sententious, than conciliating or diffident. There
was nothing feminine about her; and though her opinions were
usually just, as well as delivered in language suited to give them force,
yet the organ which conveyed them was not soft or harmonious.'

He disliked her taste in dress and hated the diamond necklace and
brooches which she wore unfailingly every evening. 'I used to think',
he said maliciously, 'that these glittering appendages of Opulence
sometimes helped to dazzle the Disputants, whom her arguments
might not always convince, or her literary reputation intimidate.'

Her literary reputation had in fact already suffered, for in 1769 she
had published anonymously her essay on Shakespeare in answer to
Voltaire's attack on him. Although the authorship was soon public
knowledge, Dr Johnson condemned it before he knew the identity of
the writer, saying that it contained no real criticism, but it sold well
and at the time was much applauded by many of the circle, including
Joshua Reynolds and David Garrick.

It promoted a coolness between Mrs Montagu and Johnson, even
though there were others, who, with justification, criticised the essay
adversely. But she still invited Johnson to her parties, the real quarrel
coming in 1781, when he wrote disparagingly of Lord Lyttelton's
poetry, Lord Lyttelton having died in 1773.

Wraxall admired Johnson's intellect but heartily disliked his manners, saying that 'I will freely confess that his rugged exterior and
garb, his uncouth gestures, his convolutions and distortions, when
added to the rude or dogmatical manner in which he delivered his
opinions and decision on every point, rendered him so disagreeable
in company, and so oppressive in conversation, that all the superior-
ity of his talents could not make full amends, in my estimation, for
these defects. In his anger, or even in the warmth of argument, where
he met with opposition, he often respected neither age, rank, nor
sex; and the usages of polished life imposed a very inadequate restraint on his expressions, or his feelings.'

Horace Walpole had an even lower opinion of the Doctor. He
thought he was an odious and mean character, with a feminine
bigotry.

'His manners were sordid, supercilious, and brutal, his style ridicu-

lously bombast and vicious; and, in one word, with all the pedantry
he had all the gigantic littleness of a country schoolmaster.'

Even the sweet-natured Garrick avoided him as much as possible,
if they were attending the same party, for Johnson did not attempt to
conceal his opinion that Garrick contributed nothing to the interpretation of Shakespeare; but there was one memorable autumn evening
in 1776 when Garrick held the stage at Hill Street by enchanting his
audience with recitals from Macbeth and Lear. The French Ambassador and Mme de Noailles were present on that occasion, and Mme
de Noailles was so profuse in her thanks, as she descended the stairs
at the end of the party, that Mrs Montagu afterwards said that she
was afraid she was going to miss her footing, fall down the stairs and
break her neck.

Edmund Burke was occasionally to be found at the parties, although his presence was more often 'coveted than enjoyed'. The
Dowager Duchess of Portland, a girlhood friend of Mrs Montagu's,
and the young Georgiana, Duchess of Devonshire, also came from
time to time. With the passing years, Sir Joshua Reynolds became so
deaf that he could not join in the general conversation. Rather sadly,
Wraxall says that 'with his Trumpet held up to his ear, he was grati-
fied by the attention of those who addressed to him their discourses;
a notice which the resources of his mind enabled him to repay with
interest'.

All through these years, in addition to her Blue Stocking parties,
Mrs Montagu found time to take part in the social life of Mayfair,
during the short season that every one was in London, before retiring
to the country for the summer and autumn. She attended the drawing-rooms at St James's Palace and she wrote dozens of letters describing all that was happening, as did her sister, Mrs Sarah Scott.

In 1761 they were all busy with the preparations for the marriage
of the young George III with Charlotte of Mecklenburg. Mrs Scott
wrote saying she had heard that the bride was very far from handsome. 'Her mouth fills a great part of her face' and a friend who had
seen her in passing, when the Princess was laughing and talking,
'which would shew it in its full dimensions' had said that 'she could
see no other feature'.

An immense amount of scaffolding went up in London to give
people an opportunity to see the procession. Mrs Scott said there was
enough to hold two millions of people.

Almost all the kingdom will be in London . . . and the finery of every one who intends to appear at court is beyond imagination. The queen's clothes are so heavy, that by all accounts, if she be not very robust, she will not be able to move under the burden; but I hope her constitution is not very delicate, for she did not arrive in London till three o'clock; and besides the fatigue of her journey, with the consequences of the flutter she could not avoid being in, she was to dress for her wedding, be married, have a Drawing-room, and undergo the ceremony of receiving company, after she and the king were in bed, and *all* the night after her journey and so long a voyage. Nothing but a German constitution could have undergone it . . .

As people drove into London for the wedding, the highwaymen lurking about the approaches to the city, on the lonely heaths of Hampstead and Wimbledon, the woods of Highgate and the forest of Epping, had a field-day and dozens of parties were held up and robbed. West of Charing Cross the crowds were so dense that it was literally a fight to get through, with no quarter given, and to add to the confusion the press-gangs were busy picking up likely lads for service in the Navy while after dark the mob surged through the streets, rampant and drunk and picking up whatever spoils came to hand.

The following night there was a court ball, grander than anything that had ever before been seen in England. The Duke of Ancaster, who was living at Number 39 Berkeley Square, with his Duchess, the mistress of the Queen's robes, appeared at the ball in the costume which the King had worn the whole day before and which he had presented to the Duke as a memento of the occasion.

Mrs Scott recorded in her letters much the same gossip as Horace Walpole, such as the proposed marriage of Lady Raymond, of Number 41 Berkeley Square, with Lord Robert Bertie – 'an union wherein no acid will enter; for they are both famed for good temper'; but she also writes on more strictly feminine matters, such as the new Court dress decreed by the Queen, 'which greatly distresses the old ladies, who are quite clamorous on the occasion, and at a loss how to cover so much neck as the stiffened-bodied gowns are made to show, and which they are sensible is not very appetissante after a certain age; as likewise how to supply the deficiency which churlish time has made in their once flowing tresses . . . The consumption of pearl-powder will certainly be much increased; for where there is such a resource, even fourscore will exhibit a snowy breast, and the corpulent dowagers will unite the lilies of the spring with all the copious abundance of a later season.'

Though she pretended to laugh at it, Mrs Montagu had always been as interested in fashion as her sister and as a girl, back at the beginning of the 1740s, she had written to her:

'I do not know what will become of your fine shape, for there is a fashionable make which is very strange. I believe they look in London as they did in Rome after the Rape of the Sabines!'

In May 1762 Mrs Montagu, writing to her brother, records that 'the king has purchased Buckingham House, and is going to fit it up elegantly for his retired hours. Her majesty promises to give us an heir very soon.' She also described 'a cold and fever in town, as universal as a plague', during which ten of her servants were ill at the same time.

And in regard to the enormous number of honours bestowed by the King at the outset of the new reign, Mrs Scott says to her brother:

'You will find few commoners in England. We make nobility as fast as people make kings and queens on Twelfth Night and almost as many . . . Lady Townshend says that she dare not spit out of her window for fear of spitting on a lord.'

The Duke of Newcastle resigned and Lord Bute took office as Prime Minister. The King gave Dr Johnson a pension of £300 a year and Wilkes in the *North Briton* hastened to remind the world of all that Johnson had written with bitterness against the royal family in former years and hoped he would be forgiven 'by the true friends of the present illustrious family for what he has been writing and saying for many years'.

In that same month, August 1762, the Prince of Wales was born and the Chancellor and the Archbishop of Canterbury must have had a fatiguing office, for the Queen was brought to bed at seven in the morning and 'they must have attended her labour all night, for fear they should be absent at the critical moment of delivery'.

Lady Mary Wortley Montagu, a connexion by marriage to Elizabeth Montagu, returned to England this year, on the death of her husband, from whom she had been estranged for years. She stayed in various parts of Mayfair – Hanover Square and Berkeley Square – but it was at Lady Bute's home in South Audley Street that Mrs Montagu called on her. She seemed perfectly well at the time, but a few weeks later she developed a virulent cancer which killed her in less than three weeks and she was buried in the Grosvenor Chapel.

A scandal which caused a great deal of chatter in Mayfair was the strange affair of Kitty Hunter, a maid of honour, who ran off with Lord Pembroke, Lord of the Bedchamber. He left behind a letter for his wife, who was a daughter of the Duke of Marlborough, applauding her virtues and charms but confessing that he found Miss Hunter irresistible. A few weeks later he had second thoughts and invited her to join him and Miss Hunter in Holland, where they might form a very happy society, if she would bring over her guitar, two servants to play on the French horn, and his dog, Rover.

The Duke of Marlborough put his foot down on behalf of his daughter and before long Lord Pembroke was writing again to his wife, saying that he would never be happy till he lived with her again. He was preparing to abandon Kitty Hunter and some said he had advised her to turn nun. 'To be sure he best knows how fit she is to take a vow of chastity,' remarked Mrs Scott.

By the following year Kitty Hunter was back in England, deserted by her lover. 'Shame and a fatherless babe she had brought back.' But before long she was happily married to someone else and lived for nearly another fifty years, 'in the odour of fashion'.

The marriage market was a never-ending source of interest, and many a hard bargain was struck. 'The Duke of Marlborough and Lady Caroline Russell were married eight and forty hours after his grace had declared himself a lover. The Duke of Bedford was always known to be a man of business, but he never despatched a matter quicker than this. He gave to Lady Caroline £50,000 down, and is to give as much more at his death', reported Mrs Montagu.

In 1764 Mrs Montagu lost one of her dearest friends, the Earl of Bath, on whom Anne Pitt and Lady Isabella Finch had so doted and who was believed to have been the richest man in England.

Although she disliked politics, she could not help commenting on the state of the country during the troubled year of 1769, when the letters of Junius were causing so much disturbance.

'I hope I shall see all my friends safe and well at my return to town', she wrote, 'but, indeed, a wicked mob and a foolish ministry may produce strange events. It was better in old times, when the ministry was wicked and the mob foolish . . . Ministers, however wicked, do not pull down houses, nor ignorant mobs pull down government. A mob that can read and a ministry that cannot think are sadly, matched.'

Two years later, 'the Duke of Bedford died of a fit of the asthma. He departed singing the 104th Psalm. This shows he had some piety but I think his grace sang out of tune.'

In the 1770s she seemed to be growing weary of her letter writing, finding it 'idleness without ease, and fatigue without purpose'. 'When newspapers only told weddings, births, and burials, a letter from London bore some value; but now that the public papers not only tell when men are born and dye, but every folly they contrive to insert between these periods, the literary correspondent has nothing left. Lies and dulness used to be valued in manuscript, but printing has assumed a right over the lies of the day and the amusement of the hour.'

She was in low spirits that winter of 1773 and on New Year's Day of 1774 she was writing that 'many persons go at this dreary season to their dreary mansions to keep their Christmas, who will not laugh till they return to London'. But her husband was in failing health and sinking into senility. He does not seem to have featured in her literary parties but the marriage remained perfectly happy until his death in the following year, 1775.

In due course she recovered her spirits, however, and was soon writing as amusingly as ever.

A scandal that was causing much gossip in Mayfair at this time was the shameful affair of the Reverend William Dodd, who for many years was a very popular preacher in London. He was particularly successful in preaching for charities, for he had more than a touch of the actor about him and knew how to put his message across so that it had the desired effect of 'extracting tears and loose cash' from his listeners, particularly the women. In 1758 he had preached the inaugural sermon at the opening of the Magdalen House for Fallen Women in Goodman's Fields, to which he had been appointed chaplain, and even Horace Walpole admitted that he preached 'very elegantly and touchingly'. The 4th Earl of Chesterfield appointed him tutor to his godson and successor, who was to become the 5th Earl, and he was made a chaplain of George III.

With money which his wife had won in a lottery, he invested in a proprietary chapel in Pimlico, where he quickly attracted large and fashionable congregations and began to mix with the upper crust of society. But it all went badly to his head. He took to the gay life and high living, far beyond his means, and was soon head over heels in debt.

The living of St George's, Hanover Square, was a rich prize, and in 1774, at a time when it was falling vacant, he caused an anonymous letter to be sent to Lady Apsley, wife of the Lord Chancellor, promising a down payment of £3,000 for the appointment. It sounds an extraordinarily naïve trick, born of desperation, and by some accounts it was sent by his wife, but it was soon traced to its source and Dodd was straightaway struck off the list of royal chaplains. He departed hurriedly to Switzerland, hoping that the storm would eventually blow over and the disgrace be forgotten. Here he met his old pupil again, now the 5th Lord Chesterfield, who befriended him and presented him with the living of Wing in Buckinghamshire. So Dodd returned to England, but he was still in dire money troubles, even after he had sold his chapel in Pimlico.

In 1777 he took the fatal step of offering a bond of £4,200 in the name of Lord Chesterfield, to a stockbroker who handed over the money, on the strength of a forged signature. The forgery was quickly discovered and Dodd was arrested. Although he at once repaid the money, and Lord Chesterfield was reluctant to prosecute, the matter had gone too far. He was committed to Newgate, tried for forgery and condemned to be hanged.

At the time of the trial, Mrs Montagu was writing that 'some suppose that, for want of some formality, he will escape hanging. Lord Chesterfield has behaved with great kindness to the doctor's brother, who is a worthy man, and to Mrs Dodd's nephew . . .'

Dr Dodd must have had a compelling personality, for there were many petitioners for his reprieve, but George III would not grant him a pardon. Among his many supporters was Dr Johnson, who wrote for him not only his final speech from the dock, before his sentence, but his valedictory sermon to his fellow-prisoners before his execution, for by this time the fire of his native eloquence must have been quenched in mortal fear and utter hopelessness.

Yet plans were laid for his escape, even to the making of a wax model to be laid in his bed, in order to fox such gaolers who were not in the plot, and Dr Johnson told Boswell that £1,000 had been provided for any warder who would help. But the plans miscarried and on 27 June 1777 Dr Dodd took the last grim journey to Tyburn, along Holborn and the Tyburn road, passing close to aristocratic Hanover Square, and watched all along the route by crowds of Londoners, to whom the Monday morning hangings at Tyburn were a regular entertainment.

In a letter to George Selwyn, Anthony Storer, who was always fascinated by executions, wrote:

> The doctor, to all appearance, was rendered perfectly stupid from despair. His hat was flapped all round, and pulled over his

eyes, which were never directed to any object around, nor even raised, except now and then lifted up in the course of his prayers. He came in a coach and a very heavy shower of rain fell upon his entering the cart, and another just at his putting on his night-cap.

He was a considerable time in praying, which some people standing about seemed rather tired with; they wished for some more interesting part of the tragedy ... There were two clergymen attending him, one of whom seemed very much affected; the other, I suppose, was the ordinary of Newgate, as he was perfectly indifferent and unfeeling in everything that he said and did.

The executioner took both the hat and wig off at the same time. Why he put on his wig again I do not know, but he did, and the doctor took off his wig a second time, and then tied on a nightcap which did not fit him; but whether he stretched that, or took another, I could not perceive. He then put on his nightcap himself ... very soon afterwards there was an end of all his hopes and fears on this side the grave. He never moved from the place he first took in the cart; seemed absorbed in despair, and utterly dejected, without any signs of animation but in praying.

But Mrs Montagu soon had other affairs to write about and later that year she was describing Lady Strathmore, during the election campaign for her husband, Stoney Bowes.

'Lady Strathmore's conduct at Newcastle, in the election, is, perhaps, not generally known. Her laydship sits all day in the window of a public-house, from whence she sometimes lets fall some jewels or trinkets, which voters pick up, and then she gives them money for restoring them – a new kind of offering bribes.'

After all this it is surprising to see her writing that 'of all the vices of the human disposition, a love of scandal and detraction is the most contemptible', but she was angry with the newspapers who had 'let fly their pop-guns at the Duchess of Devonshire's feathers' for she was fond of Georgiana. 'Her grace is innocent, good-humoured, and beautiful: but these adders are blind and deaf, and cannot be charmed.'

That year she told Garrick that she was 'hurried to death with assemblies' and in the following winter life was just as gay. 'The town is now full of company; full of bustle. Real business and serious occupation have their hours of retreat and rest, but the pursuits of pleasure have no intermissions ... As to me, I am, like other light and insignificant matters, whisked about in the whirlwind.'

At the beginning of March in 1781, just before she left Hill Street, she said that she had on her chimney-piece a multitude of cards for assemblies for every day till near the end of Passion Week.

After she moved to Portman Square the Blue Stocking parties were never the same. Some of the original group of friends had died, Benjamin Stillingfleet as early as 1771, and Mrs Montagu now invited many more people, being far less discriminating than in the old days. Yet she was very generous and helped a great number of young and aspiring authors.

The eating-habits of Mayfair society were odd. They seem to have consumed a prodigious amount of bread and butter and this seems to have been the staple refreshment offered even at Almack's. The Duke of Dorset, British Ambassador to France, had brought back the custom of serving tea at eight o'clock, which was reasonable enough in France where people dined at two o'clock, but strange in London where the hour for dinner had become established at six o'clock. Mrs Montagu took to this new form of entertainment and Hannah More described how she would have fifty to a hundred guests seated either at a long table or in parties at small ones, and in addition to tea, they were served hot buttered-rolls, muffins, bread and butter and wafers. 'Of all nations under the sun, as I take it, the English are the greatest fools', said Hannah, 'for what wit could there be among people eating buttered muffins two hours after a heavy dinner and strong port wine?'

She was genuinely fond of Mrs Montagu but in the last years, as she grew visibly frailer, the parties were 'not to be had in the usual style of comfort'. 'Everything', said Hannah More, 'is grand, and vast, and late, and magnificent, and dull.'

Wraxall, in fact, said that the genuine Blue Stocking parties lasted only from 1770 till 1785, for after that time Mrs Vesey was too old and Mrs Thrale had married Mr Piozzi and left London. Although Mrs Montagu continued to hold the parties, the charm and impulse had disappeared, particularly after the death of Dr Johnson in 1784.

It was was during these years that the notorious Elizabeth Chudleigh was causing a flutter in Mayfair. She was born in 1720 and came to London with her widowed mother in 1741, to settle in Conduit Street. One of the susceptible Hamiltons, the young Duke, fell in love with her and made an offer of marriage, but then he went off on the Grand Tour and she heard no more of him, for it was said that his relations intercepted his letters. She was appointed maid of honour to Augusta, Princess of Wales and accepted an offer of marriage from Augustus, younger son of John, Lord Hervey, but as he was just off to the West Indies and she did not want to lose her position at Court, she insisted on the marriage being kept secret. When she was not at Court, amusing herself with all and sundry, including King George II himself, she continued to live in Conduit Street with her mother, until the King appointed Mrs Chudleigh housekeeper at Windsor.

Lady Mary Wortley Montagu's nephew, the young and profligate Duke of Kingston, fell in love with Elizabeth and made her an offer of marriage. She prevaricated and lived with him for a time at the splendid villa she had built for herself in Kensington Gore.* When Augustus appeared on the scene, demanding a divorce as he wished to marry again, she denied that they had ever been married at all, took legal action and was successful in being declared a spinster, where-upon she married the Duke of Kingston at St George's, Hanover Square, in March 1769. Four years later he died, leaving her a life interest in his large estates, to the fury of his family, who began an action against her.

Meanwhile, Augustus Hervey had succeeded to the Earldom of Bristol. He petitioned the King for a new trial and Elizabeth was convicted of bigamy and perjury. She claimed the privilege of her peerage which, unaccountably, was accepted, and escaped with a fine. Still wealthy, she fled to France and bought herself an estate near Paris, but in 1788, on receiving news that a French lawsuit had gone against her, she flew into a rage, burst a bloodvessel and died.

Many interesting characters came to live in Lord Burlington's new streets in the south-eastern corner of Mayfair during the early eighteenth century. James Ralph described the houses in Burlington Street as 'in the finest taste of any common buildings that we can see anywhere; without the least affectation of ornament or seeming design at any remarkable elegance'.

In Cork Street, named after Lord Burlington's brother, Lord Cork, there stood on the east side, stretching back to Burlington Street, the little house which Lord Burlington built and presented in gratitude to General Wade, after his success against the Jacobite Rebellion in 1715. Ralph described it as 'small but chaste and simple in design, though rather overladen with ornament', but added that 'it is the only fabric in miniature I ever saw where decorations are perfectly proportioned to the space they are to fill, and do not by their multi-plicity, or some other mistake, incumber the whole'.

* See *Two Villages* – Mary Cuthcart Borer.

But Lord Chesterfield said it was too small to live in and suggested that the General took the house opposite, so that he could admire the elegant exterior of his gift in comfort.

During the nineteenth century General Wade's house became the Burlington Hotel, where Florence Nightingale often stayed, before she settled into her house in South Street; and close by was the grim-looking charity school which was endowed by Lady Burlington 'for the maintenance, clothing and education of eighty female children'.

Lady Masham lived in Cork Street for a time and also Queen Anne's physician, Dr Arbuthnot.

On the north side of Burlington Gardens, between Savile Row and Old Burlington Street, once stood Queensberry House, built for the Duke of Queensberry, cousin of 'Old Q', and his wife Catherine Hyde, who was a granddaughter of Lord Clarendon.

The Duke and Duchess were good friends of Gay, and after the production of *The Beggar's Opera* and its sequel *Polly*, which the Lord Chamberlain suppressed, they invited him to live at Queensberry House, and here he remained for the last few years of his life.

The Duchess was so indignant at the suppression of *Polly* that she organised a subscription list for its publication, and for her pains George II forbade her the Court. Lord Hervey tells the story in his *Memoirs*.

> One Gay, a poet, had written a ballad opera, which was thought to reflect a little upon the Court and a good deal upon the Minister. It was called *The Beggar's Opera*, had a prodigious run, and was so extremely pretty in its kind, that even those who were most glanced at in the satire had prudence enough to disguise their resentment by chiming in with the universal applause with which it was performed.

Gay had been disappointed of a place at Court and was delighted that his barbs had struck those whom he felt were responsible for his rejection. *Polly*, however, was less subtle, and Sir Robert Walpole, not enjoying the prospect of being depicted on the stage as a high-wayman, persuaded the Lord Chamberlain to forbid its performance.

When the King found the Duchess soliciting subscriptions for its publication even in the Queen's drawing-room, it was not un-reasonable for him to send her a message to stay away, but she sent him the most outrageous reply, beginning: 'That the Duchess of Queensberry is surprised and well pleased that the King hath given her so agreeable a command as to stay from Court, where she never came for diversion, but to bestow a great civility on the King and Queen . . .': so it is not surprising that it was another eighteen years before she appeared there again.

As a building, Queensberry House pleased even the critical Ralph, who said that it had no other faults but its bad situation, 'over against a dead wall in a lane that is unworthy of so grand a building . . . This fabric is evidently in the style of Inigo Jones, and not at all unworthy the school of that great master.'

But later in the century the house came down and on the site Uxbridge House was built for the Earl of Uxbridge, and ultimately this house became the West End branch of the Royal Bank of Scotland. Between Old Burlington Street and Cork Street stood another mansion, which for a long time was a home of members of the Cavendish family, and in the middle years of the nineteenth century this was turned into the exclusive Bristol Hotel, which survived until, during the 1890s, its glory waned before the rising star of Claridge's and it was closed.

During the late 1740s Lady Jane Coke had her town house in Savile Row. She was born in 1706 and as a young widow married, in 1733, John Coke, brother of the 1st Earl of Leicester, whose son married Lady Mary Coke, so Lady Jane and Lady Mary were connected by marriage, but Lady Jane was a kinder, gentler character than Lady Mary, and in her letters to her friend Mrs Eyre there is no hint of the spitefulness and malice which one finds in so many letters of this period. In fact Lady Mary Wortley Montagu described Lady Jane as 'the agreeablest girl on earth'.

She was widowed again in 1750 and moved to a smaller house in Savile Row, but after the period of mourning was over and she had paid visits to her husband's relatives, the Finches and Winchilseas, she was soon writing again to Mrs Eyre, answering her questions about fashion and the affairs of London and doing small commission for her, for Mrs Eyre lived in Derby, which was three or four days' journey in a lumbering post-chaise from London.

'. . . there has been no balls nor any entertainment but cards, assemblies in abundance, and really the love of play seems the ruling passion of both sexes. Bragg flourishes as much as ever, and I believe ruins half the women in town,' wrote Lady Jane.

The death of Frederick, the Prince of Wales, in 1751, 'put an end to all fashions, and I do not believe there will be any change in the mourning till they go into white gloves.' But when the mourning period was over, sacques became all the rage. These were loose gowns, open in the front, hanging from the shoulders in a deep pleat and falling over the hoop.

'You ask me whether sacks are generally worn,' she wrote. 'I am so partial to 'em that I have nothing else – a sack and apron with a very small hoop, when I am undress'd, and the whole ones when I am to be set out. The short caps you mention are only worn by young people who curl their hair after the French Ambassadress' fashion and is very difficult to do well.'

She writes of the elder Miss Gunning's marriage to Lord Coventry and of the plays she enjoyed at Drury Lane. While she was spending the summer at Windsor, Lady Mary Coke spent a week with her and 'entirely took up my time'. She was induced by Lady Winchilsea and Mrs Finch to attend the ball at Windsor after a Garter Installation, where 'you will easily imagine there was a great deal of finery'. During a visit to Tunbridge Wells she saw Miss Chudleigh 'so altered, I was surprised to see her by daylight'.

In 1752 she went to Lady Betty Germain's to see some of the ladies show off their new dresses before going to Court for the King's birthday celebration. 'Lady Coventry, Lady Caroline Petersham and Mrs Watson (who was Miss Pelham) were allowed the finest: their clothes had all silver grounds and coloured flowers with silver mixed, and a great quantity of jewels in their hair. Mrs Watson had a diamond bird, with the wings stretched out, and in its beak held a diamond drop; her necklace comes down in rows and covers her neck.'

Later she was writing:

'As for fashions in dress, which you sometimes inquire after, they are too various to describe. One thing is new, which is, there is not such a thing as a decent old woman left, everybody curls their hair, shows their necks, and wears pink, but your humble servant ... we try to outdo our patterns, the French, in every ridiculous vanity.'

In a postscript, she mentions: 'I am in black gloves for Sir Marmaduke Wyvill,* but forgot black paper and wax till this minute.'

She buys lute-string for Mrs Eyre, which was a fashionable corded silk – but complains of the price, which has risen to 13/- a yard – and has it made up for her by Mrs Manroi, the mantua maker. She explains the mystery of a sack-handkerchief, which she considers 'very pretty and vastly decent'.

In January 1755 'Everybody wears flounced sleeves, and all the

* Her brother-in-law.

sacks are made open, with an apron very full trimmed, and as to caps, they are the same as last year.'

A few weeks later she is sending Mrs Eyre patterns of more silks, all from mercers in the streets round Covent Garden – the Hen and Chickens in Henrietta Street and the Wheat and Sheaf in King Street – but Mrs Dantin, the sacque maker, lived in Mount Street, Grosvenor Square.

Shortly after this Lady Jane left London to live at Sunbury and she died in 1761.

Half a century later Sheridan was living out his last years in Savile Row. He died in 1816 and even on his death bed his house was besieged by bailiffs and creditors, one of whom forced his way into the house when the servant opened the door to the doctor. But the doctor was a good friend to the dying Sheridan and helped the servant to throw the man out again.

At this time poor old Lady Cork, once the brilliant Miss Monckton, was living at Number 6 New Burlington Street, and giving her renowned receptions to Mayfair society, but the parties were more famed for the old lady's embarrassing tendency to kleptomania than for the elegance of the entertainment. She died here in 1840, when she was nearly ninety, but by now this corner of Mayfair was no longer so fashionable as the streets and squares to the west. The aristocrats were moving away and this became a favourite quarter for eminent doctors. In 1870 Wheatley, writing of Savile Row, said that it was 'now almost entirely inhabited by eminent physicians and surgeons, who occupy nearly every house in the street'. And when the doctors moved northwards, to Harley Street and Wimpole Street, the exclusive tailors moved in, to achieve world-fame for their skill and workmanship.

Very few of the old Georgian houses have survived in this part of Mayfair, to remind us of the architect Earl, and such as are left are fast disappearing.

During the early 1770s a small girl, Mary Darby, was sometimes to be seen in Berkeley Square calling on her godfather, Lord Northington, whose house was two doors from Hill Street, where Lord Robert Spencer was later to live. If life had not taken such a strange and tragic twist for Mary she might well have grown up to be included in the Blue Stocking parties, for she was intelligent and gifted as well as outstandingly beautiful, and she had been carefully educated at the school which Hannah More's sisters had established at Bristol, the city where Mary was born. Her family was well connected, her father prosperous and their home large, elegant and happy. But when she was only eight years old, her father went off to America, having been inveigled into a wild scheme for establishing a whale fishery in Labrador.

The original trip was intended to last for only two years but Mr Darby found a mistress in America and never returned to his wife. Worse still, the whale fishing venture failed, he fell into debt, gave a bill of sale on the Bristol house, and Mrs Darby and the two children were turned out.

Three years after leaving England Darby arrived in London with his mistress and ordered his family to come up from Bristol. He told his wife that Mary and her brother were to be educated near London and he would pay for her to live in respectable lodgings near their schools.

He crossed the Atlantic two or three times and while in London he lived with his mistress in Green Street, Grosvenor Square. Mary went to several schools but ended up at Oxford House, Marylebone, where the dancing-master was also the ballet-master at Covent Garden Theatre. He and Mary's schoolmistress had both noticed her literary gifts, her acting ability and her beautiful speaking voice. Mr Darby was in money troubles again and the payments from America were erratic and small. The school suggested that Mary would do well on the stage and the ballet-master gave her an introduction to David Garrick, who was then about to retire. Mary was only fifteen, but Garrick recognised her outstanding qualities and said he was prepared to train her.

Mary's mother moved to lodgings in Villiers Street, to be near the theatre, but she was not happy at the prospect of Mary going on the stage. It was hardly respectable and she was mortally terrified of what her husband might say. Though she saw him so seldom, he treated her abominably. He had forced her to close the small school she had opened, considering it unbecoming that the world should know she was a schoolmistress because he was not paying her an adequate allowance, and she remembered his parting words at their last meeting, ordering her to preserve his daughter's honour and threatening to 'annihilate her' if any harm befell the girl.

Mary already had several suitors and Mrs Darby, playing as she thought for safety, persuaded her to accept the offer of Mr Robinson, a law student who appeared to be a young man of fortune and certainly moved in a circle of extremely rich friends. In fact, he was the illegitimate son of a wealthy merchant who had given him a start in life by having him articled to a lawyer, but refused any other help, or to pay his debts when he ran into trouble.

However, Mrs Darby, who seems to have been a simple, un-suspecting soul, foresaw none of this. Robinson took Mary to live in the newly built Hatton Garden, furnished the house expensively, from his fast-dwindling resources, bought a smart phaeton and drew her into the gay life of the town, with visits to Ranelagh, the Pan-theon and Vauxhall. His legal studies were forgotten.

One of his friends was the young Lord Lyttelton. This was the second and wicked Lord Lyttelton, a very different character from the gentle and intellectual father who was a friend of Mrs Montagu, and he was living in Hill Street. He tried to seduce Mary, who was terrified of him, and when she successfully resisted his advances he seduced her husband instead, enticing him into his circle of vicious, libertine men and profligate women.

Mary's mother had taken her young brother back to Bristol for a time and Mary was left alone, night after night, while Robinson amused himself at the disreputable parties given by Lord Lyttelton in Hill Street. Robinson was soon hopelessly in debt and Mary was pregnant.

She began to write poetry to console herself, but soon after her baby, Maria, was born Robinson was arrested for debt and commit-ted to lodgings of the King's Bench prison. Mary, still only seventeen, went with him, and for the next nine months did all the work of cleaning their quarters, cooking and caring for the baby, while Robinson, even in confinement, was unfaithful to her and went with prostitutes who were brought in to the lodgings by the wife of a fellow prisoner.

Mary heard that Georgiana, the Duchess of Devonshire, was a patron of poetry and literature and sent her some of her work. The Duchess was interested and asked Mary to visit her at Devonshire House, which she did, on several occasions. Then Robinson managed to borrow enough money to obtain his release from the King's Bench, and they moved to lodgings at Lyne's, the confectioner in Old Bond Street.

Yet they had no means of livelihood. Robinson had not completed his articles of clerkship and at first Mary tried to earn for all three of them by writing; but one day, by chance, she met Brereton, an old friend from Drury Lane, who persuaded her to try again for a career on the stage. She agreed and he introduced her to Sheridan, who had just taken over from Garrick. He heard her read some passages from

Shakespeare and was enthusiastic about her prospects. Garrick again offered to coach her and gave her a careful training for the next few weeks. Her début was on 10 December 1776, when she played Juliet to Brereton's Romeo. Following the convention of the theatre at this time, she appeared in pink satin spangled with silver and a white feather headdress for the part of Juliet and she was at once a brilliant success. Within the next few months she went from strength to strength, playing all the great Shakespeare rôles and many of Sheridan's.

Night after night the green room at Drury Lane was crowded with admiring and illustrious visitors, including Charles James Fox and the Earl of Derby, who had come to meet the new and radiant star. She moved to a house in Covent Garden Square, next to the Hummums, to be near the theatre. She was still only eighteen, maintaining her small daughter and also her husband, but Robinson, though living under her roof, was quite indifferent to her by now, accepting her money but living his own squalid life with gamblers, drunkards and prostitutes.

In 1779 she was commanded to play before the royal family. The play chosen was *The Winter's Tale*, and as Perdita she conquered the heart of the young Prince of Wales. She was twenty-one, the Prince, her Florizel, seventeen – and he wooed her secretly but urgently, his go-between being the Earl of Essex, who arranged romantic and clandestine meetings for them in the grounds of Kew Palace, where the Prince was receiving his education.

At first she was reluctant to become his mistress but the young Prince was persuasive. The temptation was strong, her marriage was an irreparable disaster, and she at last agreed.

This was the year that the wicked Lord Lyttelton, who had brought such disaster to her marriage, died, presumably of fright, at the age of thirty-six. It was not at his house in Hill Street, where his parties had grown ever more profligate and decadent, but during a house party at Pit Place, near Epsom. One night, shortly after he had gone to bed, he heard the fluttering of a dove at his bedroom window. The next moment he saw a woman in white approach the foot of his bed. She told him that he would be dead in three days and then vanished.

All the Lyttelton family believed in ghosts and Lord Lyttelton, with a guilty conscience, was terrified, for he was convinced that the woman in white was Mrs Dawson, whom he had recently forsaken after taking all her money. For the next three days he was depressed and nervous. On the third night he went to bed as usual, but suddenly sat up to take some medicine. He called for his valet to bring him a spoon, and when the man returned Lord Lyttelton was dead. And his stepmother, the Dowager Lady Lyttelton, living in Grosvenor Square, duly painted a picture of the whole strange scene, as related to her by the valet, including the dove at the window and the woman in white at the foot of the bed.

Perdita cannot have failed to feel his end was well deserved but for her life had taken a new course. When the Prince reached his eighteenth birthday, a few months after their first meeting, he was given a wing of Buckingham House for his own use and a substantial income. Perdita left the stage and the Prince established her in the Countess of Derby's former house in Cork Street, Burlington Gardens.

For the next two years she was his mistress and they lived in the grand manner, wildly extravagant and seen everywhere, both of them beautifully dressed and Perdita riding in a magnificent coach which had cost the Prince nine hundred guineas. They were both running into debt but they were young and in love and the Prince, after all, was heir to the throne and when he came of age would be given a larger allowance.

For Perdita the future seemed all happiness and security, for the Prince had given her a miniature on which was inscribed: 'Unalterable to my Perdita through life.'

When he was twenty-one he was allowed his own establishment at Carlton House, and in addition to an income of £63,000 a year his debts amounting to £30,000 were paid. Their money troubles seemed to be over, but just as the Prince was preparing to move into Carlton House came, without any warning, the fatal note for Perdita – 'We must meet no more.' The bitter truth was that the Prince had fallen for Miss Crouch of Berkeley Square and had heartlessly abandoned Perdita.

She was left with no money and a pile of tradesmen's bills. Charles James Fox acted as intermediary with the Prince and secured her a pension of £500 a year, but she had to leave her house in Cork Street. She went to France for a time, where she was received by Paris society and also by Marie Antoinette, but back in England she settled in St James's Place, with her mother and daughter. The beautiful Perdita did not attempt to return to the stage and tried to eke out her income by writing poetry, articles and novels of a kind, but when she was only twenty-four she caught cold and developed rheumatic fever. She never fully recovered from this illness and became a semi-invalid, gradually losing the use of her limbs. She tried her hand at writing a play which was given a production, the Duke of Clarence's Mrs Jordan generously offering to take the lead, but it was a failure.

Her mother died, but her daughter remained devoted to her. With failing strength, she struggled on with her writing but in 1800, when she was only forty-two, Perdita, still beautiful and much loved by her small circle of literary friends, died almost penniless.

XI

Mayfair Mansions of the Eighteenth Century and the Regency

By 1718 the 3rd Earl of Burlington had made his alterations to his great-grandfather's red-brick house, designed by John Denham and John Webb. The front was encased with stone and the height of many of the first-floor rooms was raised, in order to convert them into impressive rooms of state. Colin Campbell had built the colonnades. The street wall with its great gate was rebuilt.

Horace Walpole was entranced by the colonnade.

'Soon after my return from Italy, I was invited to a ball at Burlington House,' he wrote. 'As I passed under the gate by night it could not strike me. At daybreak, looking out of the window to see the sun rise, I was surprised with the vision of the colonnade that fronted me. It seemed one of those edifices in fairy tales that are raised by genii in a night-time.'

The general public seldom caught a glimpse of all this, for the high street wall completely blocked the view. Ralph, in his *Critical Review* said that from Piccadilly 'we are entertained with a sight of the most expensive wall in England, namely, that before Burlington House'. However, he was impressed with what he saw once he was inside the gate. 'The grand entrance is august and beautiful', he said, 'and by covering the house entirely from the eye, gives pleasure and surprise at the opening of the whole front, with the area before it, at once.'

Yet in the fashionable Palladian tradition, the comfort of the house had been sacrificed to the magnificence of the splendidly decorated reception rooms. In comparison, the rooms on the ground floor were rather small and cramped and provoked many criticisms, Lord Chesterfield resorting to verse:

> Possess'd of one great hall for state
> Without a room to sleep or eat;
> How well you build let flattery tell,
> And all the world how ill you dwell.

Nevertheless, the 3rd Earl – the architect Earl – entertained lavishly and was a generous patron to men of letters, musicians and theatre people, and whether or not the house was comfortable according to the standards of Lord Chesterfield and the other critics, it was a happy haven for innumerable people who were to achieve fame in their own particular fields.

The Earl's wife, Dorothy Saville, was as well liked as her husband and shared the responsibilities of the entertaining. One of the people she took to live at Burlington House for a time was Eva Violetti, the dancer, who later married Garrick and became a friend of Mrs Montagu and the Blue Stocking circle. Dr Doran quotes an unpublished letter in the Cathcart collection from the Earl of Strafford, dated March 1746, describing Eva Violetti's first appearance on the London stage.

'She surprised her audience at her first appearance on the stage; for at her beginning to caper, she showed a neat pair of black velvet breeches, with roll'd stockings; but finding they were unusual in England, she changed them the next time for a pair of white drawers.'

Another distinguished visitor at Burlington House, who lived there for three years, before moving to Brook Street, was Handel, whom George II had appointed Court musician. Many of his oratorios and operas were performed at the King's Theatre in the Haymarket, the first oratorio ever to be heard in England being his *Esther*, which was produced at the theatre in 1732 and soon followed by *Acis and Galatea*. Handel was a great admirer of the voice of Susannah Cibber, Colley Cibber's daughter-in-law, and wrote the part of Galatea especially for her, as well as some of the arias in the *Messiah*, but after a time she tired of opera and oratorios and joined Garrick at Drury Lane. Some ten years after her death, when Perdita Robinson arrived there, Garrick assured the newcomer that her voice was as good as Susannah Cibber's and in some ways similar.

Pope was a frequent visitor at Burlington House in the 3rd Earl's day and also Swift.

Lord Burlington died in 1753 and the house passed to Lord Hartington, the 4th Duke of Devonshire, who had married Lady Charlotte Boyle, Lord Burlington's daughter. Their daughter, Lady Dorothy Cavendish, married the 3rd Duke of Portland, who became the next inheritor of the house, and in 1783, when he was serving as the First Lord of the Treasury under Charles James Fox, Burlington House became an important meeting-place for the Whigs.

The Duke of Portland died in 1809, and six years later the 6th Duke of Devonshire sold Burlington House to his uncle, Lord George Cavendish, for £70,000. Lord George proceeded to make many alterations and improvements to the old house, using for his architect Samuel Ware, whom he also commissioned to build the Burlington Arcade.

He maintained the tradition of hospitality which had always been associated with Burlington House but after his death the house fell empty, and in 1854 the Cavendish family sold it to the Government.

At first various learned societies were housed there and then, after many discussions and rejected plans, the main building was given over to the Royal Academy of Arts, which had been founded in 1766, with the newly knighted Sir Joshua Reynolds as president. The Academy moved in from Somerset House. Smirke designed the first-floor exhibition galleries. The private rooms of the academicians are above them and the building also houses the Royal Academy schools. Wings were built to house the learned societies who sought accommodation there. Today the headquarters of the Geological Society, the Chemical Society and the British Academy are in the east wing, those of the Society of Antiquaries, the Royal Astronomical Society and the Linnean Society in the west wing. The back wall, facing Burlington Gardens, came down in 1866 and here, on the site of the garden, Sir James Pennethorne built the administrative building of the University of London, which recently became the Museum of Mankind, housing the British Museum's ethnographical collection. The colonnades and the Piccadilly wall were demolished in 1868 and the present Piccadilly frontage built to the courtyard.

Lord Chesterfield's house-warming for Chesterfield House was in 1752, when Burlington House was nearing the end of its great days under the reign of the 3rd Earl, for he died the following year, but Lord Chesterfield had been superintending the building of his palace for at least six years before then.

Chesterfield House, standing where South Audley Street and Curzon Street meet, was sited to face across the desolate Tyburn Lane to Hyde Park, of which it had an uninterrupted view, and its garden stretched back all along the north side of Curzon Street to the garden of Crewe House, the long white garden house, which Shepherd had built for himself opposite the Mayfair Chapel.

Chesterfield House was composed of a central block, joined by colonnades to two large wings. The central part comprised two main floors and an attic storey, above a basement which was protected by iron railings. On the ground floor there were two windows on either side of the front door, which was approached by three shallow steps. The five long sash-windows on the first floor were pedimented and each had a wrought-iron balcony.

On 13 August 1747, Lord Chesterfield was writing to a friend:

'My house goes on apace, and draws upon me very fast. My colonnade is so fine, that to keep the house in countenance, I am obliged to dress the windows of the front with stone, those of the middle floor too with Pediments and Balustrades.'

By 12 December he was writing again:

'My new house is near to opening its door to receive me; and as soon as the weather shall be warm enough I shall get into the necessary part of it, finishing the rest at my leisure. My eating room, my dressing room, mon Boudoir, and my Library will be completely finished in three months. My court, my Hall and my staircase will really be magnificent. The staircase particularly will form such a scene, as is not in England. The expense will ruin me, but the enjoyment will please me.'

It was a double staircase of white marble, each step made from a single block twenty feet long. The two branches of the stairway swept upwards from the main approach to meet again at a triple-arched landing, and the baluster was of the most delicate ironwork. The staircase and the columns of the screen facing the courtyard had been bought at the sale of the Duke of Chandos's possessions at Canons, when the house was demolished in 1744. A beautiful copper gilt lantern, made to hold eighteen candles, had come from a sale of Sir Robert Walpole's Houghton Hall, and furniture and hangings had been collected from all over Europe.

By 1749 Lord Chesterfield was writing to Dayrolles:

'I have yet finished nothing but my Boudoir and my Library; the former is the gayest and most cheerful room in England; the latter the best. My garden is now turfed, planted and sown, and will in two months more make a scene of verdure and flowers not common in London.'

There were six reception rooms on the ground floor. French looking-glasses hung on the pale blue walls of the boudoir and the chairs were covered with petit point embroidery of flowers on a white background.

The library was 'stuffed with easy chairs and easy books'. The bookcases reached only as high as the tops of the doors and above them hung portraits of English poets in white painted, stucco frames, for, said Lord Chesterfield:

'I have determined to have no gilding at all in it, as the constant fire and candles in that room would so soon turn it black, whereas by having it new painted once in four or five years, it will always be clean and cheerful.'

The Italian drawing-room had an outstandingly beautiful marble mantelpiece. An organ was built in the music-room. In the white and gold great drawing-room, with its crimson flowered silk hangings, was exquisite French furniture, and the china cabinets were filled with Sèvres and Chelsea porcelain. The picture collection included the works of Titian, Rubens, Van Dyck, Poussin, Canaletto, Guido, Salvator Rosa and Tenier.

To complete this picture of abounding luxury, Lord Chesterfield, who was an epicure, employed as his chef La Chapelle, a descendant of Louis XIV's famous chef, and his dinners and suppers were superb, Chesterfield being one of the first to introduce the skills of French cooking to London.

All the most amusing people of Mayfair society were invited to Lord Chesterfield's parties – the Gunning sisters, the Duke of Hamilton, the Duke of Newcastle, Lord Bath, Selwyn, Horace Walpole, the Duke of Queensberry – their names crop up over and over again. The Duke of Hamilton who fell in love with Elizabeth Gunning at the first house-warming party, and was in such a hurry to marry her, ran into difficulties even after they had decided on a midnight marriage at Keith's Chapel, for Keith himself was in prison by this time and his deputies were either otherwise engaged or not considered suitable, but the Duke's cousin, Old Q, was sympathetic and offered the services of his private chaplain, Kidgell, who duly performed the ceremony. Why Old Q should have needed a chaplain at all no one could say, but despite his frightful reputation for profligacy, he was at heart a kindly, generous soul. Kidgell had been at Winchester with him. He was hard up and needed a job.

Sad to relate, the Duke of Hamilton and Elizabeth did not stay in love for long. They parted and, after his death, Elizabeth soon married the 5th Duke of Argyll; and in the end as well as being the wife of two Dukes she became the mother of four, while her sister Maria, who was as beautiful as Elizabeth, married Lord Coventry.

Lord Chesterfield had twenty years to enjoy his splendid house but as he grew older and increasingly deaf he withdrew more and more from society, content in the seclusion of his library and his garden.

During these years Lady Chesterfield lived apart, still devoted to good works and the evangelism of John Whitfield. But when her husband lay dying she brought the Reverend Rowland Hill to his bedside, to pray over his departing spirit. Lord Chesterfield's stylish good manners never left him, but at this time, even if he had been prepared to receive Mr Hill's ministrations, he was far too deaf to hear what he had to say.

In 1743, only a few years before Chesterfield House was built, the author of the *History and Present State of the British Isles* had written:

> Between Portugal Street in the south and Grosvenor Buildings in the north, was a great open space, bordering on Hyde Park towards the west, where, not long since, May Fair (now suppressed) was held and which still retains the name of May Fair. Here some enterprising people ventured to build, hoping for the like success of those met with, who had built more to the eastward; but most of the buildings are running to ruin, some unfinished, and very few inhabited. But as this was formerly the case with the new buildings in Little Lincoln's Inn Fields and Red Lyon Fields, the first undertakers thereof were ruin'd, I'm inclined to think that May Fair will e'er long rise into buildings not much inferior to those of Grosvenor Square and Hanover Buildings, and lying not so far from St James's as Grosvenor and Hanover Squares do.

He was quite right, for although when Lord Chesterfield chose the site for his house it was on the western fringe of Mayfair and seemed lonely and remote, he lived to see the development of streets all round him.

The drive from the gates of Chesterfield House to the Park was soon lined with mansions which were every bit as grand as those of Grosvenor Square. It was known as Stanhope Street and later as Stanhope Gate.

Nathaniel Curzon, the ground landlord of much of this land, had granted John Phillips a building lease of 988 years and Phillips, in his turn, had disposed of his leaseholds in separate building plots, with strict insistence that the houses should be completed within twelve months and built to specified high standards, so that the aristocratic tone of the street should be maintained; and by 1761 Stanhope Street was one of the 'fine new streets' described by Defoe, 'near Berkeley Square and May Fair, in a place which herds and herdsmen, very few years ago, only inhabited. But now the residence of many of the first gentry equally splendid and convenient.'

For the next generation or two all the residents of Stanhope Gate were members of the aristocracy, and not until the 1830s did the intrusion of high finance into high society occur, with the arrival of the Baring family at Number 12.

With the death of the Earl of Chesterfield in 1773 Chesterfield House passed to his cousin, the 5th Earl; and during his time Mrs Fitzherbert was living at a house in Park Street. Here the Prince of Wales used to 'fly upon the Wings of Love', entering 'by the back way through the Stables and the Garden' and in 1785 they were married in the drawing-room. Ten years later she bought Number 6 Tilney Street, 'within sight of Park Lane and Stanhope Gate' and it remained her London home until her death in 1837. Her house in Park Street has long since disappeared but Number 6 Tilney Street remained until 1927, when it was pulled down and Fitzherbert House, a block of flats, was built on the site.

South Street and Mount Street were built gradually, throughout the eighteenth century, developing westwards as Park Lane was built, but Mount Street was one of the blots on Mayfair until, to-wards the end of the last century, the old eighteenth-century houses were pulled down and blocks of exclusive flats built above the new shops. Mount Street had been a dirty, unkempt street, once the short-cut from Tyburn to the Fair, past the parish work-houses and the old St George's burial-ground, and the shops were 'irregular in plan and size, and by no means of the first calibre'.

'Dear to me art thou, May Fair', wrote the satirist in 1823:

> Though many a stable scents the air,
> Though many a butcher's glowing shambles
> Startle the beauty's morning rambles.'

Mayfair was a mixture but the builders saw to it that the necessary, seamier side of existence was kept under control.

The 5th Earl of Chesterfield was succeeded in 1815 by his son, the 6th Earl. This was the Earl who sold Chesterfield House to Charles

Magniac for £150,000. But Magniac was soon in money troubles. He sold off some of the garden and on the site the houses of Chesterfield Gardens were built. He then demolished the wings of Chesterfield House and lived in the main block for some time, but then he went bankrupt. Lord Burton bought the house, lavishing great care on it and restoring it to something of its former grandeur, although many of the Chesterfield treasures had long since been returned to Bretby, where that earlier Lady Chesterfield, the daughter of the Duke of Ormonde, had been immured by her doting husband and Colonel James Hamilton, of that very susceptible family, had wooed her in vain.

Soon after their marriage, the late Princess Royal and Lord Harewood took Chesterfield House for their London home, but when they left it, in 1932, the house was demolished and has vanished without trace. The crowning indignity was the fate of the beautiful staircase, of which the 4th Lord Chesterfield had been so proud, for it was bought and installed in a cinema at Broadstairs, where, during the last war, it was bombed.

Crewe House, the elegant white house, with its portico of Ionic columns and its semicircular bays, standing back from Curzon Street amidst its beautifully tended lawns and plane trees, is one of the very few survivors of Mayfair's great mansions. Edward Shepherd built the original house during the reign of Queen Anne at a time when there was hardly any building of importance between its garden and Piccadilly, and he died here in 1747. Lord Fane bought it and lived here for a number of years and then, in 1792, it came into the possession of Lady Reade, who made extensive alterations to the house, which were undertaken by Sir John Soane. After her death the house was acquired by James Stuart-Wortley-Mackenzie – later Baron Wharncliffe of Wortley – grandson of Lord Bute and great-grandson of Lady Mary Wortley Montagu, whose letters he edited. He held some amusing literary parties here and often entertained his fellow members of the Owls club – the literary club which was called the Owls because of the late hours kept by its members. The house, by this time known as Wharncliffe House, remained in the Stuart-Wortley family from 1818 to 1899. It was then sold to the Earl of Crewe for £90,000.

At this time it had a high wall in front, like all the big town houses of the day, as well as a hedge and a creeper-covered lodge, but now that the old wall has given place to a new low wall and railing, with some splendid wrought-iron gates, every one can enjoy the sight of this beautiful house which, like the Grosvenor Chapel, is quite out-standing in its refreshing simplicity and grace.

In its heyday, after the rebuilding by Sir John Soane, the house had a magnificent collection of pictures, including the work of Romney, Hoppner, Lawrence, Gainsborough, Stubbs and Landseer, while from the library on the east side to the dining-room on the west, with the two drawing-rooms and the boudoir in between, the rooms were filled with beautiful French furniture.

Lord Crewe bought the house at the time of his marriage to the beautiful eighteen-year-old Margaret, daughter of the 5th Earl of Rosebery and Hannah, daughter of Baron Mayer de Rothschild, two families who had long been part of Mayfair.

Lord Crewe was already a prominent Liberal and Crewe House became an important social centre for the Liberal party, for during his lifetime he was Secretary of State for the Colonies, Lord President of the Council, Secretary of State for India, and, from 1922 to 1928, British Ambassador in Paris.

Lady Crewe performed her duties as a political hostess in the tradition of the Duchess of Devonshire and Lady Holland and it was at one of her dinner parties that the young Winston Churchill met his future wife.

During the First World War Lord Crewe lent the house to the Government, for the headquarters of Lord Northcliffe's propaganda department, which produced and distributed propaganda to the enemy countries, but with the end of the war he and Lady Crewe returned here for a time. But Crewe House had fifty-one rooms, with stables and garages and a vast basement. As so many owners of London mansions were to find, during the post-war years, the time had come to sell.

It was bought in 1937 by Thomas Tilling Limited and is no longer a private residence. The firm made certain obviously necessary altera-tions, but in essentials the lovely old house has been beautifully pre-served; and it is elegantly maintained, so that the eighteenth-century atmosphere still lingers.

The stables and garages behind have been pulled down and con-verted into offices. A few windows have been put in on the second floor, to give more light. The domed ceiling of the ballroom has gone and the room is now the board-room. The yellow room and the north room have been divided, but the Adam ceilings and marble fireplaces have been preserved. The vaulted ceiling over the entrance-hall is still there and also the black and white marble floor, though this is now covered by a fitted carpet. The spiral stone staircase has been replaced by a more practical one, hidden away under an arch at the back of the hall, but the marble-floored courtyard, around which the house is built, is the same as it was when Sir John Soane planned it nearly two hundred years ago.

Throughout the last quarter of the eighteenth and the early years of the nineteenth century, particularly during the lifetime of the vital brilliant, auburn-haired Duchess Georgiana, William Kent's Devonshire House remained an important centre of the Whig party.

George IV, as Prince of Wales and Prince Regent, was a frequent visitor at the Devonshire House parties, as were all the other important Whigs of the day, including Sheridan, Grey, Whitbread, Lord Robert Spencer, George Selwyn, Lord and Lady Grenville and Charles James Fox.

Georgiana, the daughter of Lord Spencer and great-granddaughter of the Duchess Sarah, had married the 5th Duke when she was only sixteen, and as she grew up she became a livelier personality than her husband, though he was a man of unassailable honour. In 1805 her health began to decline and in March 1806 she died of consumption. On her death-bed she is said to have begged her husband's forgiveness for her long devotion to Fox, knowing that he himself had been in love with Lady Elizabeth Forster, another close friend of Fox's, for many years.

'We have lost the best-bred woman in England', said George, Prince of Wales, when he heard of Georgiana's death, and Fox said, more simply, 'We have lost the gentlest heart'. Fox, already a sick man, died later that year, only a few months after taking office from Pitt, who had also died that year.

As for the Lady Elizabeth, Mrs Creevey, in a letter to Miss Ord, written in September 1806, just before Fox's death, tells a story about her which came from Sheridan. Sheridan told Mrs Creevey he had had a note from Lady Elizabeth, giving an account of Fox's health and ending: 'try to drink less and speak the truth'. 'Sheridan was very funny about it', wrote Mrs Creevey, and said: ' "By God! I speak more truth than *she* does." Then he told us how she had *cried* to him the night before, "because she felt it her severe duty to be Duchess of Devonshire!" '

It was in 1809, nearly three years later, that the wedding finally took place and Lady Elizabeth had nearly left it too late to become the new Duchess of Devonshire, for within two years of the marriage the Duke was dead.

Devonshire House was a two-storeyed, long, low building, plain and simple, still hidden from Piccadilly by Hugh May's original brick wall with its heavy wooden gates at either end. In Georgiana's day the entrance from the courtyard was by a double stairway which led straight into the first-floor reception rooms, but the 6th Duke changed this plan as well as making many other alterations to the house. This work was undertaken by James Wyatt in 1811 and at the same time many of the long range of beautifully proportioned rooms on the first floor, with their domed ceilings, gilded and painted like some Venetian palace, their vast mirrors and chandeliers, their aubusson carpets and tapestries, were redecorated.

The entrance was now made on the ground floor, with a plain pillared porch under which carriages could drive and passengers alight under cover. There was a balcony above the porch but the main doorway led straight into the hall, which was thrown out on the north side in a semicircular bay, overlooking the garden with its wide lawns and fine old elm trees. This bay contained the famous circular staircase made of marble and alabaster, with a baluster of gilded ironwork and a solid crystal handrail.

In the great white and gold ballroom, hung with blue and gold brocade, were paintings by Veronese and Rubens, cabinets of porcelain and Venetian furniture. There were Rembrandts in the red drawing-room, Tintorettos in the green drawing-room, pictures by Lely, Van Dyck and Frans Hals in the dining-room, and in Georgiana's blue and silver boudoir, which her son left as it had been during her lifetime, there was more work by Frans Hals and a number of Canalettos.

The 6th Duke was a handsome and attractive man, clever and amusing, and he maintained the great traditions of hospitality which his parents had established. During the junketings which accompanied the visit of the Allied Sovereigns to England, in 1814, he entertained the Emperor of Russia, the King of Prussia and all the important people who had come with them, and shortly afterwards the Prince of Orange, on the eve of his departure from London after Princess Charlotte had broken off her engagement to him. Lady Brownlow declared in her *Reminiscences* that she had seen the Princess and the Prince at a party at Carlton House a few days before, which the Russian Emperor and the King of Prussia had attended, and they were sitting together and walking about arm-in-arm, looking perfectly happy and lover-like. She wondered what intrigues had been taking place to make the Princess break off the engagement so suddenly, but the Princess herself was perfectly clear on the matter. Not only had she found that the Prince was a drunkard but she had decided that she did not want to spend a greater part of her life in Holland.

When, in the mid-nineteenth century, Bulwer Lytton and Charles Dickens were trying to raise money to establish their Guild of Art and Literature, it was the next Duke who offered them the use of Devonshire House to stage the two plays they had written – Bulwer Lytton's *Not So Bad As We Seem* and Dickens' farce *Mr Nightingale's Diary*. A movable stage was set up in the drawing-room and the library was turned into a green room. Queen Victoria and the Prince Consort saw a performance here on 27 May 1851, in which Douglas Jerrold, John Leach and Maclise all took part. The plays were repeated several times at the Hanover Square rooms and were well received, but the Guild never materialised.

There were many complaints about the unsightly Devonshire House wall all through the nineteenth century. George Augustus Sala defended the Devonshire family's right to privacy and in 1878 described the house as 'a perfectly unpretending building with low-pillared entrance hall', saying that 'the winding marble staircase with wide shallow steps is admirably suited to the princely hospitalities of the Cavendishes'; but in 1897 the Duke of Devonshire came to terms with the critics. He removed the old wooden gates and placed the armorial gilded iron gates from Chiswick House in the middle. This gave a grand approach across the courtyard to the main entrance of the house, which at last became visible from Piccadilly.

Chiswick House was a Palladian mansion which had been built by the architect Earl of Burlington during the reign of George II and had been inherited by the Devonshires. The gates had been designed by Inigo Jones for Beaufort House in Chelsea which had once been Thomas More's house. Sir Hans Sloane bought Beaufort House from the Beaufort family in 1737 and ultimately demolished it, but for many years it stood empty, and Lord Burlington, seeing the gates in danger of falling into ruin, begged them from Sir Hans for Chiswick House. And when Chiswick House was sold to a doctor and turned into a lunatic asylum, the gates came to Piccadilly.

The Devonshire family sold Devonshire House shortly after the First World War. The elm trees in the garden came down first. Then, in 1924, the grand old mansion which had seen so much history and on which consummate art and skill had been lavished was razed to the ground and in its place the twelve-storey block of the

present Devonshire House was built. All that is left of old Devonshire House is the pair of beautiful armorial gates, which have been
set up on the opposite side of Piccadilly, giving on to the Green
Park.

Adam had originally planned Lansdowne House as a long, low
building similar to Devonshire House, but as it had to be built facing
eastwards, with little ground at the back and the garden in the front,
divided from the Devonshire House garden by the Lansdowne
Passage, the design was changed to a taller house with a shorter frontage.

When Lord Shelbourne bought it from Lord Bute he ordered
certain alterations to be made by the Adam brothers to Lord Bute's
original design, but it remained a typical Palladian mansion, with the
intercommunicating state rooms on the first floor, decorated by
Cipriani, Zucchi and Perfetti; but with the disregard for creature
comforts which was to be found in so many of these houses, Lord
Shelbourne's bedroom was on the ground floor and his dressing-
room on the first floor, on the opposite side of the house, while the
servants' bedrooms were little more than cupboards.

After Lady Shelbourne died, in 1771, Lord Shelbourne made a
journey to Italy, where, with the help of Gavin Hamilton, who
supervised the excavations of an archaeological site near Rome, he
began his collection of Classical sculpture for which the house became famous.

He was created the 1st Marquess of Lansdowne in 1784 and when
he died, in 1805, his son the 2nd Marquess kept the statuary but sold
off all his father's pictures, books and manuscripts, for which he
seemed to have no feeling and little appreciation of their value. The
British Museum bought the manuscripts, but the books and pictures
were dispersed to the highest bidders.

However, he lived for only another four years and his half-
brother, the 3rd Lord Lansdowne, not only made a fresh collection
of pictures and books for the house but bought back the statuary,
which the 2nd Marquess had bequeathed to his widow.

In the early years of the nineteenth century, the 3rd Marquess
established Lansdowne House as yet another Whig stronghold and
the sumptuously furnished state rooms were the scene of many a
brilliant entertainment and important political gathering.

Much of the furniture and many of the pictures of these Mayfair
mansions were acquired in the course of the Napoleonic Wars.
either by purchase or loot. Thomas Creevey, who was a friend of the

Marquess, and a frequent visitor at Lansdowne House, was writing to Miss Ord in May 1823:

'My Lord Lansdowne was *affable* beyond measure yesterday. He had had a special messenger from Marshal Soult offering him in the first instance, and before anyone else, his Murillos, taken by him when in Spain and only asking as the price of them *one hundred* thousand pounds! My lord said Soult had shown them to him when he was last in Paris, and certainly they were the finest things ever seen – great altar pieces etc. . . .'

In addition to the work of Velasquez, Murillo, Rembrandt and Reynolds, including the Reynolds' portraits of Kitty Fisher, David Garrick, Horace Walpole and Sterne, the Marquess had collected examples of the Italian, Dutch and early English schools and was also a patron of contemporary English artists, such as Calcott, Collins and Wilkie.

His home became a meeting-place of the Holland House circle – Allen, Sydney Smith, Luttrell, Macaulay and Rogers, as well as Lord Holland, 'truly kind and agreeable' and Lady Holland 'very gracious – or intending to be so', and he offered entertainment as generous to poets and painters, musicians and men of letters. These parties were all glitter and glamour, with a fair measure of intrigue not far below the polished surface, as one can read in the diaries and letters of Creevey, Greville, Tom Moore and George Tickney, the New England traveller and Harvard professor.

In 1812 Creevey is telling his wife that 'Sheridan is more base in his resentment against Whitbread than you can imagine, and all from Drury Lane disappointments' but the next day, 28 May, he met Sheridan 'coming from a long interview with the Prince, and going with a message to Wellesley; so of course I walked with him and got from him all I could'. The Prince was distraught, for 'he conceived the different candidates for office to be determined upon his ruin; and, in short, I begin to think that his reign will end in a day or two in downright insanity' . . . 'Canning has been found out in some intrigue with Liverpool already . . .'

A few days later he is telling his wife that 'Prinny, Wellesley and Canning are both madmen and villains . . . In the meantime, we must have the Bank made to pay us in specie . . . which would give you and me £700 per annum more than we have. This would be something like, so we shall see what we shall see.'

'Is one to laugh at our poor foolish party having so obviously and so fatally for themselves played the game of these villains Wellesley and Canning, or is one to cry at the never-failing success of rascality in this country?' he exclaims, and in 1824 he was writing to Miss Ord: 'Would you believe it? Lady H. would not let Lord Holland dine with Lord Lansdowne last week – a dinner made purposely for Mina,★ 'merely because she thought it might not please the King if he heard of it! Nor will she let Mina or any Spaniard approach Holland House for the same reason. Was there ever such a ——?'

Moore's diary is full of descriptions of the parties at Lansdowne House, including the occasion when he found himself sitting next to the eccentric Lord Dudley and noted his 'mutterings to himself; his fastidious contemplation of what he had on his plate, occasionally pushing about the meat with his fingers, and uttering low-breathed criticisms upon it' and came to the conclusion that he was 'on the verge of insanity'.

The 4th Marquess of Lansdowne married the daughter of Count Flahaut, French Ambassador to London during the Second Empire, and Count Flahaut was generally believed to be the natural son of Talleyrand, so the 5th Marquess was Talleyrand's great-grandson.

The glories of Lansdowne House faded after the First World War. Early in the 1920s the house was let to Gordon Selfridge for a time, at a rental of £5,000 a year. The garden remained until 1925 but then, after Devonshire House had disappeared and there was no longer any bar to building along the south side of Berkeley Square, it disappeared under the new Lansdowne House and Morris House. In 1935 old Lansdowne House was cruelly mauled so that Curzon Street could be joined to Berkeley Square. The front of the house was removed to a depth of some forty feet and the original façade built on to what was left. The two wings were demolished and two storeys added to the central portion for its present use as the Lansdowne Club.

Two of the rooms from the front of the house were sent to America, the main drawing-room, which has been reconstructed in the Pennsylvania Museum of Art in Philadelphia, and the dining-room, which can now been seen in the Metropolitan Museum in New York, while one of the Adam chimney-pieces was presented to the London Library. And all that is left of old Lansdowne House is a sad travesty of Lord Bute's magnificent dream.

While Lord Chesterfield was enjoying his last years at Chesterfield House and the Cavendishs were living in Burlington House,

★ General Mina was a Spanish soldier who commanded a corps under Wellington during the Peninsular War.

William Douglas, the 4th Duke of Queensberry, known to all the world as Old Q, was living in Piccadilly. He was born in 1725 and built Number 138 Piccadilly for himself in 1768; and here he lived until his death in 1811. His father had died in 1731, and his mother, who was yet another member of the Hamilton family, in 1748, so while he was still very young he was left on his own, with an immense fortune. As a young man he had a passion for racing and was a founder member of the Turf Club. He bred bloodstock and owned one of the largest studs in England. To his lasting regret he never won either the Derby or the Oaks, but throughout his lifetime he is thought to have won a quarter of a million pounds on the turf.

He was an inveterate gambler, as the betting book at White's shows, and would wager on anything, from the number of children a couple were likely to have to how much a man could eat at a sitting – Old Q's man winning on that occasion 'by a pig and an apple pie'.

But this kind of betting was a common habit in Mayfair. Some men ruined themselves by it. Both Lord Montford and Sir John Bland bankrupted themselves and committed suicide and Horace Walpole, writing in 1752, said:

'I did not doubt you would be struck with the death of poor Bland. I t'other night at White's found a very remarkable entry in our very – very remarkable wager-book: "Lord Montford bets Sir John Bland twenty guineas that Nash outlives Cibber." How odd that these two old creatures, selected for their antiquities, should live to see both their wagerers put an end to their own lives . . .'

Old Q had countless love affairs and was a womaniser all his life, which gave him a bad name among the more puritanical members of society, of which there were not, at this time, a great many, but he was kind-hearted, a loyal friend, particularly to George Selwyn, and he had his own strict code of honour.

He never married. For seven years he had admired Frances Pelham, daughter of the Prime Minister, but Pelham did not approve of him as a son-in-law and he eventually abandoned the chase. Whatever Frances may have thought about him, she never married and ended up in poverty, having gambled away the whole of her considerable fortune at cards.

After Lady Mary Coke, another gambler and a bad loser, was widowed, he proposed to her, but she turned him down flatly, though they remained good friends. He tried several other young women, including Gertrude Vanneck, when she was living next door at Number 139, but she, too, refused him. After that he made do

Barbara Castlemaine, Duchess of Cleveland.

Cambridge House, Piccadilly, the town residence of Lord Palmerston, 1865.

Clarges House, Piccadilly.

Bath House, Piccadilly, as it stood in 1820,
before being rebuilt by Lord Ashburton.

Devonshire House, about 1800.

The ballroom at Devonshire House.

Piccadilly in the late nineteenth century;
the view towards Hyde Park Corner.

Piccadilly, looking towards the City from Old Bond Street;
the Egyptian Hall (now Jackson's) is on the right.

Burlington House, Piccadilly.

The Albany, Piccadilly. A T. H. Shepherd print.

The Albany in 1925, drawing by Hanslip Fletcher.

Regent Street, looking towards the Duke of York's column.
A nineteenth-century view by T. S. Boys.

with a succession of singers and actresses, largely drawn from the Haymarket Theatre.

In his early years his title was Lord March and he did not become Duke of Queensberry until 1778, being given the English title of Lord Douglas of Amesbury in 1786.

There was a more serious side to his character for although he played no great part in the debates in the House of Lords, he took a keen interest in them and attended regularly for forty years. He was a staunch Tory and his most notable activity was rousing the House to the activities of Wilkes and helping to put him on trial for his *Essay on Woman*, which the Peers declared 'a most scandalous, obscene and impious libel ... and a most wicked and blasphemous attempt to ridicule and villify the person of our Blessed Saviour'.

He had several homes, including a house at Richmond, where he kept the pictures he had inherited from Clarendon House, but Piccadilly was always his favourite house and after he had given up racing and his house at Newmarket, during the 1780s, he seldom left it. It took two years to build and was magnificent, the first-floor drawing-room having a ceiling painted by Angelica Kauffmann.

'March's great room is gilding, and when finished he is to give a dinner to Lady Sarah (Bunbury), and a concert to a great many more,' wrote George Selwyn to Lord Carlisle in February 1768, and Lady Mary Coke, who was one of the guests at that party, wrote in her diary on 12 March of that year:

> The house is very fine and fitted up with a great deal of taste. There were three and twenty people; the Duchess of Grafton, the Duchess of Hamilton, the Duchess of Buccleugh, Lady Coventry, Lady Essex, Mrs Fitzroy, Mrs Pitt and Lady Susan Stewart. The rest were all men. The supper was fine but not tedious. When it was over there was music and five couples danced. Some time ago I should have liked it very much, but now nothing entertains me. At a quarter after one o'clock, the Duchess of Buccleugh and I called for our chairs and all the party seemed breaking up.

It was an illustrious party, even though Lady Sarah seems not to have put in an appearance after all. She was born Lady Sarah Lennox, a daughter of the Duke of Richmond, who was a grandson of Charles II and the Duchess of Portsmouth: she was the girl with whom the young George III had been so much in love, when his mother and Lord Bute quickly married him off to Charlotte of Mecklenburg, at a time when Lady Sarah had every justification for thinking that she was about to become Queen of England herself. Shortly after the coronation she married Sir Charles Bunbury, but before long she left him, and after the divorce she married Colonel George Napier.

The Duchess of Grafton was on the eve of a divorce and about to become Lady Ossory. The Duchess of Hamilton, whose marriage to the Duke at Keith's Chapel had been helped forward by Old Q offering the services of his chaplain Kidgell, was by now the Duchess of Argyll, but this fact Lady Mary seems to have preferred to overlook. Her sister, who had married Lord Coventry, was already dead, and the Lady Coventry of Lady Mary's account was the 2nd Lady Coventry, while Mrs Pitt was the half crazy Anne Pitt who was always turning up at Mayfair parties.

Old Q was a great lover of music and the opera and made full use of his box at the Haymarket Opera House; and apart from the young women who became his mistresses, he was a generous patron to a great many singers and musicians.

Sunderland House, to the east of Burlington House, was never so grand as its neighbour, although when it came into the possession of the 1st Lord Melbourne, in 1770, it was altered and enlarged by William Chambers. It remained a plain and unostentatious brick house, elegant in its simplicity, and separated from the street wall by a wide courtyard; but inside it was beautifully appointed and the ceiling of the ballroom was painted by Cipriani. It was in 1791 that Lord Melbourne exchanged his house with the Duke of York for the Duke's house in Whitehall, but the Duke did not live there for long and in 1803, a few years after he had left it, Melbourne House was converted into the present chambers, which were called Albany, the Duke's second title.

The garden, stretching back to Burlington Gardens, was built over to form extra accommodation and a covered way was made leading into Vigo Street, to give an alternative entrance. About the same time, the wall dividing the front courtyard from Piccadilly was demolished and four shops built on either side of the gateway.

At first Albany, comprising sixty sets of apartments, was occupied entirely by bachelors or widowers. The residents were mostly Members of Parliament or of the services, with a fair sprinkling of literary men, including Byron, Macaulay and also Bulwer Lytton, who sought sanctuary there for a time, from his impossible wife. No one engaged in trade or commerce lived there and no woman was expected to cross the threshold, unless she were a close relative paying a brief visit.

Rooms in Albany have always been coveted, for with the increasing busyness and noise of Piccadilly it came to be, and has remained, a delightfully peaceful and secluded backwater, yet Arthur Dasent was one who confessed that he found it rather a gloomy place.

West of Devonshire House was Bath House, standing on the western corner of Bolton Street. The original Bath House, where Mrs Montagu's friend William Pulteney, Lord Bath, lived, was an early eighteenth-century house, flat fronted and plain, comprising a ground floor with two floors above. Two short wings enclosed the front courtyard and the garden stretched back to Curzon Street.

William Pulteney moved into it from Arlington Street in 1740, but it did not have a very long life, for after one or two generations of extremely wealthy Pulteneys had lived there and the direct line became extinct, it came into the possession of Alexander Baring, the 1st Lord Ashburton, head of the house of Baring Brothers, who in 1821 demolished the old house and built Ashburnham House on the site, filling it with his splendid collection of Dutch and Flemish paintings.

Three more generations of Barings lived here and then Sir Julius Wernher, who died in 1912, since when the house has been demolished.

On the east corner of Bolton Street stood Coventry House which Sir Henry Hunloke built in the early 1760s, on the site of the old Greyhound Inn and sold in 1764 to the Earl of Coventry. This was the Earl who had married one of the Gunning sisters. They had lived at Number 3 Grosvenor Square, but she died young and when he re-married he took his second wife to live at his beautiful new house overlooking the Green Park, with its double staircase, its Adam decorations and Angelica Kauffmann ceilings. The only drawback was the noise of the Fair taking place almost at his back-door, and after he had succeeded in bringing it to an end, many more mansions were built in this western part of Piccadilly, down to Hyde Park Corner, displacing the drovers' taverns and the stonemasons' yards, which for many years had been turning out very bad statues.

'Among a hundred statues, you shall hardly see one even tolerable, either in design or execution; nay, even the copies of the antique are so monstrously wretched, that one can hardly guess at their originals,' wrote Horace Walpole.

The Coventry family lived in Coventry House for nearly a century and when the house fell vacant, in 1854, it was taken by Count Flahaut, who from 1860 to 1864 was French Ambassador for Louis

Napoleon and used the house as his Embassy. In 1869, a few years after his return to France, the house was acquired by the St James's Club, which has been there ever since.

Cambridge House, Number 94 Piccadilly, and now the Naval and Military Club, is another eighteenth-century survival. The architect is not certain but was probably William Chambers. The house was built about 1760, on the site of an old inn, for Charles Wyndham, the 2nd Earl of Egremont, and was first known as Egremont House. Dodsley in his *Environs of London* described it at this time as the last house in Piccadilly. 'It is of stone, and tho' not much adorned, is elegant, and well situated for a town house, having fine views over the Green Park, which would be still more extended if the houses on each side were set further back.'

Lord Egremont, who served as Secretary of State under Greville, was a man of great wealth and an important member of the Cocoa Tree Club; but he was also a great eater and unfortunately carried his favourite pastime to such excess that he died of apoplexy only two years after moving into his fine new house.

His son and heir was a very different character, but equally odd in his way. He was less interested in politics than the arts, of which he was a generous patron; and he entertained generously, both in Piccadilly, where he lived for the next thirty years, and at Petworth.

He was very fond of children and had a great many, but he disliked the prospect of marriage and dispensed with the ceremony. At least six of his children lived happily with him at Egremont House and Petworth, calling him their father, but mother remained a mystery, though she was thought to have been the wife of a master at his old school, Westminster.

He lived until 1837 but he left Egremont House in the 1790s for a house in Grosvenor Place and the Marquess of Cholmondeley moved in from Gloucester House, Hyde Park Corner, where he remained until his death in 1827. The next arrival was Adolphus Frederick, the Duke of Cambridge, son of George III, who like his two brothers the Duke of Kent and the Duke of Clarence, had abandoned a mistress to make a hurried and respectable marriage after the sudden death of Princess Charlotte, which had made the line of succession to the throne so much closer. If not particularly intellectual, he was a cheerful, hearty soul, much given to talking aloud to himself, and he and his German wife – a Princess of Hesse – lived here until his death in 1850. The widowed Duchess, who survived him for nearly forty years, moved to York House, St James's Palace, and the next important arrival at Cambridge House was Lord Palmerston, who moved here from Number 144 Piccadilly, in 1857, for the last eight years of his life.

In Lord Palmerston's day, during the stormy years of controversy before the passing of the second Reform Act of 1867, Cambridge House was a brilliant Whig stronghold and invitations to the beautiful Lady Palmerston's parties were greatly prized. She made a point of writing all her invitations personally, and scorning the penny post, they were always delivered by hand.

Lord Palmerston was Prime Minister from 1855 until 1858 and again from 1859 until his death in 1865, an aristocratic Whig of the old school and the last Prime Minister to ride to the House on horseback.

The Naval and Military Club had been formed a year or two before his death and had first opened in a small house in Clifford Street. The next year, as their numbers increased, they had moved to Number 22 Hanover Square, but when, with Lord Palmerston's death, Cambridge House fell vacant, they bought it. Within the next few years they built several extensions, including the coffee-room over part of the garden at the back, but left an attractive enclosed courtyard. The street wall still stands and the In and Out gates at either end have given the club its nickname. It was sorely damaged by bombs during the last war but has been beautifully restored and still looks very much like the charming house which Lord Egremont built more than two hundred years ago.

While the Duke of Cambridge was living at Cambridge House, during the second quarter of the nineteenth century, his sister, Princess Mary, who had married her cousin, the Duke of Gloucester, was living at Gloucester House, farther west in Piccadilly, at the corner of old Park Lane.

Princess Mary had been the beauty of George III's six daughters, but was probably the least romantically inclined. When she was quite a young girl she had decided to marry the Duke of Gloucester, but the affair had dragged on for years, for her father hated the thought of any of his daughters marrying, and had been known to burst into tears when the subject was raised. At last, in 1816, when she was forty but still beautiful, the wedding took place; but by this time both her parents were ill. The mad old King lingered on at Windsor and the Queen, who was to die two years before him, was living out her last years at Kew. With her sisters, Princess Elizabeth and Princess Augusta, Princess Mary spent a good deal of her time with her sick mother, while Princess Sophie devoted herself to the King at Windsor. In the first years of her marriage, Princess Mary seemed happy, but after a time the Duke is thought to have become jealous of her devotion to her parents and was said to have ill-treated her, although she would never admit as much.

Gloucester House had originally been built for the Cholmondeleys in the 1770s. When they moved the house was bought by Lord Elgin and it was here that he stored the Elgin marbles, including the wonderful sculptures from the Parthenon of Athena at the Acropolis in Athens, which he had brought back to England in 1802. At this time he had been Ambassador to Constantinople and he had bought the marbles to save them from destruction by the Turks. Some years later he sold them to the British Museum for less than half the £75,000 he had paid for them.

The Duke of Gloucester bought Gloucester House from Lord Elgin at the time of his marriage to Princess Mary. It was a comparatively small but charming house of three storeys, with a wide balcony along the first floor which had a pagoda-like curving green roof supported by iron posts, more like a Regency house at Brighton than a Piccadilly mansion: the small courtyard in front was protected by a high street wall, its entrance gate being in Park Lane.

Queen Charlotte, the Duke's aunt, had always been fond of the Duke when he was a small boy and nicknamed him Silly Billy. And Silly Billy he remained all his life, for he was not over bright and no conversationalist, although he became a Field-Marshal in the Army and was elected Chancellor of Cambridge University.

His father, George III's brother, had made a morganatic marriage with Maria, the Dowager Countess Waldegrave, who was beautiful and charming but in King George's view, socially unacceptable, since not only was she illegitimate, her father being Sir Edward Walpole, but her mother was the daughter of the postmaster at Darlington. For six years the marriage was kept a secret and the Duke lived alone in another Gloucester House, which had been built for him in Park Lane, when it was still Tyburn Lane. Then he took his wife to Italy and Silly Billy had been born in Rome in 1776, but when they returned to England shortly afterwards and made their marriage public, King George was completely won over by the Duchess's charm and tact, and they were forgiven.

Silly Billy spent his childhood at the Gloucester House in Park Lane and when his father died the house was sold to the Grosvenor family and was known as Grosvenor House.

Silly Billy died in Gloucester House, Piccadilly, in 1834 and Princess Mary lived on there alone until her death in 1857. The Duke of Cambridge, who had died at Cambridge House in 1850, had always been her favourite brother, and since she had no children of her own she made her nephew, the new Duke of Cambridge, her heir, leaving him Gloucester House and all its contents, pictures, porcelain, furniture and family treasures which the Duke of Gloucester had inherited from old Gloucester House in Park Lane.

The Duke was, of course, first cousin to Queen Victoria, and he now took up his abode in Gloucester House, Piccadilly, a fine, upstanding young man who became Commander-in-Chief of the Army. But he had a guilty secret. Despite the Royal Marriage Act of 1772, which his exasperated grandfather had insisted upon when he found that two of his brothers had married without his consent, and which stipulated that no such marriage should be considered legal, the young Duke of Cambridge had been married for ten years to Louisa Fairbrother, an actress from the Covent Garden Theatre.

She retired from the stage at the time of her marriage in 1848 and it remained a closely guarded secret for many years. The Duke lived at Gloucester House and his wife at Number 6 Queen Street, where their three sons were born. It is still standing, an interesting old terrace house, narrow and tall, with four storeys above the ground floor, a basement and a rather wide front door. There is a balcony on the first floor on to which open three tall windows from the drawing-room, the central window being pedimented, and there is a stone balustrade below the attic floor.

Here Louisa was content to live in peaceful obscurity, but when Queen Victoria at last came to hear of the marriage she was highly indignant. She allowed Maria to be given the name of Mrs Fitzgeorge, and the three boys bore this name, but she insisted that they should be debarred from inheriting the Dukedom of Cambridge.

Mrs Fitzgeorge seems to have been an extraordinarily understanding woman, as well as very beautiful and intelligent. She entertained a wide circle of friends in Queen Street, which included Mr Gladstone and Lord Burnham, and the Duke always spent Sundays with her and his family, driving round from Gloucester House in his phaeton. Yet they were never seen together in public, except when they all went to church at the Mayfair Chapel.

This strange marriage continued happily until Louisa died in 1890. Then, although the Queen had never met her, she sent the Duke a note of condolence; and the Duke sadly noted in his diary that the

Queen's affectionate message 'would have been such a joy to my beloved had she known the fact'.

The lonely old Duke survived his wife by many years, living alone in the bleak grandeur of Gloucester House until his death in 1904: then the old house was pulled down and a block of flats built in its place, which in their turn have disappeared to make way for an office block.

His son, Sir Augustus Fitzgeorge, inherited Number 6 Queen Street on his mother's death and lived there until he died in 1933. Then Queen Mary visited the house to examine the royal treasures which over the years had come there from Gloucester House. They included prints and signed portraits of all George III's children as well as other portraits and family mementoes, together with relics of the Duke of Cambridge's foreign campaigns. Some of these went to the royal collections but others remain in the Fitzgeorge family.

When the immensely rich 2nd Earl of Grosvenor acquired old Gloucester House in Park Lane, soon after the Duke of Gloucester's death in 1805, he proceeded to enlarge and embellish it, to make it a home fit for a man who owned nearly half Mayfair and whose descendant, Henry Lupus Grosvenor, was, in 1874, to be created the 1st Duke of Westminster.

Grosvenor House occupied two and three-quarter acres. It stood at the corner of Upper Grosvenor Street and Park Lane and its garden ran down to Mount Street. The entrance was in Upper Grosvenor Street, by way of a majestic stone screen composed of eight columns, with lamp-posts in between each, and a carriage entrance at either end, protected by magnificent metal gates surmounted by pediments bearing the family crest.

This colonnade was designed by Thomas Cundy, who was also the architect of the new west wing of the house, containing the picture gallery. The Grosvenor House pictures had mainly been collected by the 1st Earl, who had succeeded in 1755, and who, in addition to buying old masters, had commissioned work from many contemporary artists, including Reynolds, Gainsborough and Richard Wilson.

Grosvenor House, with its pictures and French furniture, was truly magnificent, and by the time it was a ducal residence it had probably the finest collection of Rembrandts in the country, as well as pictures by Salvator Rosa, Claude Lorraine, Murillo and Velasquez. In the dining-room there were five Rembrandts and a Rubens, as well as seven pictures by Claude. In the saloon there were Italian, French, Spanish, Dutch and Flemish pictures. In the small drawing-room hung Gainsborough's Blue Boy and Joshua Reynold's portrait of Mrs Siddons.

All the doors of the house were of solid mahogany picked out in gold. There were mantel-pieces of Carrera marble, Louis XIV cabinets of exquisite porcelain, tables of lapis lazuli mounted on ormolu.

In 1926 it all came down. The picture collection was dispersed and on the site of the old house was built the Grosvenor House Hotel.

Close by was Dorchester House. Little is known about the old Dorchester House, which had once been the London residence of the Earls of Dorchester, except that it was here that the 3rd Marquess of Hertford, the husband of Maria Fagniani and the original of Thackeray's Lord Steyne, in *Vanity Fair*, lived for the last few years of his life, dying in 1842.

The old house was bought by R. S. Holford, who in 1852 rebuilt the new Dorchester House on the site – a Venetian palace by Vulliamy. It had a triangular forecourt enclosed by a massive stone wall, and a lodge at the entrance, which was where Deanery Street now runs into Park Lane. He built it as a setting for his pictures and books, and it was all on the grand scale of Grosvenor House, with its vast state rooms – the saloon, the green drawing-room, the red drawing-room and the state drawing-room. The life of the house belonged entirely to Victorian times and the first quarter of the twentieth century and in 1931 it was demolished and the present Dorchester Hotel built in its place.

Brook House, at the corner of Brook Street and Park Lane, had an even shorter life. It was a tall, red-brick house built in 1867 for Lord Tweedsmuir by T. H. Wyatt. Sir Ernest Cassel bought it and spent even more money on it, importing tons of Italian marble for the grand staircase and the hall, but in 1931, by which time Sir Ernest's granddaughter, Lady Mountbatten, had inherited it, it was pulled down and the present block of flats built in its place.

Londonderry House stood on the corner of Hertford Street and Park Lane, a huge, square, corner house with three storeys and a basement, and a stone balustrade round the roof. It was originally Holdernesse House, built by 'Athenian' Stuart for the d'Arcy family, the Earls of Holdernesse, at the beginning of the reign of George III. The last peer of the Holdernesse line died in 1778 and the house stood empty for some years, until it was bought , in the 1830s, by the 3rd Marquess of Londonderry, half-brother of Lord Castlereagh. The Marquess had fought with Wellington in the Peninsular War and also during the decisive 1814–15 campaign. He married the immensely rich heiress, Lady Frances Anne Vane-Tempest and engaged Benjamin and Philip Wyatt to re-model the house, although a good deal of Stuart's work was preserved, including two of the first-floor rooms overlooking the Park.

The magnificent double staircase with the gilded balustrade, designed by the Wyatts, led straight into the great gallery and ballroom, which was probably the finest of all the superbly furnished rooms in the house. Here, in niches built into the walls, the Marquess displayed his collection of Canova statuary. It had no windows but was lighted from above, by a skylight running the entire length of the room. The state drawing-rooms, with their domed and painted ceilings, silk hangings and French furniture, their pictures and their cabinets full of porcelain, led from one to the other in the manner of nearly all these vast palaces.

The study, a long room divided half-way by pillars, looked out on to Hertford Street, but the white dining-room, with its Canalettos and Guardis, had a view of the fountain which used to stand at the corner of Hamilton Place and Park Lane; and for all its magnificence, its grandeur did not overwhelm it, for the house was comfortable and homelike.

The 3rd Marquess died in 1854 but three generations of his family succeeded him at Londonderry House and for more than a century it was a centre of the world of fashion, philanthropy and politics, becoming an important social meeting-place for the Tories. After the First World War receptions were held here on the eve of the opening of Parliament, with the leader of the party standing with Lord and Lady Londonderry to receive the long procession of distinguished guests who mounted the splendid staircase.

With the 1920s, the expenses of maintaining the house became too great. It was occasionally let for important wedding receptions and fashionable dress shows, given for charity, but it became an increasing burden. When the near-by towering Hilton Hotel was opened in 1963, overlooking and casting its shadow over the elegant Londonderry House, it was sold to the developers, and now the Londonderry House Hotel has risen on the site of the historic old house.

It was in 1770 that the 'weak but worthy' Chancellor of the Exchequer, the 2nd Earl Bathurst, who had become Lord Apsley, took a fancy to the plot of land at the corner of Hyde Park, where Apsley House was to be built. He met with several difficulties but at last succeeded in obtaining from the Crown the land where a gatekeeper's lodge stood and another site, where Mrs Allen, a widow, kept an apple stall and had built herself a small cottage. The land had been granted to her late husband by George II, after he had fought with him at Dettingen, and Lord Apsley had to pay her handsomely before she would budge.

He also managed to buy some of the land which had been granted to the Duke of Hamilton and his widow late in the seventeenth century, on which stood the old inn the Hercules Pillars, where Squire Western had stayed when he was chasing Tom Jones.

These problems solved, the Earl proceeded to build himself a plain, red-brick house, which cost him £10,000. The Adam brothers supervised the interior decorations but Lord Bathurst did not allow them much say in the general plan of the house, preferring his own ideas, which nearly ended in disaster, for he forgot to allow for a staircase from the first to the second floor and also left no room for stabling. However, the first difficulty was overcome, and after demolishing the Hercules Pillars he had space to build his stables.

Lord Apsley died in 1794 and his son, the 3rd Earl, lived there for a time, but in 1807 he moved and the Marquess of Wellesley, eldest brother of the future Duke of Wellington, lived there, after his return from India.

Throughout 1815 and 1816, the Duke of Wellington was living in a rented house in Hamilton Place, but when the Marquess was appointed Viceroy of Ireland, the Duke acquired the leasehold of Apsley House from him, and ultimately bought the freehold, while the estate of Stratfieldsaye was bought for him by a grateful nation.

At Apsley House the Duke commissioned Benjamin Wyatt to make many alterations and extensions. The old red-brick house was encased in Bath stone, the Corinthian portico was added and the west wing built, which contained the Waterloo room, where the Waterloo banquet was held each year, for the Duke's fellow officers, who had fought with him at Waterloo. Although, as the century lengthened, the numbers inevitably dwindled, the Duke held this banquet every year until his death in 1852.

The Duke acquired many treasures during his campaigns, including some beautiful porcelain and pictures, the most outstanding being the Murillos and Velasquezs, which are still there, for the public to enjoy. These pictures had been looted by Joseph Bonaparte and were on their way back to France, during his retreat in 1813, after the Battle of Vittoria. However, the English captured his baggage train and the Duke, with characteristic honesty, made arrangements for their return to Spain, but King Ferdinand VII insisted on presenting them to the Duke, as a token of gratitude for his victories.

Yet despite the grandeur of much of Apsley House – the Waterloo gallery, the picture gallery, the striped drawing-room and the yellow drawing-room – the Duke's personal taste was for simplicity. His small bedroom on the ground floor, overlooking the little garden which divides the house from Hyde Park, had spartan furnishing – a small iron bedstead and a plain writing table, with a few books – as plain as the room in which he died at Walmer Castle, his home as Warden of the Cinque Ports.

During the Reform Bill riots of April 1831, Apsley House was one of the many houses in the West End which had its windows broken by the angry crowds, but when they learnt that the Duchess had died a day or two before, and that her body was still in the house, they disappeared, for despite his temporary unpopularity over his opposition to the Bill, the Duke was greatly loved and honoured. However, like all good soldiers, he learnt from experience and took no unnecessary risks. After that night he had bullet-proof shutters put up at his windows, which remained there until after his death.

His son, the 2nd Duke, made certain alterations to the house after his father's death, which were undertaken by Philip Hardwick, but in essentials the Apsley House which today stands in isolation at Hyde Park Corner, is much as the old Duke knew it. In 1952 the 7th Duke presented it to the nation, retaining only a few rooms for private residence, and it has become the Wellington Museum.

XII

Piccadilly

These great mansions of the late eighteenth century and the early nineteenth were not the whole story of Mayfair's grandeur, and in Piccadilly, as building gradually extended westwards, and the old inns and artisan dwellings disappeared, many large houses were built for the aristocracy, and also for the rich, whether they were aristocratic or not. The sites opposite the Green Park were particularly sought after, once the Fair had been abolished.

None of the houses had a very long existence as a private residence. Many became clubs or hotels and others were demolished for flats or offices, but in their day they played an important part in the social life of Mayfair and maintained its tradition of grandeur and social distinction.

The house on the corner of Stratton Street and Piccadilly was built in the early 1760s for Lord Eglinton, a friend and schoolfellow of Old Q, but Lord Eglinton died young. He was murdered on his Scottish estates by a poacher, who hanged himself in prison to escape the gallows.

There were several aristocratic occupiers of the house during the next few years, who made minor additions to Matthew Brettingham's original design, and in 1795 it was bought by Thomas Coutts, the banker, who made a small garden at the back and added a library and some extra bedrooms by incorporating properties round the corner in Stratton Street.

Thomas Coutts had married a servant maid of his brother James, but three months after her death, by which time he was close on eighty years old, he married the Drury Lane actress, Harriet Mellon, who had made her name in 1795, as Lydia Languish.

Coutts died in 1822 and Harriet, by this time approaching fifty, married the young Duke of St Albans, ninth in the line, who was only twenty-six.

Coutts' youngest daughter by his first marriage, Sophie, had married Sir Francis Burdett, and their youngest daughter, Angela, who was in later life to be created Baroness Burdett-Coutts, was born in this large corner house in 1814.

Sir Francis – Old Glory – was a champion of free speech and shortly before Angela's birth he had been seized at his Piccadilly home and imprisoned in the Tower for a spell. He was again imprisoned in 1820, for an alleged libel against the Government, and after that he became more circumspect in airing his views and for the next thirty years was a respectable Member of Parliament, representing the City of Westminster as a democrat, after which he was a Tory county member.

Number 80 Piccadilly, next to the corner house, was built by Sir Richard Lyttelton in 1764, on the site of an older house built by a Mr Boswell, on land granted to him by Lord Berkeley of Stratton. Thomas Coutts had bought this house in 1802 and various members of the Coutts family lived in it, the last being Angela, the Baroness, but after her stepmother died – the Duchess of St Albans who had been Harriet Mellon – the Baroness moved round the corner to Stratton Street and Number 80 became part of the Royal Thames Yacht Club for a time.

Number 81 Piccadilly, on the east corner of Bolton Street, had been built in the mid-eighteenth century but by about 1805 it was standing empty. One day about this time the Prince Regent asked some of his friends what the food was like at their clubs, White's and Brooke's. They said it was passable but dull and monotonous, whereupon the Prince summoned his chef, Watier, and suggested that he take a suitable house and open it as a dining-club. Watier agreed and took a lease of Number 81; and in partnership with Maddison, the Prince's page, and Auguste Labourie, another royal chef, the club was duly opened.

The food was excellent but the dining-club was a thin disguise for the real business of Watier's, which was gambling. Stakes were very high and Byron, Sheridan and Beau Brummell were among the dozens who lost a great deal of money there.

'The play at Watier's is *tremendous*,' wrote Sir Harry Featherstone to Arthur Paget in 1811. 'Charles Manners has won £3,000 to £4,000, which he was much in need of.'

In her Memoirs, Harriette Wilson describes the famous masked ball given by the members of Watier's to 'all the nobility of England', in honour of the peace between Great Britain and France in 1815, a magnificent affair which all Mayfair seems to have attended: and Harriette and her friend Julia bought their costumes from Mr Stultze, the German regimental tailor in Clifford Street, who combined this occupation with the equally accommodating one of money-lender.

But the betting at Watier's was ruinous and the pace grew too quick to last. Only five or six years after it had been opened Watier retired from the fray, and most of the original members were either dead or ruined, although as late as 1823 Labourie was still paying the rates of the house.

John Maddocks cut his throat, Brummell left hurriedly for France, nearly bankrupt, and died there in 1840, almost penniless, and Byron departed for the Continent never to return, for by 1823, at the age of thirty-five, he was dead.

In 1824 Joshua Taylor took the house and entered into partnership with Crockford, who had started life as a fishmonger near Temple Bar. They set up a hazard bank and during the first year made a great deal of money. Then they quarrelled and Crockford moved to St James's Street, where he prospered and built the sumptuous Devonshire Club. Alone at Number 81, Taylor's luck forsook him and he failed. He departed and the house was privately occupied again until the Thames Yacht Club took it over for additional premises.

But in 1925 this house as well as the Coutts' houses, comprising the corner block of Numbers 79 and 80 Piccadilly, and Number 1 Stratton Street were all demolished for office buildings.

To the west of the Naval and Military Club, Number 95 was a Cubitt house built in 1886 on the site of an old house built in 1765. Number 96, on the corner of White Horse Street, was built on the site of the seventeenth-century White Horse Inn, and Charles Dumergue, surgeon dentist to the royal family, was living here early in the nineteenth century, one of his distinguished visitors being Sir Walter Scott, who stayed here several times, in 1809, 1815 and 1820.

Number 97 next door had been built on the site of Carter's statuary yard, which had been there since 1734, for Sir John Irwin, the friend of Lord Chesterfield, but Sir John overspent and departed hurriedly from England to avoid bankruptcy. Tom Panton of

Newmarket fame, friend of the Prince Regent, Old Q and the 3rd
Marquess of Hertford, lived here from 1784 to 1805 and then came
the widowed Lady Pulteney. Both these houses were pulled down at
the end of the nineteenth century and the club-house of the Junior
Naval and Military Club built on the site.

Numbers 101 to 104 were all houses built in the late eighteenth
century. The first occupant of Number 102 was Sir Thomas Lawrence, who lived here from 1796 to 1798, and half a century later it
was the home of Lord Granby. Number 103, built in 1797, was taken
by yet another member of the Hamilton family, who had been
associated with Mayfair since the beginning. This was Sir William
Hamilton, who lived here with Emma from 1801 until his death in
1803. So much has been written about Nelson and Emma that Sir
William's personality has been overshadowed. Not only was he a
distinguished classical scholar, but in his heyday he had been a great
sportsman, and like so many of the Hamiltons, he had a streak of
wild and endearing gallantry in his make-up.

Nathaniel Wraxall described a celebration at the house in Piccadilly, when news arrived from Nelson 'with his remaining hand' of
the victory of the Battle of Copenhagen. At this time Sir William
and Emma had been married for ten years. Wraxall called at the
house with Sir John Macpherson, about ten o'clock on an evening in
April 1801 and found there, among others, the Duke of Gordon, the
Duke of Queensberry, Lord William Gordon, Charles Greville –
Sir William's nephew who had kept Emma for a time, when she was
plain Emma Hart, before sending her off to his widowed uncle, then
British Ambassador to Naples – John Kemble of Drury Lane and his
wife, and a Neapolitan nobleman, the Duke of Noia.

They were all in high spirits, Emma playing on the harpsichord
and singing, until she at length began to dance the tarantella. This
dance, derived from the classical Bacchanalia, was performed by a
satyr and a nymph, and the sort of thing she had been performing at
the Temple of Health years before, when Charles Greville first met
her.

Although he was thirty years older than Emma and approaching
seventy, Sir William began to dance the part of the satyr to Emma's
nymph, and, said Wraxall, 'maintained the Conflict, for such it
might well be esteemed, during some Minutes. When unable longer
to continue it, the Duke of Noia succeeded to his place; but he, too,
though nearly forty years younger than Sir William, soon gave in
from Extenuation. Lady Hamilton then sent for her own Maid

servant; who being likewise presently exhausted, after a short time, another female Attendant, a Copt, perfectly black, whom Lord Nelson had presented her, on his return from Egypt, relieved her Companion.'

Wraxall was obviously shaken by the performance. 'The Voluptuous features of the dance' with the 'Screams, Attitudes, Starts, and Embraces, with which it was intermingled, gave it a peculiar Character,' he wrote, and rendered it 'too Powerful over the Imagination and the Senses.' 'It was certainly not of a nature to be performed, except before a select Company,' he concluded, rather primly, perhaps contrasting it with the very different parties he had attended at Mrs Montagu's in Hill Street a generation earlier.

Later that year Nelson joined the Hamiltons in Piccadilly for a few days, before returning to duty. Two years later Sir William was dead, and in another two years Nelson had fallen at Trafalgar. Emma moved to rooms in Clarges Street and a few years later old Lady Keith, one of the patronesses of Almack's, moved in to Number 103. She was Mrs Thrale's daughter – Johnson's 'Queenie' – and she lived there until 1832, when she moved to Number 110 Piccadilly.

Number 105 was originally built in the 1780s for the young Lord Barrymore, on the site of John Van Nest's figure yard, from a design by Michael Novosielski, but he could not afford to live in it, for young as he was he was gambling wildly and losing. He took a much smaller house to the west, on the site of Number 114, but by 1792 he was bankrupt, and a year later, still only twenty-three, he died, having lost £300,000 in five years.

Number 105 stood empty for many years and then was acquired by Jean Escudier, a French chef, and opened, in 1812, as the exclusive Pulteney Hotel, one of the very few in existence at this time. Two years later, in 1814, when Louis XVIII was recalled from exile to the French throne, the Grand Duchess Catherine, sister of Alexander I of Russia, was staying at the Pulteney, and was able to watch Louis's state entry into London from Hartwell House near Aylesbury, where he had been living since 1808. The Prince Regent had joined the triumphal procession at Bushey and Louis stayed for a day or two at the other important Mayfair hotel, Grillion's in Albemarle Street, which had opened in 1803 at Number 7.

The Pulteney was very expensive, for it cost the Grand Duchess £210 a week, no doubt because her entourage was large and occupied a great deal of space, but she liked it so much that she induced Alexander, who had planned to stay at St James's Palace, to join her there. 'J'ai un hôtel garni, le plus beau de la ville . . .', she wrote to him and went on to describe with enthusiasm 'certain arrangements *de commodité*' which referred to the hotel's newly installed water closets, some of the first to be seen in London. The hotel was close to the Piccadilly dip, under which the Tyburn, by this time covered, flowed from Brick Street across to the Green Park, and the sewage from the Pulteney must have flowed into it.

The story goes that the Grand Duchess did not want the Princess Charlotte to marry the Prince of Orange, preferring an alliance with Prince Leopold. She therefore invited the Prince of Orange to the Pulteney and filled him with so much champagne that he became hopelessly drunk and disgusted the young Princess. Prince Leopold was then produced, exerting all his charms, and the Princess quickly fell for him and broke her engagement to the Prince of Orange. Lady Brownlow may have had an inkling of all this, which caused her veiled hints of subtle scheming behind the scenes, but Princess Charlotte was a strong-minded young woman and quite capable of deciding, within the circumscribed limits of her position as heiress to the throne, whom she would marry.

About 1823 the Pulteney Hotel moved to Albemarle Street and the building became a private house again, bought by the 3rd Marquess of Hertford. It seems doubtful whether he ever lived there but the house was now called Hertford House. His mother was the Lady Hertford for whom the Prince Regent deserted Mrs Fitzherbert, after their brief reconciliation following his disastrous marriage to Princess Caroline. She was also a friend of Old Q and it seems probable that between them they had arranged the marriage of her son, the 3rd Marquis, with Maria Fagniani.

Maria's parentage was a mystery. She was born in 1771, the daughter of the Marchesa Fagniani, but no one ever knew who her father was, except that it was certainly not the Marchesa's husband. It could have been Old Q, Selwyn, or Selwyn's butler, but when the Fagnianis returned to Italy, shortly after Maria's birth, it was George Selwyn who took care of her and brought her up, at his house in Cleveland Row. When she was six or seven years old, he sent her to the school in Kensington which had been opened in one of Queen Anne's old homes – Campden House – but she was not there for long, for her Italian grandparents, not knowing the story of her birth, were puzzled that she was still in England and arranged for her to be brought to them in Italy. Shortly afterwards, when Maria, whom the doting Selwyn always called Mie-Mie, was only ten years old, Count

Fagniani went hopelessly mad and the Marchesa took her to Paris, leaving her in a convent.

From here Selwyn rescued her and brought her back to London. When he died, in 1791, leaving her £30,000, Old Q took full responsibility for her, and on her marriage in 1798, at the age of twenty-seven, to the twenty-one-year-old Lord Hertford, who until his father's death in 1822 bore the title of Lord Yarmouth, he cut down an oak wood six miles long, on his Scottish estates at Drumlanrig, to provide her with a suitable dowry; and he also took a large house in Piccadilly adjoining his own, for her and her husband. They now had two houses in Piccadilly but they were seldom or ever there and shortly after the marriage they went to France.

The marriage was a disaster, for young Lord Yarmouth was a dissipated young man, a member of the Prince Regent's circle and too fond of wine, women and gambling. He found himself a prisoner of war of Napoleon for a time and only by Fox's especial plea to Talleyrand was he released, in 1806.

By this time he and Mie-Mie had three children, but she had had enough of her young husband and when he returned to England she remained in Paris, finding her own diversions and lovers.

Lord Yarmouth had inherited his father's love of pictures and had made some valuable additions to the collection housed in the family mansion, Hertford House in Manchester Square, but he spent very little time either in Manchester Square or his houses in Piccadilly. He wandered abroad again for many years and when he eventually came back to England, as the wicked Lord Hertford, the original of Thackeray's Marquis of Steyne in *Vanity Fair*, he lived alone in old Dorchester House. Despite his bad reputation, Harriette Wilson admired him for his brilliant conversation, his impeccable manners and his profound knowledge of pictures, and infinitely preferred him to the Duke of Devonshire, Georgiana's husband.

He was an excellent host and kept a cow in Hyde Park, just opposite his windows, to ensure a supply of fresh cream. And between Dorchester House and Park Lane he built a small retreat for the entertainment of his paramours, which could be approached from the house or by a secret entrance in Park Lane.

'A small, low gate, of which he always kept the key, opened into Park Lane, and a little, narrow flight of stairs, covered with crimson cloth, conducted to this retirement,' wrote Harriette. 'It consisted of a dressing-room, a small sitting-room, and a bed-chamber. Over the elegant French bed was a fine picture of a sleeping Venus. There were a great many other pictures, and their subjects, though certainly warm and voluptuous, were yet too classical and graceful to merit the appellation of indecent. He directed our attention to the convenience of opening the door himself to any fair lady who would honour him with a visit *incognito*, after his servants should have prepared a most delicious supper and retired to rest.'

All she had to do was to feel her way through the dark, deserted and dangerous Park Lane to the little low door, which looked like the entrance to a cellar, knock three times and be admitted by his Lordship, down the winding staircase, to the fairyland he had prepared for her.

The Marquis seems to have been an unhappy, restless soul, with far too much money, for when he died, in 1842, he was worth two million pounds, a generous amount of which he left to Mie-Mie, still amusing herself in Paris, where she died in 1856.

Her son, the 4th Marquess of Hertford, was an even more ardent collector of pictures than his father or grandfather. Having spent much of his life in Paris, he had acquired a collection of eighteenth-century French paintings and some superb French furniture, as well as some Dutch pictures, which he had bought at The Hague. All these he brought over to England. He let Hertford House, Manchester Square to the French Embassy and turned his attention to Number 105 Piccadilly, which, in the 1850s, he engaged Cubitt to rebuild, with a gallery on the first floor to house his pictures.

However, he took a dislike to the house because of the frightful smell which pervaded it from time to time. This was not surprising as the Tyburn sewer was so close and the long overdue rebuilding of London's sewerage system had not yet been undertaken. And even to this day, if there is any fog about, it settles most densely in this part of Piccadilly, over the submerged Tyburn, which flows only a few feet below the surface of the road, as it crosses underneath the Green Park to the Thames, by way of the vicinity of Buckingham Palace.

Lord Hertford eventually sent his pictures and furniture to Hertford House, Manchester Square, and departed again for France. When he was only eighteen, he had had an illegitimate son, Richard, by a Scottish girl called Agnes Wallace, and Richard Wallace was brought up in Paris by his grandmother, Mie-Mie, though at first he was treated as an unwanted waif and was not allowed to take his meals with the rest of the family. As he grew up, he, too, developed a love of pictures and a discerning judgment, and his father became devoted to him, eventually making him his principal heir. The 4th

Lord Hertford died in 1870 and when the Franco-Prussian War was over Sir Richard Wallace returned to London with all his pictures and other art treasures, which he arranged in Hertford House, Manchester Square. When he died, in 1897, his widow bequeathed them to the nation. The Government bought the freehold of Hertford House and the Wallace Collection was opened to the public in 1900.

Number 105 Piccadilly was sold to Sir Julian Goldsmid, who remained here until his death in 1896, when the Isthmian Club acquired the lease: and when, at the end of the First World War, the Isthmian Club came to an end, the house was remodelled to become the Green Park Hotel for a few years, and from 1968 this building has become the new headquarters of the Arts Council.

Number 106 Piccadilly, Lord Coventry's house, became in 1869, as we have seen, the St James's Club, which had been established in St James's Street in 1858 for members of the diplomatic service.

At Number 107 old General Blücher lived for a time and became a familiar figure, for he liked to sit in an armchair on the top of the steps leading to his hall door, smoking his pipe, watching the world go by and acknowledging the greetings of passers by. In 1825 Nathan Rothschild, father of the English branch of the family, came here to live, after seventeen years in England, the first few of which he had spent in Manchester, studying the cotton trade, and the next ten in the City of London, building up his business in St Swithin's Lane. He died in 1836 and his son, Lionel, the first orthodox Jew to be elected to the House of Commons, moved to Number 148 Piccadilly, next door to Apsley House, while Number 107 passed to his youngest brother, Mayer. In 1885 the house became the Savile Club headquarters. The house of the Junior Athenaeum, at the east corner of Down Street, was first built in 1848 for Henry Thomas Hope, who sold it to the club in 1868.

The houses between Down Street and Old Park Lane, most of which were fairly new buildings, were nearly all clubs by late Victorian times, including Number 127, the Cavalry Club, which was established in 1890.

During George III's first bout of madness, Old Q allied himself with the Prince of Wales over the Regency Bill, and the Prince, the Duke of York and Charles James Fox spent a great deal of time at Number 138 Piccadilly, sampling the new wine called champagne which had just been introduced to England, though at this time it was probably a still champagne.

When the King recovered, Old Q left the Court party for a time and retired to Brighton, where the Prince and Mrs Fitzherbert held court, but during the celebrations for the King's recovery, in 1789, he joined in unreservedly, for he was always a loyal subject.

During his last twenty years, Old Q had a French doctor living permanently in the house, at a salary of £600 a year, with John Fuller, an apothecary of Number 34 Piccadilly, on permanent call. He would drive through the West End in his dark green coach, drawn by two, long-tailed black horses, with two servants behind him and his favourite groom, Jack Radford, bringing up the rear. He was always immaculately dressed and to the end wore a tricorn hat, though they had passed out of fashion by the 1790s. He was a lonely old man in the last years, with Selwyn dead and Mie-Mie living abroad, but he still had some good friends and was a great admirer of Nelson, whom he had met through the Hamiltons; but he was in his late seventies when he went to their party at Number 103 Piccadilly, to celebrate the victory of Copenhagen.

In his last years he was a familiar figure sitting in the bay window of his house, watching the world go by, or on warm days sitting out on the balcony, shaded from the sun by a powdered footman, who held a parasol above his head. On the pavement below, Jack Radford waited, ready to take any messages or run after any passer-by for whom the old Duke had a fancy to chat.

After the death of Sir William Hamilton and Nelson, though both had left money to Emma, she soon found herself in trouble, for her finances were hopelessly mismanaged. She moved from Piccadilly to rooms in Clarges Street and when Old Q heard about her difficulties he ordered his chef to send meals round to her every day and placed one of his carriages at her disposal.

He also left her an annuity of £500, but after his death there was so much litigation over the disposal of his enormous estate, much of it instigated by Lord Yarmouth, who questioned the legality of the codicils of the will, that poor Emma never received it and became destitute. In 1812 she was arrested for debt and committed to a sponging house of the King's Bench prison. After nearly two years friends managed to raise enough of her money to pay for her release and, practically penniless, she escaped to Calais with her small daughter Horatia, whose father was Nelson, in order to avoid further writs. And here, six months later, she died in a shabby rooming house, almost destitute.

Old Q's will was not settled until the following year. He had prided himself on always having £20,000 in cash in the house and a balance of £100,000 at Coutts's bank and he left about a million pounds, more than a quarter of which went to Lord and Lady Yarmouth, the rest being divided into various legacies to friends and charities.

He died on 23 December 1810 and lies buried under the communion table of St James's, Piccadilly.

The Duchess of Devonshire took both his houses, herself living in Number 138 and letting Number 139 to Byron for a time. This house had a number of distinguished occupiers and was bought after the First World War by Baron d'Erlanger, while Number 138 became the home of the Lyceum Club, both houses having been refronted with stone at the turn of the century, in compliance with the Crown leases.

The row of houses which once stood to the west of Hamilton Place as far as Apsley House were known as Piccadilly Terrace. Number 140, on the east corner of Hamilton Place, was at one time inhabited by Dudley North and ultimately became the short-lived Bachelors' Club. Until 1871 Hamilton Place was a cul-de-sac and at the end of the seventeenth century there was nothing here but seven small houses, a stable and a brewhouse. In 1773 Lord Shelbourne acquired the land, intending to build a mansion here for himself, but he changed his mind, so the site stood empty for many years. Eventually Number 141 Piccadilly was built on the west corner, occupied in 1818 by the Lord Chancellor, the 1st Earl of Eldon, and subsequently by his son and grandson. Then George Herring bought the house, the man who, starting from nothing, made one fortune on the turf as a bookmaker and a second as a City financier, and ended up a millionaire, leaving the bulk of his fortune to charity.

Number 142 was built in 1812 for Peter Burrell and remained in his family until 1865. The family fortunes had been founded by his great-grandfather, as a City of London merchant and financier. His grandfather had married an heiress from Hackney, which enabled him to build Gwydyr House in Whitehall, and his three youngest daughters all married into the aristocracy, one becoming yet another Duchess of Hamilton, who, when the Duke divorced her, married Lord Exeter, while his son Peter married Lady Priscilla Bertie, eldest daughter of the 3rd Duke of Ancaster of Berkeley Square, who brought him a splendid fortune. He was knighted in 1781, when only twenty-seven years old and in 1796 was raised to the peerage as Lord Gwydyr. And it was his son, the 2nd Lord Gwydyr and another Peter Burrell, who built Number 142 Piccadilly, living here with his bride

Clementina, daughter of the Earl of Perth, who annoyed Lord Eldon next door with the sound of her pipers.

'I am sometimes tormented by the noise of Lady Gwydyr's Scotchmen playing under my windows upon the Scottish instrument called the bagpipes,' he wrote, 'but there is music in that droning instrument compared to the babel of lawyers' tongues.'

After the death of the 2nd Lord Gwydyr and his wife, within a few months of each other, the house was bought by Miss Alice Rothschild.

Number 143, designed by the Adam brothers in 1795, was first occupied by Sir Nathaniel Holland, but after his death, in 1811, the house came into the possession of Ferdinand Rothschild, the creator of Waddesdon Manor, and this was his London home for more than thirty years.

Numbers 144 and 145 were also Adam houses. Number 144 was first occupied by Sir Drummond Smith of Tring Park, the mansion which Lord Rothschild was to buy, and it was here that Lord Palmerston lived for a short time, before moving to Cambridge House. Number 145 was built for Sir John Smith-Burges and after his death was purchased by the Marquess of Northampton, ultimately being bought by Baron Albert Rothschild, and it was here that the Duke and Duchess of York lived, before the Duke moved to Buckingham Palace as George VI, and that the Princess Elizabeth and Princess Margaret spent many years of their childhood.

Numbers 146 and 147 were originally one large house, occupied at the end of the eighteenth century by the French Ambassador, the Count d'Adhémar, who entertained here in the grand manner, particularly on Sunday evenings, until he had a stroke and had to be replaced. The house, no longer the French Embassy, was then considerably improved and Charles Calonne moved in, having been banished from France for mismanaging the country's finances. He was no more skilful with his own money and by 1793 he was bankrupt. He returned to France almost penniless and died in 1802.

The house was then divided, the eastern part, Number 146, being taken by John Craufurd, a Whig Member of Parliament and friend of Charles James Fox, who died unmarried in 1814; and then by Sir Edmund Antrobus, a partner in Coutts' bank. The western part of the house, Number 147, was bought by Sir Charles Cockerell and then, in 1851, by Sir Fitzroy Kelly, but a few years later Lionel Rothschild acquired the remainder of the lease, and in the early 1860s made it into one house with Number 148 to the west, which had been built for the 5th Earl of Dysart in 1782.

But during the last few years one by one these old houses in Picca-dilly Terrace have been pulled down to make way for faceless, monolithic hotels, and today Apsley House alone remains, at the western extremity, firm but solitary, dwarfed by the tall new build-ings but stalwartly maintaining its dignity.

XIII

How They Lived – I

When Old Q was born in 1725 George II was on the throne of England and Charles II had been dead for only forty years. Only four years earlier, in 1721, the turnpike in Piccadilly, which had stood just to the east of Berkeley Street, had been moved to Hyde Park Corner.

In Mayfair the Fair was being held regularly during the first fortnight in May. Clarendon House had gone. Old Burlington House and Berkeley House were hidden behind their high street walls, and westwards along Piccadilly to Hyde Park Corner were the stonemasons' yards and the drovers' inns, the Triumphal Chariot, the Red Lion, the Golden Lion, the Swan, the Horse Shoe, the Running Horse, the Barley Mow, the White Horse and the Half Moon, with the Hercules Pillars by Hyde Park and close to the toll-gate which was to stand for another hundred years.

In front of the Triumphal Chariot was a bench where porters could rest their loads and another where the barbers waited, on Sundays and review days, for the red-coats to have their hair dressed and powdered.

The year 1725 was the one in which St George's, Hanover Square was consecrated and that Sir Richard Grosvenor gave the party to his first tenants of the streets around Grosvenor Square. Old Bond Street had been built and work had begun on the extension to New Bond Street, towards the Tyburn Road, along which the death cart to the gallows still trundled each month.

Yet it was to be another five years before Keith's Chapel was built and the land where Berkeley Square and its surrounding streets were to arise was still open fields.

The streets in the eastern part of Mayfair were newly built but it was to be another twenty-five years before Lord Chesterfield contemplated his house on the western fringe of Mayfair, looking across the lonely Tyburn Lane to Hyde Park.

And after the gallows at Tyburn had been removed, in 1783, and Tyburn Lane became Park Lane, there was a great deal of development and new building in western Mayfair – in Upper Brook Street, Upper Grosvenor Street, Park Street, South Street, the western parts of Hill Street, Charles Street, Curzon Street and Hertford Street, North and South Audley Street.

The English aristocracy, so many of whom took houses in these streets and squares during the middle years of the eighteenth century, were secure in their wealth and power, a position which they took for granted as part of the Divine order which had created the rich and the poor, the titled and the humble. It was all God's will, a splendid arrangement for some, if highly inconvenient for others.

The Seven Years War did not alter their view of life or change their manner of living it. Nor did the significance of the American War of Independence make any deep impression.

In Mayfair they still dressed formally, the fashions among the nobility and the rich being very much the same in London and Paris, as well as the other capitals of Europe, irrespective of which of them happened to be fighting each other at the time.

In 1760 men of fashion were wearing a small tricorn over a neat wig, with close-rolled curls under a short queue. Coats, waistcoats and breeches were all well cut and elegant. For Court occasions they were made of satin, silk and velvet, but gradually plain cloth became more fashionable, particularly during the day.

The early seventies were the years of the Macaronis. These were the young men who, having made the Grand Tour, founded a club, mainly for gambling, where macaroni, for which they had acquired a taste in Italy, always appeared on the dinner menu.

The Macaronis adopted even smaller tricorns, tilted far down over their foreheads and worn over very small wigs. They took to carrying gold-topped cane walking-sticks, their jackets were short and skimpy and their breeches tight to bursting point.

A rival group to the Macaronis were the Bucks, who cultivated, by way of contrast, a slovenly appearance in their dress, scorning not only the foppishness of the Macaronis but also the simple refinements of soap and water, for they were seldom clean, and are an interesting parallel to the drop-outs of the 1970s.

The final blow to powdered wigs came in 1795, when Pitt imposed his powder tax, but they had been slowly disappearing long before that, and as early as 1763 peruke-makers were complaining that gentlemen were crippling their business by taking to their own hair, just as a few years later, with the first appearance of shoe-laces, it was feared that 'many shoe buckle manufacturing families will be wiped out'.

Women's dress throughout the middle years of the century grew increasingly stiff and formal. From the attractively simple dress of Queen Anne's time, with its side panniers, they took to circular hoops which grew ever more unwieldy. The hoop was a petticoat stiffened with whale bone and worn over a crippling, whale-boned corset. It meant that women were able to dispense with the underpetticoats they had previously worn, and as knickers had not yet been devised, they sometimes wore nothing at all under the hoop but gartered stockings, with a plain linen shift which went under the corset.

As thin silks, muslins and cottons arrived from the East, they discarded their heavy damasks and brocades, and when the English manufacturers protested, and the import of the fashionable lighter materials was for a time forbidden, they overcame the problem by highly successful smuggling. Mrs Montagu was one who once remarked in a letter, 'I am lucky with smuggling'.

The sacque or 'sack', mentioned by Lady Jane Coke in her letters to Mrs Eyre, was a wide overdress, usually of silk, hanging from the shoulders and sometimes fastened in front with ribbons, worn over the dress and hoop, a graceful fashion which lasted through the middle years of the century.

Their hairdressing was simple at this stage and they wore small lace caps, with cloaks and hoods out of doors, which at first were scarlet but later were nearly always black. Then they took to milkmaid straw hats, tied with ribbons over their lace caps, and the hoops tended to be a little smaller, but there was no essential change in fashion until after the end of the Seven Years War, when English women began visiting Paris again and French milliners and dressmakers arrived in London.

The most practical fashion the French brought with them was an adjustable farthingale, which could be raised on either side when two women tried to pass each other in a narrow doorway and was also useful when trying to climb into a carriage. The lampoonists had already suggested various devices to ease the lot of women wearing this awkward fashion, one of which was a coach with a removable roof, through which they could be dropped from above, by means of a frame and pulley, rather like a gibbet. But from France also came the ridiculous fashion of immensely high headdresses, which reached its ultimate stupidity in the 1770s, when they became monstrous. The hair was frizzed over a large wire frame which had been filled with tow or wool. This was then greased and powdered and adorned with flowers, fruit and feathers, and a few extra curls pinned on for good measure. All this took a hairdresser three or four hours hard work and the headdress was often left untouched for weeks on end, until it became verminous.

A correspondent in the *London Magazine*, wrote in 1768:

> I went the other morning to make a visit to an elderly aunt of mine, when I found her pulling off her cap and tendering her head to the ingenious Mr Gilchrist, who has lately obliged the public with a most excellent essay on hair. He asked her how long it was since her head had been opened and repaired. She answered not above nine weeks. To which he replied: that *that* was as long as a head could well go in summer, and that therefore it was proper to deliver it now; for he confessed that it began to be a little *hazardé*.

The ladies of Mayfair supplied themselves with little long-handled ivory claws, to relieve the intolerable itching they endured, during the weeks between the visits of their hairdressers. Today the antique dealers often call them back-scratchers, for which purpose they were no doubt often used as well, but primarily they were head-scratchers.

'False hair to supply deficiency of native hair, pomatum in profusion, greasy wool to bolster up the adopted locks and grey powder to conceal dust. Thus my lady is dressed for three months at least during which time it is not in her power to comb her head,' wrote one fashion critic.

Others complained that women were overdoing the cosmetics and that their necks and bosoms were too bare. In 1770 one exasperated and disenchanted man tried, though in vain, to introduce a Bill into Parliament:

'That all women of whatever rank, profession or degree, whether virgins, maids or widows, that shall from and after such Act, impose upon, seduce and betray into matrimony, any of his Majesty's subjects by the scents, paints and cosmetic washes, artificial teeth, false hair, Spanish wool, iron stays, hoops, high-heeled shoes, and bolstered hips, shall incur the penalty of the law now in force against witchcraft and like misdemeanours, and that the marriage upon conviction shall be null and void.'

It was Georgiana, Duchess of Devonshire, who introduced the fashion for tall feathers to increase the height of the headdress and in the spring of 1775 Mrs Harris wrote to her son:

'The Duchess of Devonshire had two plumes sixteen inches long, besides three smaller ones; this has so far outshone all other plumes, that Mrs. Damer, Lady Harriet Stanhope, etc, looked nothing.'

One woman, desperate to outdo the Duchess, searched London in vain for long feathers, until she at last persuaded an undertaker to sell her some from a hearse.

Hannah More complained of young women who had on their heads 'an acre and a half of shrubbery, besides slopes, garden plots, tulip beds, clumps of peonies, kitchen gardens and greenhouses' and Fanny Burney described a young lady she had met at a party, 'her head erect and stiff as any statue . . . her hair higher than twelve wigs stuck one on each other . . .'

Hats grew as large as the headdresses, until they became the Gainsborough hats with wide, sweeping tilted brims and huge ostrich feathers, in which Gainsborough painted the Duchess of Devonshire and Mrs Siddons.

Mayfair took their hats very seriously. Horace Walpole complained that Lady Somerset wore a hat 'over her nose, so that I only fell in love with her chin' and in 1777 Mrs Delaney was warning her niece that propriety 'will never suffer you to wear your hat *one edge* to touch your *nose*, and the other edge perpendicularly in the air'.

Huge caps to cover the piles of hair now came into fashion and in 1780 the Prince of Wales' lovely Perdita was wearing the 'Bird of Paradise' cap – a vast, cylindrical creation of goffered muslin.

Then the Duchess of Bedford invented the black silk 'calash', which was a cap shaped like the hood of a carriage and strengthened with whalebone hoops. By means of a string it could be pulled forward to shield the face, like a poke bonnet, without disturbing the headdress, or thrown backwards to expose the coiffure in all its glory.

Either way it was very strange and ugly, but it was worn well into the 1780s.

Every woman now wore a hat out of doors. Sophie v. La Roche noticed this when she visited London in 1786.

'Women here may not go without a hat,' she wrote. 'So the land with the greatest freedom of thought, creed and custom is yet to some measure fettered by convention. Meanwhile I am very glad that women of my age* wear caps under their hats, and that I shall not have much trouble or expense with my coiffure.'

Hoops gradually disappeared, and after a short fashion for pads worn on the hips they were replaced by a single pad in the small of the back, forming a preposterous bustle. To balance this and their enormous hats, English women copied the Parisians and puffed out their bodices in front with folds of linen and gauze, so that they all looked like pouter pigeons.

By 1787 bosoms, bustles and hats were larger than ever and one cartoonist drew a woman with a bustle and hat so enormous that she was able to shelter her entire family underneath them, from the rain.

All this changed with the French Revolution and the troubled years which followed. Watching the fate of their counterparts across the Channel, the sublime confidence of the English aristocracy in their heaven-bestowed invulnerability was, for the first time, rudely shaken.

Nathaniel Wraxall said that the change in dress had begun in the 1780s, when Mr Fox 'first threw a discredit on Dress'. From the House of Commons and the clubs of St James's the contagion spread through the rest of London, but 'dress never totally fell till the Era of Jacobinism and of Equality – which began in 1793'.

> It was then that pantaloons, cropped hair and shoe-strings as well as the total abolition of Buckles and Ruffles, together with the disuse of Hair-Powder characterised the men: while ladies, having cut off those Tresses, which had done so much execution ... exhibited Heads rounded 'à la Victime et à la Guillotine,' as if ready for the stroke of the Axe. A Drapery, more suited to the Climate of Greece or of Italy, than to the temperature of an Island situated in the fifty-first Degree of Latitude; classic, elegant, luxurious, and picturesque, superseded the ancient female attire of Great Britain; finally levelling or obliterating almost all external distinction between the highest and the lowest of the Sex, in this Country.

* Sophie was in her fifties.

These fashions all began in France. During the Revolution silks, satins and brocades were forbidden and women dressed as plainly and as much like each other as possible, in simple cambrics and cottons, but when the Directory was formed, in 1795, with the upper bourgeoisie in power, the mood changed, and life became gay again. After Napoleon's campaigns in the eastern Mediterranean and Egypt, women adopted a classical style of dress and began to look like the women on Greek vases. They put away their corsets and wore dresses of the flimsiest white muslin, very plain and full, confined by a single ribbon tied high under the breasts.

These were the days of the Merveilleuses, who worshipped antiquity, and in dressing themselves like the women of Ancient Greece and Rome went to the extreme limits. Their sleeveless muslin dresses were transparent, cut very low and often slit up the side to the waist. Underneath them they sometimes wore flesh-coloured tights and a garment called a 'Carthaginian chemise' and sometimes no chemise at all. They cropped their hair and wore it à la Greque or à la Victoire and sometimes à la Sacrifice, brushed up at the back and forward over the top of the head, like that of a woman who had been decapitated by the guillotine.

Developing the fashion to its logical climax, some young women took to exposing their breasts – and then came the streakers. A young man wearing a loin-cloth walked through the streets of Paris with two girls who were stark naked. But Paris was not ready for them. They had to run for their lives and never risked a second venture.

Few English women dared to go as far as the French, but they discarded their corsets and adopted a high-waisted dress made of the thinnest white muslin, which was worn over a very flimsy petticoat. And like the ladies of Paris, they caught shocking colds, which all too often developed into pneumonia.

The fashionable headdress over their cropped hair was now a muslin turban or classical bandeau, which for important occasions was adorned with an ostrich feather or group of feathers rising vertically into the air, the higher the better. Georgiana, Duchess of Devonshire, who was seldom beaten at this kind of game, managed to find one which was three feet long.

These flimsy dresses, which were worn by all levels of society, were made of English cotton and muslin, and it was now the turn of the East India Company to complain that they were losing business, but this time the taste for English materials prevailed.

In France it was Napoleon who objected to the transparency. At a reception at the Luxembourg he ordered the fires to be stoked higher and ever higher, and when the footmen said it was impossible to cram any more logs on to the fireplaces, he said in a loud voice, for all to hear:

'I wanted to be sure to get it warm enough, because the weather is cold and these ladies are practically naked.'

A week or two later a note appeared in *Le Moniteur* that 'Bonaparte has voiced his displeasure at the sight of naked women in his salon.'

In England the exceptionally cold winter of 1799 is said to have put an end to the fashion. Women took to an overdress with puffed sleeves, and then, in comforting succession, fichus and cashmere shawls, large fur muffs and short-fitted coats, known as spencers. Stays came back, and the poke bonnet appeared, together with ankle boots, furs and heavier cloaks. And very early in the nineteenth century long, tight-fitting, lace-trimmed drawers were designed.

Men of fashion did not change their appearance so much as the women but they grew tired of their tricorns during the 1780s and 1790s. Some punched them into a mitre shape like Napoleon and others wore them fore and aft like Nelson. By 1800 the tricorn had disappeared entirely, except among the diehards like Old Q, who wore his to the end.

Among the upper crust it was replaced by the tall, silk hat. The first to appear was designed by a London haberdasher, and when he wore it for the first time he caused such a commotion that he was charged with a breach of the peace, for it was alleged that the 'Tall structure, having a shining lustre' was 'calculated to frighten timid people'. The *St James's Gazette* reported that several women fainted at the sight, children screamed, dogs yelped and a small boy had his arm broken.

Despite this initial setback, the tall hat, wide-brimmed and with the crown broader at the top than the base, had come to stay, and with it men wore at first a tail-coat, waistcoat and breeches of fine woollen cloth, plain but impeccably tailored; but the fashion for breeches soon gave way to tightly-cut trousers, and in winter they wore heavy overcoats with two or three overlapping capes.

The dandies of the early nineteenth century wore their coat collars so high that they touched their cheeks and they padded their chests and hips. Beau Brummell launched the fashion for the starched cravat and the *Mirror* of 7 May 1825, reporting this latest fashion, said that at the sight of it 'dandies were struck dumb with envy and washerwomen miscarried'.

These were the fashions of the people of Mayfair in its heyday. The women's clothes were made at home by visiting seamstresses and sewing maids but for the men there were plenty of tailors available, some already established in Savile Row.

Although English women were always influenced to a certain extent by Paris fashions, young Frenchmen copied the English dandies and the Incroyables of Paris took to the huge cravats and high-collared coats which were being worn in Mayfair and St James's.

The furniture for the mansions of Mayfair underwent similar changes of fashion, but it was easily available, for throughout the eighteenth century there was a flourishing cabinet-making industry in London; and in Mayfair, as elsewhere throughout the city, there were plenty of furniture makers from whom furniture could be bought or ordered.

William Kent was one of the first architects to design furniture to match his Palladian mansions, and his cabinets and bookcases were pillared and pedimented in the manner of his buildings. But he was also fond of ornate baroque designs, a fashion which had originated in France.

His marble-topped console tables, with their elaborately carved and gilded legs, were often built against a wall as permanent fixtures, needing therefore no back legs, and they were usually surmounted by wall mirrors in ornately carved and gilded frames, flanked by candle stands.

By 1748, the year that William Kent died, a young cabinet-maker, Thomas Chippendale, had opened a workshop in Long Acre, where all the coachmakers lived and worked, but in 1753 he moved to St Martin's Lane. The following year he published a trade catalogue – *The Gentleman and Cabinet-Maker's Director* – which contained many furniture designs, some already in use, some new, with directions for making them. These engravings showed an enormous variety of designs, including rococo and Gothic, as well as those showing a Chinese influence, which Mrs Montagu favoured for her salon in Hill Street.

At the beginning of Georgian times walnut veneer on beech, or some similar, relatively inexpensive wood, was used for the better kinds of furniture, although solid oak was still used in country districts. Soon the supply of English walnut was not sufficient to meet demands and for a few years it was imported from France, but after one particularly hard winter French walnut trees were badly affected and France forbade the export of walnut. For a short time England imported it from North America but then the first mahogany was brought to London from the West Indies. It was found to be heavy, hard and reliable and was imported in increasing quantities. By the 1750s it had become far more popular than walnut and was being used almost exclusively, both in the solid and as a veneer.

Much of the furniture for the royal households and the aristocratic mansions of Mayfair was made by London craftsmen, but at the same time they and the provincial members of the industry were turning out plainer but very handsome furniture, in huge quantities, for the wealthy upper classes of squires and merchants, while the needs of the farmers and cottagers were usually supplied by the village carpenter.

Chippendale made armchairs with padded seats and mahogany arms, back and legs, which were still similar in shape to those of Queen Anne's time, but the cabriole legs were lighter and the knees higher, and they were often carved with acanthus leaves and finished with a simple, turned club foot. The back was only slightly curved and the top rail straight. Chairs without arms were similar, but stretcher rails were introduced again and the legs were sometimes plain or moulded very simply.

The Chinese influence did not affect the basic design of his furniture but decorative Chinese motifs were introduced and delicate lattice-work carving. Its most popular phase was during the 1760s, after Sir William Chambers had returned from his visit to China and published his book on Chinese art. And with 'Chinese Chippendale' furniture the enthusiasts for interior decoration took to hand-painted Chinese wall-paper, porcelain and hangings.

A few years after Chippendale had established his workshops, Hepplewhite opened his business in Cripplegate, and he also wrote a catalogue – *The Cabinet-Maker's and Upholsterer's Guide* – though it was not published until two years after his death.

Hepplewhite's furniture was as elegant as Chippendale's but rather simpler. He introduced new types of decoration, including painting and gilding and inlaid bands of satinwood, rosewood and ebony, while his carving included classical motifs such as vases, swags of draped cloth and husks.

Chairs with serpentine top rails and shield or heart-shaped backs, or backs in the form of hoops or ovals, were Hepplewhite designs which many cabinet-makers adopted. Mahogany side-tables, writing tables, bureaux, chests of drawers, tallboys and wardrobes were all restrained and graceful, and very like the work of the Sheraton school, which was to come a few years later.

Robert Adam was purely a designer of furniture and passed his drawings to a practical cabinet-maker, much of the furniture for the mansions he built being made in the Chippendale workshops. Adam was responsible for the first sideboard as we know it today. About 1780 he designed pedestal cupboards to stand on either side of the side-table, fitted with plate-warmers and wine bins and surmounted by large Greek urns of zinc-lined mahogany for storing cutlery, and it was only a short step to making these three pieces into one composite piece of furniture.

He used classical motifs in the carving, including acanthus leaves, the Greek honeysuckle, chains of husks, the key pattern, vases, drapery and plaques carved with subjects from Greek mythology; he sometimes used inlay, and occasionally marquetry, with decorative woods such as satinwood, tulip wood and rosewood.

Some of Adam's furniture was painted with flowers on a cream or pale green ground, work for which, during the late 1760s and throughout the 1770s, Angelica Kauffmann was often employed, for she was living in London at this time, in Golden Square, and making far more money than Canaletto ever did, when he was living round the corner in humble lodgings in Beak Street.

Thomas Sheraton arrived in London from the north of England in 1790, and a year or two later published *The Cabinet-Maker and Upholsterer's Drawing Book*, with still more furniture designs, together with instructions for their manufacture. His work was in many ways similar to Hepplewhite's, but his chairs were lighter. He used inlay but not a great deal of carving, and some of his furniture was painted, with the floral patterns which Angelica had made popular.

He designed a bow-fronted sideboard and made long, swinging mirrors which came to be known as horse or 'cheval' glasses, as well as small, vase-shaped mirrors swinging on curved supports, attached to a bow-fronted stand fitted with a small drawer.

One of the most useful pieces of furniture made during the first half of the eighteenth century was the mahogany press. The upper part consisted of a cupboard fitted with trays which slid forward on runners and the lower part was a chest of drawers, comprising two small drawers above two long ones. The doors were panelled, as the old solid oak furniture had been, and the drawers were surrounded with a narrow beading to keep out the dust.

Throughout the century the chest was an important piece of furniture too, the tallboy of the earlier years, with two small drawers and three long drawers, giving place to the double chest, composed of a base with three long drawers, standing on four bracket feet, and the older type of tallboy above it.

Bureau bookcases were to be found in every wealthy household. The upper part, holding the books, at first had wooden doors and then glass doors, and the base was a chest of drawers, while sometimes a writing-table was built in between, with a sloping lid.

After the Restoration a separate room for dining had become fashionable, but for many years to come the old Jacobean oak gate-legged table was still being used. It was either rectangular or circular, two of the legs moving out on hinges to support the extensions. Even in Queen Anne's time, when so much walnut was being used for fine furniture, there were no large walnut dining-tables, probably because of the difficulty of cutting a sheet of veneer for such a large surface.

Variations of the old gate-legged style of table developed throughout the 1730s and 1740s, but by the middle of the century mahogany dining-tables with a central pedestal were being made.

Although Chippendale used mahogany in the solid he also re-introduced veneering for tables. His mahogany veneer was thicker than walnut and sometimes comprised three or four layers, glued together for extra strength.

There were small tables in abundance – side-tables for the dining-room as elegant as the dining-table itself, and a variety of occasional tables for the drawing-rooms and boudoir, including the circular-topped table with a pie-crust edging, supported on three cabriole legs, which were often carved in a pattern of acanthus leaves. Later the three legs were made shorter and fixed to a vertical pillar, and the table often had a small gallery of turned spindles round the edge. Both of these tables were used by guests for wine-glasses or tea-cups.

There were corner cupboards for the display of porcelain, canter-buries for newspapers and journals, and among the numerous kinds of writing-desks and tables were the neat little davenports, often fitted with a secret drawer.

At the end of the century and during the early 1800s, when Henry Holland was both architect and furniture designer for the Prince Regent, giving a classical flavour to so much of his work, the chaise-longue and similar long-seated pieces of furniture were fashionable.

At the same time the sofa- table was designed, to stand over the end of the long seat.

In the bedrooms, the four-poster beds were lighter and made of mahogany. The gorgeous hangings of velvet, silk and cloth of gold which had been used during the seventeenth century gave way to curtains which were lighter and less voluminous. During the Chinese craze a few beds were made with a pagoda-like canopy and tent beds were also sometimes used, in which the curtains hung from a light iron framework, but on the whole the wealthy preferred their mahogany four-posters, with their carved canopies and posts.

As well as presses and chests of drawers, bedrooms were furnished with dressing-tables. Some had three drawers and were surmounted by a small toilet looking-glass. Others looked like plain cabinets when they were closed, the top opened out from the middle to form two projecting leaves. Inside was a mirror, which could be pulled upright, and a number of small compartments for bottles and boxes. These little tables, delicately made, were fitted with a drawer and sometimes a recessed cupboard below.

There was also a variety of washing stands, for by the beginning of the eighteenth century washing had become a daily routine for most of the leisured classes. Toothbrushes had been devised and gentlemen shaved regularly. By the 1740s stands to hold basins and jugs were made, fitted with drawers to hold toilet articles and recesses for soap or wash balls, and some had a shelf below for the wig stand. The other article of furniture to be found in the bedrooms of the wealthy was the night table or pot cupboard, which came in an astonishing variety of designs.

Early in this century, walls in the wealthy houses were covered with oak panelling, tapestry, silk, damask or velvet, but smaller and newer houses had either plain, plastered walls or walls covered with wainscoting of painted deal. Chinese and other hand-painted wall-papers were at first very expensive, but by the middle of the century they were being printed and became very popular.

There seems to be no record of the wallpapers Walpole chose for his house in Berkeley Square, but at Twickenham his choice included a straw-coloured paper printed with 'Gothic detail', a blue and white striped paper, adorned with festoons, and for his bedroom a deep purple paper.

According to Mary Frampton, writing in the 1780s, one of Mrs Fitzherbert's rooms was hung with 'puckered blue satin, from which hangings the now common imitations in paper were taken'.

The windows of both town and country mansions were draped with elaborately fringed pelmets and curtains, usually of heavy silk. Oriental carpets and rugs were fashionable, as well as English, hand-woven needlework carpets, but at the end of the eighteenth century English carpet manufacture developed.

During most of the eighteenth century cooking was done on an open fire and a mechanically revolving spit was used for roasting. In the vast and gloomy basement kitchens of the Georgian houses of Mayfair, these kitchen fireplaces were enormous. Pots and kettles hung from large iron hooks above the fire and frying-pans and sauce-pans were set on trivets.

By about 1780, the first kitchen range was designed, with an oven built on the side of the open fire. As this meant that one side of the food cooked more quickly than the other, someone then had the idea of making oven shelves which twisted on a pivot. Early in the nineteenth century, a boiler for hot water was fitted to this design, on the other side of the fire, but it had to be filled by hand from the house water supply, which was probably a single tap. Another development for the convenience of the cook was a cover fitted over the fire, which served as a hot-plate for boiling and stewing.

Candles were used for lighting and where many-branched candelabra were used they were an expensive item. Oil lamps burning a vegetable oil were used during the 1830s but paraffin lamps did not come in until 1853.

The first experimental street lighting by gas was in 1810 but the earliest installations in private houses were highly dangerous and smelt abominably. As late as 1828, when gas lighting had been installed at the Covent Garden Opera House, there was a serious explosion in the basement and the whole installation was scrapped, wax and oil lighting being put back for a time.

There were plenty of businesses in and around Mayfair to supply all the furniture and household equipment people might need. Chippendale, Hepplewhite and Sheraton are the furniture designers and manufacturers whose names have survived, but during the eighteenth century such makers as Goodison, Jensen, Moore, Vile and Seddon were as well known. By the end of the century William Linnell was carrying on his furniture business in Berkeley Square, in a large, double-fronted house in the north-east corner, the building running right through to Bourdon Street. The firm prided themselves on their fashionable clientèle and seem to have charged accordingly, though some of their accounts did not go unchallenged. Sir

Richard Hoare of Barn Elms went through each item of his bill, adding his own comments – 'extravagant charge' – 'too much' – 'deduct' – and some items he crossed through entirely.

William Linnell's successor, John Linnell, did a great deal of work, both at Shardiloes and at his house in Grosvenor Square, for William Drake, who was another dissatisfied customer. He sent the bill to another cabinet-maker, who agreed that it was at least 20 per cent too high, but in the end William Drake paid up in full.

Apart from Linnell's, there were many other cabinet-makers and designers in Mayfair by this time, including Robert and James Adam, whose business was in Albemarle Street from 1728 to 1794. Robert Addison was in Hanover Street in 1774, and Thomas Bailey in Conduit Street, while in 1778 Edward Bevan of Air Street was advertising his 'new and peculiarly constructed Venetian Blinds' for which he charged one shilling a square foot.

There were carvers and gilders, looking-glass makers, leather gilders and screen-makers, feather-bed-makers, frame-makers, manufacturers of cabriole chairs, invalid chairs, library steps, portable writing-desks, cane and Dutch chairs, chair frames for stuffing, sea-chests, wine-coolers, cradles, sedan chairs, clock case-makers, specialists in lacquer, marquetry and Buhl inlay, japanning, ormolu and papiermâché, wallpaper manufacturers, dealers in tapestries and Oriental carpets, and an occasional carpet weaver, such as Thomas More of Finsbury, who supplied carpets to Horace Walpole.

Everything was to hand, either in Mayfair or within easy reach of it, if one had the money to buy.

Sophie v. La Roche, writing in 1786, described a visit to Seddon's, the cabinetmaker in Aldersgate, where much of the Mayfair furniture must have been bought.

> He employs four hundred apprentices on any work connected with the making of household furniture, joiners, carvers, gilders, mirror-workers, upholsterers, girdlers – who mould the bronze into graceful patterns – and locksmiths. All these are housed in a building with six wings. In the basement mirrors are cast and cut. Some other department contains nothing but chairs, sofas and stools of every description, some quite simple, others exquisitely carved and made of all varieties of wood, and one large room is full up with all the finished articles in this line, while others are occupied by writing-tables, cupboards, chests of drawers, charmingly fashioned desks, chests, both large and small, work- and

toilet-tables in all manner of wood and patterns, from the simplest and cheapest to the most elegant and expensive . . .

Charming dressing-tables are also to be seen, with vase-shaped mirrors, occupying very little space, and yet containing all that is necessary to the toilet of any reasonable person. Close-stools, too, made like a tiny chest of drawers, with a couple of drawers in, decorative enough for any room.

She described sideboards with lead-lined drawers in which wine bottles were kept cool in water, footstools in which were two tiny cupboards, one lined with sheet-iron and neat grillers, on which plates could be heated by the red-hot iron beneath them, while the other was used for storing salt-cellars and other table utensils. She wrote of 'chintz, silk and wool materials for curtains and bed-covers; hangings in every possible material; carpets and stair-carpets to order; in short, anything one might desire to furnish a house . . .'

Three years before Sophie's visit, the whole place had been burned to the ground, but so flourishing was the furniture trade in London that Seddon had completely re-established himself.

Fires were a constant danger. Humphrey Skelton, an upholsterer in the Haymarket from 1709 to 1723 suffered a similar calamity which, according to the *London Gazette* of 17 August 1723, had been caused 'by an experiment which was being carried out to smother bugs'.

And this brings us to the seamy side of life in eighteenth-century Mayfair.

By 1774 William Cauty, cabinet-maker and upholsterer, of King Street, St James's, was assuring his customers that he had found the answer.

'Bedsteads, Sophas and Chairs finished so that no vermin of any Denomination can possibly exist in either by a new and infallible method never before found out and done no where else but at the above shop,' he declared.

But he was only one of many tradesmen offering the same service. As early as 1740 Mary Southall was advertising to free 'such quality and gentry as are troubled with Buggs, and are desirous to be kept free from these vermin . . .'. Her family maintained that the bug was unknown in England until it arrived in consignments of timber imported for the rebuilding of London after the Great Fire. Be that as it may, they settled down very happily. In 1775 Andrew Cooke of Holborn boasted of having 'cured 16,000 beds with great applause' and of having 'worked at the Palace'.

In mid-Victorian days the senior partner in the firm of Tiffin and Son, who bore the proud title of Bug Destroyer to Her Majesty, assured Mayhew that he worked for the upper classes – 'that is for carriage company and such-like approaching it . . . I have noble-men's names, the first in England, on my books' and described the delight of Princess Charlotte when he had caught a bug in her bed which had been troubling her all the previous night.

How clean were the 'quality and gentry' during the eighteenth century? It would be fair to say that they became increasingly aware of the disagreeableness of dirt as the years passed. The increase in the manufacture of washstands suggests that soap and water were being used more regularly, but none of the houses of Mayfair had bath-rooms when they were first built and the earliest, primitive water closets were not installed until 1775. At first this meant that the cess-pits filled up more quickly and became even more dangerous as sources of infection, for very often their contents seeped into the leaky wooden supply pipes.

Large houses often had cesspits directly underneath the house which were seldom emptied, and when they were the contents were carried away by the night men and emptied into a large, communal cesspit or the nearest river. And it was from the rivers that the so-called fresh water supply was drawn.

In London Sir Hugh Myddleton's New River, built in 1613, had been intended to provide purer water than that of the Thames and its tributaries, but by the eighteenth century this, too, had become contaminated by the contents of the cesspools seeping into the ancient supply pipes leading to street pumps. The piped water supply to individual houses was at first irregular – each house receiving water for two or three hours, two or three times a week.

Bathrooms were devised from spare bedrooms and at first there were arrangements for heating the water in the bathroom, after it had been tipped cold into the bath. Later, when the first kitchen boilers were installed, hot water was carried up from the basement, by one or other of the army of servants, but the bath had to be emptied by hand, until waste-pipes were built, connected with the sewers.

Bathing was not easy, for it involved much planning and arduous work. As late as 1837 there was no bathroom at all at Buckingham Palace and water was carried to the Queen's portable bath in her bed-room. Moreover, for many years to come there was a strong preju-dice against the daily bath, for it was said to be debilitating.

Princess Amelia, chatting one day in 1769 to Lady Mary Coke about Lady Rochford, said:

'She was dressed so loose and so naked, that I told her I cou'd see I did not know where, upon which She pulled up two napkins that She said She always wore upon her stomack and very dirty ones they were.'

Mrs Montagu, writing to her sister, after visiting her niece at school in Chelsea during the 1770s, said:

'I was pleased to find my neice [sic] perfectly clean and neat, tho' I called on ye Saturday, which is usually the eve of cleanliness. I remember at Mrs Robartes', at Kensington, the girls used to be so dirty, sometimes one could not salute them.'

Yet Horace Walpole thought that London was cleaner than Paris. Writing from Paris in September 1765, to Lady Suffolk, he said:

'I could wish there was less whisk (whist) and somewhat more cleanliness here. My Lady Browne and I have diverted ourselves with the idea of Lady Blandford being here. I am convinced she would *walk upon stilts* for fear of coming near these floors, and that would be a droll sight.' And he complained that it was more difficult to keep one's bedchamber pure in Paris than in London – 'water not being reckoned here one of the elements of cleanliness'.

He was vitriolic in his criticism of Lady Mary Wortley Montagu, whom he had come across many years earlier in Florence, but this may have been partly because of a fundamental family antagonism. 'She wears a foul mob that does not cover her greasy black locks, that hang loose, never combed or curled,' he wrote.

Most people seemed to accept bad smells as a part of life. They indicated which way the wind was blowing and helped to forecast the weather. When the 4th Marquis of Hertford objected to the smell in his Piccadilly House, it must either have been very bad indeed or else he was unusually sensitive.

The first drains were built of brick and were not properly maintained, while all too often they were built without a proper fall, so that the sewage never reached the main sewers and became the abode of rats.

Early nineteenth-century London was undermined by cesspits and many of the drains and sewers were in a deplorable condition. This applied to Mayfair as well as other parts of Westminster, while in 1844 no less than fifty-three overflowing cesspits were found beneath Windsor Castle.

Writing in 1851 about London's drains, Mayhew said that there was so much rottenness and decay that 'there is no security for the sewers standing from day to day' and to flush them for the removal of the 'most loathsome deposit' might be 'to bring them down altogether . . . throughout the new Paddington district, the neighbouring Hyde Park Gardens, and the costly squares and streets adjacent, the sewers abound with the foulest deposits, from which the most disgusting effluvium arises . . .'

During the 1850s the Government put into operation a plan to remove the London cesspits and install sewers leading from houses to main drains, which would empty into the Thames. London streets were dug up and miles of pipes were laid, made from Doulton's newly-devised glazed stoneware. Compared with the old wooden pipes, this stoneware made for really sound drains, but in the result all the fish which had once abounded in the Thames collapsed and died. For over a century they never came back, and only in the last few years have they ventured to reappear.

Elegant as the houses of Mayfair were, few had any but the smallest patch of garden at the back and some people found them oppressive and airless. Mrs Montagu often felt this when she was at Hill Street and in 1779, when her new house in Portman Square was nearly ready for her, she wrote: 'I am impatient to have my new house fit for habitation, as I think the large and high rooms and its airy situation will be of great service to my health,' while a few years later Sir William Abdy complained to Harriette Wilson that he thought Hill Street the dullest street in all London, but his wife had just left him and he was feeling lonely in that 'nasty, dull, large house' of his.

Most people used their Mayfair mansions only for the London season, and for the remaining months of the year, when they were living on their country estates, or were staying at Bath, Tunbridge Wells or Brighton, or had gone abroad, the houses were shut and the whole district seemed dreary and dead.

In *Vanity Fair*, Thackeray wrote of Mayfair during the Napoleonic Wars, for Gaunt Square is generally considered to have been intended for Berkeley Square and Great Gaunt Street for Hill Street. In describing Becky's first arrival in Great Gaunt Street, he wrote:

Having passed though Gaunt Square into Great Gaunt Street, the carriage at length stopped at a tall, gloomy house, between two other tall gloomy houses, each with a hatchment over the middle drawing-room window; as is the custom of houses in Great Gaunt Street, in which gloomy locality death seems to reign perpetual. The shutters of the first floor windows of Sir Pitt's mansion were closed – those of the dining-room were partially open, and the blinds neatly covered up in old newspapers.

In the dining-room, 'Rebecca found that apartment not more cheerful than such rooms usually are, when genteel families are out of town . . . The turkey carpet has rolled itself up, and retired sulkily under the sideboard: the pictures have hidden their faces behind old sheets of brown paper: the ceiling lamp is muffled up in a dismal sack of brown holland: the window-curtains have disappeared under all sorts of shabby envelopes: the marble bust of Sir Walpole Crawley is looking from its black corner at the bare boards and the oiled fire-irons, and the empty card-racks over the mantel-piece: the cellaret has lurked away behind the carpet: the chairs are turned up heads and tails along the walls: and in the dark corner opposite the statue, is an old-fashioned crabbed knife-box, locked and sitting on a dumb waiter.'

Later in the story, Becky and Rawdon Crawley took a little house, Number 101 Curzon Street, where Becky could hear the bells of the Curzon Street chapels. Little George was given a famous tailor from the West End of the town – a Mr Woollsey of Conduit Street; and when Sedley took his house in Gillespie Street, he bought 'the carpets, costly mirrors and handsome and appropriate planned furniture by Seddon's'.

Lord Steyne was believed to have been the wicked Lord Hertford, living out his last years in old Dorchester House, but some of the characteristics of Gaunt House Thackeray may have drawn from Harcourt House, which occupied the whole of the west side of Cavendish Square, round which the eccentric 5th Duke of Portland had built a high wall, so that he could live in monastic seclusion. 'Gloom sat perpetually on its outward walls' – and they were so high that hardly a glimpse of the house could be seen from the outside world.

James Boswell, in his *London Journal* of the 1760s, writing of the new squares of London, including those of Mayfair, said that 'Behind these gracious houses, however, with no gardens to insulate them, were closely-ranged houses and tenements of a baser sort, so that the back windows of "the Squares" looked out on a sordid prospect and were looked in upon by many pairs of eyes, some envious, some hostile . . .': and in *Little Dorrit*, set, like Thackeray's *Vanity Fair*, early in the nineteenth century, Dickens describes this aspect of Mayfair, writing of the murky little streets which grew up behind the grand ones, though they have long since been regenerated.

'Mews Street, Grosvenor Square, was not absolutely Grosvenor Square itself, but it was very near it. It was a hideous little street of dead wall, stables and dunghills, with lofts over coach-houses inhabited by coachmen's families, who had a passion for drying clothes, and decorating their window-sills with miniature turnpike-gates. The principal chimney-sweep of that fashionable quarter lived at the blind end of Mews Street; and the same corner contained an establishment much frequented about early morning and twilight, for the purchase of wine-bottles and kitchen-stuff. Punch's shows used to lean against the dead wall in Mews Street, while their proprietors were dining elsewhere; and the dogs of the neighbourhood made appointments to meet in the same locality. Yet there were two or three small, airless houses at the entrance of Mews Street, which went at enormous rents, on account of their being abject hangers-on to a fashionable situation; and whenever one of these fearful little coops was to be let (which seldom happened, for they were in great request), the house agent advertised it as a gentlemanly residence in the most aristocratic part of town, inhabited solely by the élite of the beau-monde. This was the home of the Barnacle family, for a gentlemanly residence was essential to the blood of the Barnacles.'

When Arthur Clennam made his first visit to Mr Tite Barnacle, he came to a 'squeezed house, with a ramshackle bowed front, little dingy windows, and a little dark area like a damp waistcoat-pocket, which he found to be Number twenty-four Mews Street, Grosvenor Square. To the sense of smell, the house was like a sort of bottle filled with a strong distillation of mews, and when the footman opened the door he seemed to take the stopper out.'

'He was by no means as grand as the footmen of Grosvenor Square itself. His gorgeousness was not unmixed with dirt, and both in complexion and consistency he had suffered from the closeness of his pantry.'

As Arthur Clennam was ushered into the inner hall, another stopper was taken out, releasing 'a smell of concentrated provisions and extract of sink from the pantry'. At the end of a narrow passage, in this hutch of a house, he was left to wait in a close back parlour, looking on to a low, blinding brick wall, only three feet away from the window, until the flunkey summoned him to the first-floor drawing-room.

Later on, when Clennam and Mr Meagles went in search of the

runaway Tattycoram, whom they suspected had fled to Miss Wade, living somewhere between Park Lane and Grosvenor Square, they 'dived in among the great streets of melancholy stateliness, and the little streets that try to be as stately, and succeed in being more melancholy, of which there is a labyrinth near Park Lane. Wildernesses of corner houses, with barbarous old porticoes and appurtenances – horrors that came into existence under some wrong-headed person in some wrong-headed time, still demanding the blind admiration of all ensuing generations, and determined to do so until they tumbled down – frowned upon the twilight. Parasite little tenements, with the cramp in their whole frame, from the dwarf hall-door on the giant model of His Grace's in the Square, to the squeezed window of the boudoir commanding the dunghills in the Mews, made the evening doleful.

'Rickety dwellings of undoubted fashion, but of a capacity to hold nothing comfortable except a dismal smell, looked like the last result of the great mansions' breeding in-and-in; and where their little supplementary bows and balconies were supported on thin iron columns, seemed to be scrofulously resting upon crutches . . . the shops, few in number, made no show . . .'

It was a hot summer evening and 'everyone seemed to be out to dinner and no one giving the dinners they had gone to'. 'On the doorsteps there were lounging footmen with bright, party-coloured plumage and white polls, like an extinct race of monstrous birds; and butlers, solitary men of recluse demeanour, each of whom appeared distrustful of all other butlers. The roll of carriages in the Park was done for the day; the street lamps were lighting; and wicked little grooms in the tightest fitting garments, with twists in their legs answering to the twists in their minds, hung about in pairs, chewing straws and exchanging fraudulent secrets . . . Here and there was a retiring public house . . . where gentlemen out of livery were not much wanted.'

It was an aspect of Mayfair that few who chose to live there ever mentioned, or indeed ever saw, in all probability, but Dickens caught the atmosphere of dreary boredom which the servants must have endured when they were not on duty, spending their time in dark basements and cold attics, in cramped and dirty mews or one of the few small pubs. And however much one may deplore the steadily increasing numbers of the motor-car, the dozens of horses which were crowded into the mews, built close against the backs of the terraced houses, must have created problems at least as great.

XIV

How They Lived – II

There is a great deal of social history in fiction and later writers than Thackeray and Dickens give a dismal impression of Mayfair out of season, but with the end of the hunting season and the coming of spring, fashionable Mayfair flocked back to its town mansions. The plane trees in the squares broke into bud, the dust covers came off the furniture, the invitation cards arrived by the score and the shops stirred into renewed activity, to serve the wealthy households for all their needs.

Moreover, such residents as had felt the first doubts of their social invulnerability, during the years of Jacobinism, recovered their confidence. As the nineteenth century progressed and the years of the second British Empire dawned, along with Britain's short-lived world supremacy in trade and industry, Mayfair held its own. Servants were as plentiful as they had ever been and the standards of luxury, if not of living, were rising.

As Dickens said, there were slums in Mayfair behind the aristocratic squares and streets, particularly to the west, before Park Lane came into its own. Mount Street, with its parish workhouse, had been a short-cut from Tyburn to the Fair, past the old St George's burial-ground, and a dreary, forlorn spot until the burial-ground was closed and transformed into a garden; then, towards the end of the nineteenth century, the old eighteenth-century houses and shabby shops were pulled down and the splendid new ones built in their place, with blocks of exclusive flats above them.

Even when the Grosvenor family's land to the south of Hyde Park
and west of Chelsea – the marshy five fields – was developed during
the 1820s and 1830s by Thomas Cubitt, to become the exclusive
Belgravia, Mayfair did not lose face. There was room for both, all
through the nineteenth century, and both were equally acceptable
and fashionable as places of London residence for English society. It
was a close-knit community, very much inbred, into which it was
difficult to enter, although with the passing years wealth proved a
valuable weapon in penetrating the barrier set up by title and lineage.
Wealth could buy a title or marry one, and humble origins could
quickly become submerged in a discreet but consistent display of its
power.

When the poet wrote of Mayfair in 1827, the barricades were still
intact.

> Dear to my soul art thou May Fair
> There greatness breathes her native air
>
> . . .
>
> There all the mushroom, trading tribe
> In vain would bully or would bribe,
> The Rothschilds, Couttses, Goldsmiths, Barings,
> In other spots may have their pairings.
> We fix your bounds, ye rich and silly,
> Along the road by Piccadilly.

And thus he wrote of the Mayfair season:

> Of dinners fix'd at half-past eight;
> Of morning lounge, of midnight rout,
> Of debt and dub, of love and gout,
> Of drowsy days, of brilliant nights,
> Of dangerous eyes, of downright frights . . .
>
> Of Dice and Doctors, Bowstreets, Bards.
> Crowds, Concerts, Chat, Champagne and Cards.
>
> Of faction, flirting and quadrille;
> With all thy faults I love thee still.
> And, while I have a love to spare,
> Dear to my soul art thou, May Fair.

Throughout the eighteenth century, in addition to their horses,
many of the Mayfair households kept their own cows, which grazed

in Hyde Park during the day and were brought home at night to the stables. Berkeley Street was full of stables belonging to the aristocratic houses in Dover Street. Mexborough House, at the corner of Hay Hill, where the 3rd Earl of Orford moved for a time, in 1827, after he had gambled away Number 11 Berkeley Square to Baring, was an eighteenth-century mansion which had among its outbuildings probably the last cow-house in the West End, but as late as the 1880s the last remaining goat from one of the Rothschild stables was a well-known figure strolling up and down Piccadilly and sometimes wandering into the clubs, before returning home each night to share a stable with the horses.

As the cows disappeared, milk was supplied to Mayfair by milkmaids carrying pails on a shoulder yoke, many of them coming from a dairy in Queen Street. There were a number of shops in the streets of Mayfair supplying the daily needs of the residents, and though many of them were, as Dickens complained, unattractive and dingy-looking from the outside, with few wares displayed in their small windows, the produce they sold was good and a number of them served many generations of Mayfair families and became household names. But apart from the shops in Shepherd Market they have now mostly disappeared and the dairy with the golden cow in the window has become the Queen Street post-office.

Bond Street, like Albemarle Street and Dover Street, had first been inhabited by people of quality, in large, four-storeyed brick houses, but sooner than the other two streets, Bond Street developed into a street of shops, the shopkeepers living over their shops and letting off the extra rooms.

The Duke of St Albans, son of Charles II and Nell Gwynn, was one of the earliest residents of Bond Street, and when he died here in 1726 the house was advertised 'To be let or sold . . . A House in Old Bond Street, Piccadilly, of four rooms on a floor, with closets, good cellar and all other conveniences. Being the house in which the late Duke of St Albans lived. Inquire at the Said House.' The Duchess of Kendal took this house for a year, after George I's death, and before she moved to Grosvenor Square in 1728.

As early as the 1690s a beauty doctor was practising in the street. She lived at 'Mr Trout's in Bond Street, near Piccadilly, the second House on the left-hand side' and on her trade bill she declared herself to the world unhampered by any false modesty.

'Let every one then consider that such a Person as this Lady is, is a PEARL AND A TREASURE, for she works almost Night and

Day for the good of mankind, which a great many persons of the
first rank can testify.' Like the 'Gentlewoman who lived at the
SURGEON'S SIGN, just at the corner of Coventry Court in the
Haymarket, near Piccadilly', she sold 'Balsamick Essence, with
several other incomparable Cosmeticks' that women 'might be
pleasing to their Husbands, and that they might not be offended at
their deformities and turn to others'. There was also on the market at
this time a 'Super-super excellent paste for the SHAKING and
TREMBLING of the HANDS, after HARD DRINKING or
OTHERWISE'.

Soon after 1700 the building of New Bond Street began and by
1717 the *Weekly Journal* reported that 'The new buildings between
Bond Street and Mary-le-bone go on with all possible diligence, and
the houses even let or sold before they are built. They are already in
great forwardness.'

James Smyth opened his perfumery shop in New Bond Street, between Grosvenor Street and Brook Street, selling lavender water,
wash-balls, pomatum, perfumed powder and soap; and close by
Richard Robinson, the confectioner, sold exotic sweetmeats, including comfits, pistachio nuts, prunellos, aniseed, limes and flowered
jelly glasses.

Shops catering for all the needs of Mayfair were soon established.
The customers were rich and the shops sold only the best, and by the
middle of the eighteenth century Pennant was saying that the street
'abounded with shopkeepers of both sexes of superior taste'.

Although many of the rooms above the shops were let out as
lodgings, there were still some private houses. Lavinia Fenton, the
original Polly Peachum, was living here in 1730, before she became
the Duchess of Bolton, and at the same time Mrs Delaney, when she
was Mrs Pendarves.

The 2nd and 3rd Dukes of Grafton lived at Grafton House in New
Bond Street during the middle years of the century and the 3rd Duke
took for his mistress Nancy Parsons, the daughter of a Bond Street
tailor. When Grafton House was pulled down, Grafton Street was
built, partly on the site of the old house and partly on Ducking
Pond Row.

Bond Street became increasingly fashionable as a place for lodgings. Fielding's Tom Jones took lodgings here – 'a very good part of
the town' – with Mrs Miller, the widow of a clergyman. Gibbon,
who found in London 'crowds without company, and dissipation
without pleasure', preferred the quiet of his rooms in Bond Street to

the diversions of the town. 'While coaches were rattling through Bond Street, I have passed many solitary evenings in my lodgings with my books,' he said. Thomson took lodgings with a milliner, where 'he seldom rose early enough to see the sun do more than glisten on the opposite windows of the street', wrote Mrs Piozzi. In 1768 Laurence Sterne died in his lodgings at the silk-bag shop in Old Bond Street and the following year Boswell was entertaining Dr Johnson, Reynolds, Goldsmith and Garrick in his Bond Street rooms.

The number and variety of the shops increased and by the end of the century the street contained book and music publishers, tailors, milliners, perfumerers, including Atkinson's, which was established in 1799 and disappeared only a few years ago, jewellers, chemists and druggists, fishmongers, butchers, poulterers, dairymen, tea and coffee merchants, fruiterers, grocers, cheesemongers, pastrycooks and bakers, wine and spirit merchants, porcelain, china and glass shops, woollen drapers, linen drapers, boot and shoe-makers, tobacconists, gold and silver lacemen, carpet manufacturers, an umbrella and parasol-maker, furriers, a seedsman and florist, lamp-makers, cabinet-makers and upholsterers and a curious sounding establishment which called itself a fish sauce warehouse. There was a saddler and harness-maker, a gun-maker, carriage manufacturers and livery stables.

Until 1762 they all had their street signs hanging above their charming little Georgian, bow-fronted shop-windows, but the signs became bigger and bigger, as the shopkeepers vied with each other to attract attention, and at last became serious obstructions, blocking out the light and highly dangerous in a strong wind.

So the Government forbade them and all the Turk's Heads, Plumes of Feathers, Flaming Swords, Civet Cats, Olive Trees, Three Crowns and King's Arms had to come down and be replaced by mundane numbers, but Old and New Bond Street were numbered separately, although their personalities have merged. On the east the division comes at Burlington Gardens, but on the west Number 25 Old Bond Street adjoins Number 180 New Bond Street.

Together they formed Mayfair's principal shopping street, but these were no ordinary shops. They became increasingly elegant and many proudly displayed the Royal Warrant. By the early nineteenth century Savory and Moore, the chemist's, was established at Number 143 New Bond Street, by Thomas Savory and its beautiful Georgian shop-front, with the Royal Warrant of William IV, still stands. Thomas Savory, the apothecary, was a Gentleman of the

King's Privy Chamber and entertained lavishly in New Bond Street, in his apartments above the shop. Many of the doctors in the near-by doctors' quarter around Savile Row were his dinner party guests and the Duke of Cambridge was a personal friend and frequent visitor, who liked to play the fiddle with him.

Another interesting survival is Tessiers of Number 26 New Bond Street. This little house, so much smaller than those on either side, was one of the original private houses of Bond Street, built during the early eighteenth century, and the first record of it becoming a shop was in 1840, when it was occupied by Winfield and Sims, selling military beds and camp equipment; but by 1852 the Tessier family had taken over the premises. They were descendants of Etienne de Tessier, a Huguenot refugee who, after several years in Switzerland, arrived in England in 1712, and whose son Lewis, a merchant of the City of London, was two generations later dealing in jewellery sold to him by refugees from the French Revolution.

In 1811 his son opened business as a jeweller at Number 32 South Audley Street, and later, with his own sons, opened shops in Mount Street, Conduit Street and Number 26 New Bond Street, where their account heading announced 'Specialité for Onyx and Mourning Jewellery' and 'Artists in Hair'.

The last of the Tessiers retired towards the end of the nineteenth century and then the three Parsons brothers took over the business, which is still in their hands; and they have preserved the dignified old shop-front, while some of the Tessiers' hair pictures still hang in the shop.

The founders of Asprey and Company of 165–169 New Bond Street were also descended from a distinguished Huguenot family who fled to England at the end of the seventeenth century. The Aspreys were skilled craftsmen, watchmakers, silversmiths, weavers, leather-workers and master-smiths, and when William Asprey founded his firm at Mitcham, in 1781, his inherited skills quickly brought him success. With his son Charles he became renowned for his beautifully fitted dressing-cases and during the 1830s Charles Asprey set up his business at Number 49 New Bond Street, moving in 1848 to a larger shop at Number 166 New Bond Street.

His dressing-cases and writing-cases, his beautiful jewellery and exquisite gold, silver and leather-work, all made and designed in the workrooms above the shop, soon brought him fame and honours. The firm was given the Royal Appointment by Queen Victoria in 1861, and it has been renewed by every reigning monarch since then.

The firm spread to Numbers 165 to 169 New Bond Street, and to Number 22 Albemarle Street, and today it is world famous, for the high standard of impeccable workmanship has been unfalteringly maintained. With its high, rather narrow, arched Victorian windows, it is a beautiful, spacious shop. It still belongs to the Asprey family, the craftsmen still design and work above the shop and the tradition of friendly, personal service is unbroken.

Amidst the wide variety of shops in the street, Bond Street, both Old and New, became famous during the first half of the nineteenth century, as the headquarters of the circulating libraries and book-sellers. Their business also included the letting of theatre boxes and the selling of tickets for various fashionable entertainments, while some ventured into the book-publishing business.

These shops became the meeting-places for writers and young men about town who were interested in books and the theatre. One of the earliest was John Brindley's shop, which he opened in 1728. He was also a printer and publisher and became renowned for his beautiful bindings. He received the Royal Warrant and dedicated his first published book to Queen Caroline, although the subject was by no means romantic, being *Observations on the Small Pox*.

When he died James Robson continued the business and he also entered the proprietary chapel business, for it was he who bought the Trinity Chapel, refurbished it inside and engaged the popular preacher, Dr Beamish, who drew in the crowds each Sunday, to the spiritual benefit of the congregation and the material benefit of Mr Robson.

This shop, at Number 29 New Bond Street, lasted for over two hundred years, ending as Ellis's, but it disappeared in 1931.

Hookham, the friend of Shelley and Thomas Love Peacock, ran a book-shop at Number 15 Old Bond Street, and in 1804 he published Peacock's first poems. John Ebers's shop was at Number 27, but his interest in booking opera boxes induced him to forsake books for the management of His Majesty's Theatre, where, from 1820 to 1827, he lost more than £4,000. His son-in-law, Harrison Ainsworth, took over the Bond Street publishing business for a time and on 25 November 1826, he was writing:

> My shop is nearly ready. The partition has been erected and the library books removed, and my stock is being transferred to the vacant shelves. The customers stare and marvel at the change, but it has by no means a bad effect. My shop consists of a long, lobby-

like room, terminating in a snug room, the shelves of which are loaded with goodly tomes, and the tables covered with magazines, newspapers and new publications. When it is entirely completed it will have a very knowing appearance.

However, he soon tired of publishing and turned to writing, while the business was taken over by other members of the family, under the name of J. Ebers and Company.

John Mitchell was another important theatrical agent who, in 1834, opened a library at Number 33 Old Bond Street, at the corner of Stafford Street, and the business remained here for the next forty years. Among his customers were Lady Blessington and her lover Count d'Orsay, the husband of her step-daughter, who set up house together for a short time in Seamore Place – now named Curzon Place – before moving to the splendid Gore House in Kensington, where within a few years they had bankrupted themselves. In 1836 Mitchell opened the Lyceum Theatre for Italian comic opera and in 1842 brought over French plays and players to the St James's Theatre.

During these early years of the nineteenth century, Bond Street was essentially a man's street, particularly during the afternoons, between the hours of two and five, when it became a promenade for the elegant Bond Street loungers. The street was full of men's lodgings and the early 'sporting' hotels were beginning to appear, frequented only by men. There were the libraries with their newspapers and new books to be conned and an increasing number of specialist men's shops were opening – hatters, tailors and shirt-makers. Until the 1850s or even later, no lady would shop in Bond Street during these afternoon hours, and as it was unthinkable for her to shop after dark, although the shops were still open, it left only an hour or two in the morning for her, when she would be accompanied by a maid, a footman or a page.

Notwithstanding the booksellers and publishers of Bond Street, it was close by at John Murray's in Albemarle Street that most of the important literary figures of the early nineteenth century were meeting. The founder of the firm died in 1793 and it was the second John Murray who published Byron's work, the first two cantos of *Childe Harold's Pilgrimage* appearing in 1812. A warm friendship sprang up between Byron and John Murray, and others in the circle were Thomas Campbell and Sir Walter Scott. Byron's work made money for John Murray, but even more successful, financially, was one of his earlier ventures, *Mrs Rundell's Cookery Book*; but Harriette Wilson never forgave him for turning down her outrageous but amusing *Memoirs*, which were ultimately accepted by Allman of Princes Street, Hanover Square. Murray launched the *Quarterly Review*, as the organ of the Tory party, and under the editorship of William Gifford, the early contributors included George Canning, John Hookham Frere, Sir Walter Scott, Byron, Dean Milman and Jonathan Croker.

At his dinner parties, John Murray included politicians, statesmen, authors and artists and his 'four o'clock' visitors were as distinguished.

> The room's so full of wits and bards,
> Crabbes, Campbells, Crokers, Freres and Wards

wrote Byron.

Writing to Thomas Moore about these gatherings, Sir Walter Scott said:

> We met for an hour or two almost daily in Mr. Murray's drawing room, and found a great deal to say to each other ... I saw Lord Byron for the last time in 1815 after I returned from France. He dined or lunched with me at Long's in Bond Street. I never saw him so full of gayety or good humour to which the presence of Mr. Matthews, the comedian, added not a little.

The house where these meetings took place and the first-floor drawing-room where John Murray received his guests are little changed, although since 1928, when the fourth John Murray died, and the house ceased to be a private residence, this room has been the office of the present head of the firm.

It was the establishment in the middle of the nineteenth century of Mudie's vast circulating library in New Oxford Street, with its 800,000 volumes in constant circulation, at the very modest charge of a guinea a year, which rang the death-knell of the small circulating libraries and bookshops, but one which has survived, though not strictly speaking in Mayfair, being on the south side of Piccadilly, is Hatchard's. John Hatchard had spent his boyhood at the Grey Coat Hospital and in 1784 was apprenticed to Mr Ginger, bookseller to Westminster School, who lived in Great College Street. He did well and in 1797 opened his own shop in Piccadilly, where the firm has been selling books ever since, at one time being a meeting-place of men of letters, particularly those who were members of the Tory party.

And only a few doors away, many Mayfair residents must have shopped at Fortnum and Mason's, for Mr Fortnum had been a footman in the service of Queen Anne and set up his shop in 1707, before many of the New Bond Street shops had been established, while during the 1830s and early 1840s Chapman & Hall, close by, were publishing Dickens's first serials, *Pickwick, Nicholas Nickleby, Martin Chuzzlewit* and *A Christmas Carol*.

The Royal Institution in Albemarle Street was first established in 1799, its objective being 'to encourage improvement in arts and manufacture'. Five old houses were taken and adapted by Vulliamy to the present building, with its Corinthian façade. Count Rumford was the moving spirit and meetings began in 1800, with lectures on philosophy and science and their application to mechanical inventions.

Sir Humphrey Davy, who lived at Number 26 Park Street, was director of the Institute for many years and it was a fashionable Mayfair diversion to attend his lectures and demonstrations, particularly when he was able to produce a 'column of electric light' from a gigantic voltaic battery.

Davy died in 1829 but his young assistant Michael Faraday continued to work at the Institute and produced the first magneto-electric machine – a dynamo – which enabled electricity to be produced on a large scale and made possible the development of the telephone and telegraph.

It was during Old Q's lifetime that the public coach service developed. It had begun in a small way a century earlier, before the Civil War, when two draughty and cumbersome coaches were running each week over the appalling road between St Albans and the Bell Inn at Aldersgate, but it was with the Restoration that the service developed. By this time, though there was little improvement in the roads, the coaches were more weatherproof, with glass windows and proper doors instead of leather flaps. At first the service operated for only relatively short distances, but by the 1670s every important town within about twenty-five miles of London had a service of one or more coaches running once or twice a week, at a cost of twopence or threepence a mile.

The long-distance coach services were promoted by the innkeepers, the landlord of the Belle Sauvage on Ludgate Hill opening his service with a 'Flying Machine to Bath, taking three days (If God Permit) and running three days a week'.

At first coaches did not change horses during a day's journey, for they sometimes diverged from their published route, for the convenience of passengers, thus making it difficult to establish regular posting-houses, but by 1734 the system had changed. The proprietors of the Newcastle 'Flying Coach' announced that by arranging for eight strong horses to be stationed at proper distances he could promise to cut the journey from twelve days to nine. The idea caught on and the stage-coach was established.

Until the 1780s, the mail was still carried by post-boys, riding at about six miles an hour, but in 1782 John Palmer planned a service of mail-coaches which by changing horses every seven or ten miles would increase the speed of the post to eight or nine miles an hour; and as he pointed out, by allowing passengers on the mail-coaches, the cost of the shortened posts would be offset by their fares and the mail need cost no more.

The first mail-coach ran from Bristol to London in 1784, the London terminus being the Swan With Two Necks in Lad Lane, and the journey took sixteen hours. The mail-coach did not displace the ordinary stage-coach, for although the fact that the guard and the coachman were both armed was a reassurance to nervous travellers alarmed at the thought of hold-ups and highwaymen, and the increased speed of the journey was an attraction to anyone in a hurry, the ride itself was a fairly nerve-racking experience and there was seldom a month went by without one coach at least being overturned. Many, therefore, preferred the more leisurely progress of the stage-coach, which ensured at least a proper bed at a coaching inn each night.

By the end of the eighteenth century there were a score or more of coaching inns in the City of London, each with vast stables attached. The Belle Sauvage, for example, had stabling for four hundred horses, and it was renowned for its comfort and good food, even though Parson Woodforde, staying there in 1782, confessed that he was 'bit terribly by the Buggs'.

The London end of the coaching business was mainly in the hands of six competitors, most of whom had West End offices. All the mail-coaches, except those bound for the west, left the General Post Office every evening at eight o'clock, having collected their passengers first from their City inns; but to avoid confusion and congestion, the passengers for the West Country waited at the West End booking offices in Oxford Street and Piccadilly. In Oxford Street the Green Man and Still and the Gloucester Coffee House served passengers taking the Uxbridge road and around the area where Piccadilly Circus was later to be built stood the White Bear, the Spread Eagle, the Bull and Mouth and the Golden Cross, serving passengers travelling to Bath and Exeter by way of Hounslow.

Hatchett's was another popular coaching inn for travellers to the west, and on the other side of the road, on the site of the Ritz Hotel, stood the old White Horse Cellars.

Crowds always gathered to watch the departure of the stage- and mail-coaches in Piccadilly, and in addition to the friends and well-wishers there was always a handful of Jewish street-traders, selling oranges, pencils, sponges and anything else that they thought a traveller might be induced to buy.

It enlivened stately Piccadilly, which, as Horace Walpole had already complained to Miss Berry and her sister in 1791, was becoming congested enough with the private carriages of the gentry. The public coach services were not, of course, a method of transport used by the aristocracy. The mansions of Piccadilly, still hiding behind their high brick walls, had no part in the changing scene which was taking place on their doorsteps and it did not affect their way of life at all, but there were many changes in their own ways of travel. Each year saw the introduction of a new model. The post-chaise was popular for long journeys, for it was fairly comfortable, the body being hung by leather braces to upright springs. The back wheels were much larger than the front ones and luggage was stacked both behind and in front, while horses were changed at each posting-house.

For short distances in and around London, where the roads were better, they used lighter carriages, known as chariots. By the 1750s the landau arrived, similar to the chariot except that the upper part could be opened and pulled back. A phaeton for two, drawn by two horses, was popular at the end of the century. The perch phaeton, with the body over the front wheels, was sporting but rather dangerous. The gig drawn by one horse had only two wheels, the open body being suspended by leather braces from curved springs. A two-horse gig was known as a curricle, and if it had a hood it was a cabriolet, while another form, with a different arrangement of springs, was a whisky. The tilbury – a light, two-wheeled carriage – was invented by Mr Tilbury the carriage-builder, whose business, Captain Gronow records, was in a street leading from South Audley Street to Park Street.

This was the kind of traffic which blocked Piccadilly and the streets of Mayfair, including in particular the narrow straits of Old

Bond Street, before it opened out into the wider New Bond Street. For over two hundred years Old Bond Street was a bottle-neck for traffic but in the last year or two it has been cut off by a line of attractive trees in tubs, so that traffic coming up from Oxford Street now has to turn into Clifford Street in order to reach Piccadilly.

In 1811 several hundreds of acres of land north of the Marylebone Road reverted to the Crown and the Prince Regent asked John Nash to develop them as a fashionable residential area. Nash planned his terraces of Palladian stucco-covered brick mansions surrounding a park which was re-named Regent's Park, and then, between 1813 and 1820 he built Regent Street, to link Regent's Park with St James's Park. For the main part of Regent Street nearly all of the narrow, dingy Swallow Street had to be demolished, which was no loss, for it had an evil reputation, and several of its inns had been known as houses-of-call for highwaymen, while for the building of Lower Regent Street the old St James's market was swept away.

From Piccadilly Circus towards Oxford Street Nash built his shops, on both sides, with a Doric colonnade projecting over the pavements, to provide a covered walk, beneath a balustraded roof.

'The buildings of this noble street', wrote Tallis in 1837, 'chiefly consist of palace-like shops, in whose broad, showy windows are displayed articles of the most splendid description, such as the neighbouring world of wealth and fashion are daily in want of. The upper part of these elegant structures are mostly let as apartments to temporary visitors to the metropolis' . . . 'Its form is one of the best which could be devised for the purpose,' he continued. 'It gives an air of grandeur and space to the streets, and a free circulation of air to the houses. It affords facilities to carriages and horsemen in the turning from one street to the other, and is as elegant in form as useful in application.'

A few years later, some of the shopkeepers complained that the colonnade made their shops too dark, and to the dismay of a great many admirers of Nash's work, it was taken down in 1848 and a balcony added to the first floor of the buildings behind.

From the beginning, the shops in Regent Street were fashionable and elegant, and during the London season the street was crowded with women of fashion from Mayfair and Belgravia. But with the coming of high summer and the end of the season, they all departed again. 'There are no more lines of carriages at the kerb; no concert programmes in the music-shops; nor bouquets and lap-dogs on the pavements,' wrote Albert Smith in his *Sketches of London Life and Character*. 'Regent Street assimilates to Pompeii in its loneliness . . . All have departed – the handsome girls to recruit their somewhat jaded strength, and recover from the pallor induced by late hours and the thousand fretting emotions of society; the men to shoot, and ride, and sail; the heads of the families to retain their caste, because it is proper to do so, but all to get away as soon and as fast as they can, when Parliament is prorogued and the grouse are reported to be ready for slaughter.'

Life in high society was following a fairly rigid pattern and even the shopping hours had their fashionable times, for while the men were monopolising Bond Street it was right for women to shop in Regent Street from two until four in the afternoon. This was a gift for the satirists but the shops were splendid; and although Oxford Street did its best to copy, it never quite reached such high standards, for it catered mainly for the strata below high society, the prosperous and rising middle classes. Yet for many years its shops had been busy and flourishing, many of them tending to concentrate on women's fashions.

In 1817, while Regent Street was still being built, Oxford Street had thirty-three linen drapers, ten straw-hat manufactories, six bonnet warehouses, five woollen drapers, five lace warehouses, three plumassiers, twenty-four boot- and shoe-makers, one muslin and shawl warehouse, two silk and satin dressers and dyers, two drapers and tailors, an India muslin warehouse, three fancy trimmings and fringes manufactories, a button-maker, three stay and corset warehouses, a stocking warehouse, a ready-made linen warehouse and four umbrella manufactories.

At the sign of the Golden Lion at Number 54 Oxford Street the firm of Dickins and Smith had been established in 1790, and in 1837 they moved to Regent Street, later becoming Dickins and Jones, and here they have been ever since. The Golden Lion moved with them and hung over the door of the new shop, discreetly enough to avoid the shop-sign law, until 1927, when Regent Street was rebuilt. In 1833 Peter Robinson opened a linen draper's shop at Number 103 Oxford Street and the present store still occupies part of the original site.

Number 10 Piccadilly at the time of Waterloo was the West End office of the Bull and Mouth in St Martin's-le-Grand, the inn which catered for west-bound coach traffic. This property was bought by two young men who had kept stalls in St James's market. William Edgar, the son of a Cumberland farmer, came to London early in the century, to seek his fortune, and began by selling men's cravats, socks and haberdashery in the market.

A large part of the ordinary men's outfitting trade was conducted in this way, in open markets, both in London and the provinces. St James's market, though so close to Carlton House, had become a dirty slum by this time – a labyrinth of murky stalls and dingy, dangerous alleys, which straggled along Jermyn Street towards St James's Square. As in Covent Garden, the stall-keepers more often than not slept under their stalls. Life was hard and rough, but William Edgar began to make money, and so did John Swan, who kept a stall close by.

The two young men became friends, and when, with the building of Regent Street, the St James's market was swept away, they bought the Bull and Mouth, together with its drink licence, and opened shop. John Swan died at Number 10 Piccadilly in 1821, when he was only forty-four, but William Edgar stayed on and built up his famous business.

While Nash was building Regent Street, Lord George Cavendish was living at Burlington House and had already commissioned Samuel Ware to make many improvements and additions to the old house. He now commissioned him to build the Burlington Arcade. The *Gentleman's Magazine* for September 1812 wrote:

> It is said that after numerous deliberations, Lord George Cavendish has determined to appropriate a proportion of the grounds connected with Burlington House for the gratification of the publick, and to give employment to industrious females. A line has been marked out at the west end, extending north and south, in which will be a covered way or promenade from Piccadilly into Cork Street. This covered way will contain a double line of shops, for the sale of jewellery and other fancy articles, and above will be suites of rooms. What first gave birth to the idea was the great annoyance to which the garden is subject from the inhabitants of a neighbouring street throwing oyster-shells, etc., over the wall. The intended erections will prevent these nuisances in future and also block out the view of so delightful a place.

Clearly they were not over-enthusiastic at the idea, but the plan went ahead. The arcade was described as 'a Piazza for all hardware, Wearing Apparel and Articles not Offensive in appearance nor smell', 'piazza' being a favourite word at this time, used regardless of its etymology, to describe any covered walk.

The arcade was finished in 1819 and with its attractive little shops and its uniformed beadle, to see that people behaved themselves and to ensure that the gates were locked each night, it was successful from the outset and proved a useful source of income to the Cavendish family. It later passed to Lord Chesham, a grandson of Lord George Cavendish, and remained in the Chesham family until 1926, when they sold it to the Prudential Assurance Company. The northern end of the arcade was badly damaged by bombs during the Second World War, but it was beautifully restored and the Regency atmosphere preserved, although the gates have been removed. The Chesham coat of arms is still to be seen at either end and the Prudential have continued Lord Chesham's tradition of recruiting the beadles from his old regiment, the 10th Royal Hussars.

In 1819 the seventy-two little shops in the arcade were let at a rental of £18 a year. Whether or not there were ever any hardware shops, they did not stay for long, and it was soon filled with shops selling nothing but luxuries. One of the first men to rent a shop there, in 1819, was Lord, and the firm is still there, the business now extending from Number 66 to Number 70 in the arcade.

By 1859 George Augustus Sala was saying that there was not a shop in the arcade selling anything that we could not do without.

'Boots and shoes are sold there, to be sure', he wrote, 'but what boots and shoes! Varnished and embroidered and be-ribboned figments, fitter for a fancy ball or a lady's chamber, there to caper to the jingling melody of a lute, than for serious pedestrianism. Paintings and lithographs for gilded boudoirs, collars for puppy dogs, and silver-mounted whips for spaniels, pocket handkerchiefs, in which an islet of cambric is surrounded by an ocean of lace, embroidered garters and braces, filigree flounces, fire-work-looking bonnets, scent bottles, sword-knots, brocaded sashes, worked dressing-gowns, inlaid snuff-boxes, falbalas of all descriptions. These form the stock in trade of the merchants who have here their tiny boutiques.'

The Burlington Glove and Fan Depot was at Numbers 22 and 23 in the arcade and Madame Parsons sold her guinea bonnets at Numbers 26, 27 and 28. There was also a 'friendly bonnet shop' where the accommodating milliner allowed the rooms above to be used as a brothel, and this rendezvous became as fashionable, in its way, as the shops, so that men of affairs, who wished to avoid any breath of scandal, took care to avoid the precincts of the arcade at certain times of the day.

The bonnet shops have all disappeared now, and so have the

prostitutes, for this was once their happiest hunting-ground in all Piccadilly, but the splendid jewellers are still there and some notable leather, linen and cashmere shops; and in the grim, utilitarian world of the 1970s, it is still a place of deliciously unnecessary extravagance and luxury.

Urling's Lace Warehouse was one of the earliest shops in Regent Street, for it was established at Number 24 in 1817, and it was given the Royal Appointment by Queen Adelaide. John J. Holmes opened his Shawl Emporium at Number 171 in 1820, where they sold nothing but shawls. They also gained the Royal Appointment of Queen Adelaide and later of Queen Victoria, by which time the shop had extended to Numbers 173 and 175 Regent Street and were selling shawls of every conceivable kind, costing anything from one guinea to a thousand guineas.

There were several other shawl shops in Regent Street, as well as milliners and lace-men, shoe-makers and glovers. Mrs Huntley at Number 294 was Staymaker and Corset Maker to Queen Adelaide, conducting her business with the utmost refinement and discretion, and announcing herself as 'At Home to her clients from 12–5 daily', although invalids and those too frail – or too noble – to visit her, she called on herself.

But when Miss Weeton, the governess, paid her first visit to London in 1824, she showed no interest in the new shops, probably because she was so poor that she knew she could afford nothing they had to offer. They belonged to a different world, far out of her reach.

She tells us that on 9 July she took a walk into Piccadilly, to Bullock's Museum in the Egyptian Hall, and saw the room where specimens of modern Mexico were exhibited, but the admission was a shilling, which she could not afford, so she got no further.

The Egyptian Hall was on the south side of Piccadilly, almost opposite Bond Street, and had been built in 1812 to exhibit the collection which William Bullock had made during thirty years of exploration in Central America. Later the hall was to be used for a number of other exhibitions and entertainments, including the mysteries of Maskelyne and Cooke. Today, Robert Jackson's shop stands on the site and in the basement you can still see traces of the Egyptian décor.

When it was time for Miss Weeton to return to Liverpool she made the round of the West End coach offices, to enquire and compare prices for the journey.

'I next walked along Piccadilly,' she said, 'enquiring at several

Coach Offices the Liverpool fares; they were all £4 inside and £2 out. I next went to see the apparatus for hatching by steam (chickens): walked on to Hyde Park corner, and getting a pot of curds,* walk- up to Cumberland Gate, and turned to the right along Oxford St inquiring at various offices the fares of Liverpool coaches; they were all as in Piccadilly.'

She was anxious to see Oxford on her way home and, on 26 July, after making enquiries at Charing Cross, she went into Piccadilly again, and from the Spread Eagle office at the corner of Regent Street at last found a coach that passed through Oxford on the way to Liverpool. Two days later, she booked an outside place on the coach which was scheduled to leave the Spread Eagle at half past five the following morning.

Although she was alone and diffident and very poor, she had determination and was a dogged sight-seer, yet never once did she venture from the perimeter of Mayfair to wander through the aris- tocratic streets and squares, nor did she make any comment upon the mansions she passed in Piccadilly, perhaps because they were still hidden behind their high walls.

On the journey home she enjoyed the ride as far as Birmingham. The passengers throughout the day were few and well behaved, she said. The morning was as lovely as it could be, and the whole day's ride was most delightful. But at Birmingham they changed coaches and took up six drunk and quarrelsome Irishmen, one of whom fell asleep on Miss Weeton's shoulder, 'the brim of his hat endangering her eyes': and to escape from him, 'she spent the rest of the night on a very dangerous seat behind, backwards'.

There were few hotels in London until the early part of the nineteenth century. In fact it was not until this time that the word 'hotel' was used, and then it was applied to the more exclusive coaching inns. Public coaches still used these new-styled hotels as posting-houses, but only private coach travellers stayed at them, the others putting up at the less expensive, old-fashioned inns. Visitors to London usually stayed in rooms, where meals and service were provided.

Most of the hotels of Regency London were opened by French chefs who had been in service in England, or retired English butlers who understood the ways and tastes of the wealthy.

* The Curds-and-Whey House was a cottage attached to the entrance to Hyde Park, by the toll gate. The cottage and lodge came down in 1825, when a new stone lodge was built.

Alexander Grillion, who had been in service with the Crewe family, set up one of the first Mayfair hotels when he took the lease of Number 7 Albemarle Street in 1803 and established Grillion's Hotel. It was a splendid eighteenth-century house with a beautiful, curving staircase, rising from the entrance hall.

Louis XVIII stayed here, on his journey back to Paris, at the time of his restoration, while the Grand Duchess Catherine was enjoying the amenities of Escudier's Pulteney Hotel in Piccadilly.

Lady Crewe visited Grillion's with Fanny Burney on this occasion, to watch the King's arrival. She had booked a private room and was highly indignant when she discovered that she had been given one at the back of the building, with no view at all.

'She rang the bell for waiter after waiter, till she made M. Grillion come himself', wrote Fanny Burney. 'She then in her singularly open and easy manner, told him to be so good as to order us a front room where we might watch the arrival of the Royals, and be amused ourselves at the same time by seeing the entrance of the Mayor, Aldermen, and Common Councilmen, and other odd characters, who would be coming to pay their court to these French princes and princesses. M. Grillion gave a nod of acquiescence, and we were instantly shown to a front apartment just over the street door, which was fortunately supplied with a balcony.'

In 1813, the previous year, a group of members of both Houses of Parliament had founded Grillion's Club. They dined at the hotel each Wednesday while Parliament was in session, their aim being to meet on neutral ground, where they could talk about everything but politics. Distinguished men of both parties and all shades of opinion met here in friendship, 'the feuds of the previous day being forgotten, or made the theme of pleasantry and genial humour'; and among the members were George Canning, Lord Dudley and Ward, Lord Francis Egerton and Lord Harrowby.

Louis XVIII was not the only royal personage to be entertained at Grillion's. When the nervous Princess Adelaide arrived in England to marry the Duke of Clarence, who was soon to become William IV, she and her mother stayed here before the wedding; and when the King of Württemberg paid them a visit, a few years later, he was given rooms at Grillion's. Greville described King William and Queen Adelaide driving 'all over the town in an open calèche with the King of Württemberg' and then 'setting him down (Dropt him as he calls it) at Grillion's'.

'The King of England dropping another King at a Tavern,' added

Greville, doing less than justice to Grillion's exclusive establishment.

More than half the houses in Albemarle Street became hotels about this time, most of them run by men who had been butlers. One of the most successful was Gordon's at the corner of Piccadilly, where both Nelson and Byron stayed at times. In 1858 this became the Albemarle Hotel and in 1889 it was rebuilt and restyled the Hotel Albemarle, when for a few years it became one of the most exclusive hotels in the West End. The pinkish brick exterior is still standing, but for many years it has been converted into suites of offices.

The Clarendon in New Bond Street was in its day the biggest hotel in London. It was opened by Jacquier, the French chef who had been in the service of Louis XVIII, while he was in exile at Hartwell House. The Clarendon was said to have been the only public hotel in London where you could enjoy genuine French cooking, but it was very expensive, for in 1814 dinner was usually three or four pounds and a bottle of champagne or claret cost a guinea.

The building was at Number 160 New Bond Street, where Cartier's now stands, and it had a carriage entrance at the back, at Number 20 Albemarle Street, next to the Royal Institution, to avoid the congestion of traffic in Bond Street.

When Grillion's lease expired at Number 7 Albemarle Street, he moved to the Clarendon, and the Grillion Club moved with him. The Club lasted all through the reigns of George IV and William IV, but did not survive long into Victorian times, and the hotel itself closed in 1872. Number 7 Albemarle Street became the home of the Royal Thames Yacht Club for a time, but today it is the headquarters of the National Book League.

There were two other famous hotels in New Bond Street, both of them almost opposite the Clarendon. These were Long's and Stephen's, which together with Limmer's, at the corner of St George Street and Conduit Street, and Hatchett's in Piccadilly, were the 'sporting' hotels of Mayfair, mainly frequented by sportsmen and country squires. They were essentially men's hotels and only in the last few years of their existence did one or two women ever enter them.

Long's, a large, four-storeyed house, was the last to go, for it continued into the 1880s and its smoking-room, to the right of the entrance, was a favourite meeting-place for young men about town. The cooking was unpretentious but extremely good, and it had one or two specialities – in particular its devilled soles – while a whisky and soda as mixed by William, the head-waiter, whose secret was never revealed, was considered the best in London. Stephen's, close by, was a popular resort of Army officers and was so much like a club that any stranger who thought to dine there was usually stared at in surprise and told that there was no table vacant. It was no uncommon sight, wrote Captain Gronow, to see 'thirty or forty saddle-horses or tilburies waiting outside the doors of the hotel'. Limmer's was as popular, crowded with sportsmen, who were apparently none too fastidious, for Gronow described it as 'the dirtiest hotel in London'. Hatchett's had been built on the site of the Three Kings tavern and was an old coaching inn. The White Horse Cellars, which had stood at the corner of Arlington Street, was moved across Piccadilly and stood close by. And these two inns were where generations of country squires liked to stay when they visited London.

They were to see a great and sudden change come to Piccadilly, for during the 1840s, with the speedy spread of the railways, the old coaches were forced off the road, and within a matter of months some of the old coaching inns were ruined, their stables empty and their customers gone.

It was at Hatchett's, during the 1860s, that a group of young men, already yearning for the old days of the stage-coaches, revived the London to Brighton run. In 1866 they bought the little yellow 'Old Times' coach and managed to establish a regular summer service for a few years, which was horsed by the Duke of Beaufort and his friends.

Then the old Hatchett's was pulled down and a new hotel built in its place. It was never the same and it did not pay, so that today only the excellent Hatchett's restaurant has survived.

Just to the west of Hatchett's, between Dover Street and Berkeley Street was the Old Gloucester Coffee House and Hotel, which in 1805 was offering 'good soups, dinners, wines and beds'. This was rebuilt as the St James's Hotel and in 1898 it became the Berkeley, which lasted until the beginning of the 1970s in Piccadilly and then moved to its present site at the corner of Wilton Place and Knightsbridge. The old building in Piccadilly was demolished and the new Bristol Hotel has risen in its place.

Mayfair's first Bristol Hotel had been in Burlington Gardens and for a long time held its own as the most exclusive and expensive hotel in London, but it did not survive the competition of the luxury hotels of the 1890s, which grew up when César Ritz arrived in London to manage the Savoy.

Yet three of Mayfair's old-established hotels are still world famous: Claridge's, the Connaught and Brown's.

Claridge's began as Mivart's, when Jacques Mivart, a French chef, opened a hotel, in 1815, at a house at the corner of Brook Street and Davies Street, offering princely accommodation. He prospered and was soon able to take over four more adjacent houses, for by this time his reputation stood so high that his hotel became the usual place of residence for distinguished visitors, including foreign royalty, and the Prince Regent had a suite of rooms permanently reserved for him.

Mivart reigned for forty years and then sold to William Claridge, who had been running a small hotel close by, and whose father had learned the business of attending on the great and noble when he had been in the employ of Gunter.

Claridge maintained Mivart's high standard of decorous service and superb cooking, and the prestige of the hotel, as a place fit for kings and princes, was unassailed. He remained there until he was too old to carry on any longer. In 1881 he sold out to a company which still kept up the old traditions, but in 1895 the Savoy Company bought the hotel, which by this time was sorely in need of modernisation. The old houses were pulled down and the present building, planned as the most luxurious hotel ever known, was opened in 1897, with a staff organised by César Ritz.

The Connaught Hotel in Carlos Place was also opened early in the nineteenth century by Wauthier, and at first it was named the Coburg, in honour of the family of the Prince Consort. When Wauthier retired, the management was taken over by a member of the Grillion family, who maintained the atmosphere of elegance and unobtrusive service.

During the 1890s the Coburg was rebuilt, but lost nothing of its reputation, for it remained smaller than the mammoths which had grown up in London by this time, such as the Langham and the Grand, and had only a hundred rooms. During the First World War its name was changed to the Connaught, and it remains to this day a place of quiet comfort and privacy.

It was in 1837 that James Brown opened his hotel at Number 23 Dover Street. He had been a gentleman's gentleman and his wife a lady's maid to the widowed Lady Byron, so they knew and understood the ways of the people they planned to serve.

Their neighbours in Dover Street at this time included eight members of the peerage, three baronets, the Bishop of Ely and the Russian

Ambassador, who may have been none too pleased at this development in their aristocratic corner of Mayfair, but Mr Brown was the
soul of discretion, and his wife, though said to be 'a very tiresome
woman', had the successful hotelier's invaluable asset, a passion for
detail, and she also had the good sense to stay always in the background.

The hotel prospered and by 1844 James Brown had taken over
Numbers 21, 22 and 24 Dover Street, which represents the entire
Dover Street frontage of the present hotel.

In 1859 he sold out to J. J. Ford, who was running a hotel in
Manchester Square at the time, and during the 1880s, by which time
Ford's son Henry was managing the business, they bought the St
George's Hotel, which had been established in the 1850s in Albemarle
Street, just at the back of Brown's, and combined the two, while in
1905 three more houses were taken in Albemarle Street.

In Dover Street, the hotel still retains its Georgian frontage. There
were no public rooms in these early nineteenth-century hotels. A
visitor took a suite of rooms, which included a room for his servant,
and if he were travelling from abroad with a courier, a courier's
room was also provided. Brown's original hotel in Dover Street was
divided into sixteen suites and meals were served to visitors in their
sitting-rooms.

Henry Ford made many innovations when he returned from a stay
in Canada to manage the hotel for his father. In 1882 he installed a
lift, as well as electric light and telephones, and in 1885 introduced
the novelty of bathrooms, which were described as 'fixed baths', to
replace the zinc hip baths and jugs of hot water, placed on a towel in
front of the fire, which was the usual routine for hotel visitors. This
was a tremendous advance, for when the Hotel Victoria was opened
in Northumberland Avenue in 1890, and acclaimed as the finest
hotel in the world, it had only four bathrooms for its full comple-
ment of five hundred visitors, and no running water in the bedrooms.

Nevertheless, the guests at Brown's were by no means sure of these
new-fangled gadgets and took some time to get used to them. Oscar
Wilde complained about such 'modern improvements' at the Savoy.

'Who wants an immovable washing-basin in one's room?' he
grumbled to Madame Ritz. 'I prefer to ring for water when I need
it.'

However, Henry Ford managed to introduce all these amenities to
Brown's with great subtlety, so that his guests still enjoyed the reassurance of traditional service, with the advantages of new com-

forts. They even accepted central heating in time, instead of the open coal fires in their bedrooms and sitting-rooms.

It was not until the late 1880s that Ford introduced a smoking-room and public dining-room, and for many years after this the hotel's private butler would call each morning at the visitors' suites, to take their orders for the day's meals and enquire at what time they wished to be served.

The list of distinguished visitors to Brown's is a long one. The Comte de Paris, Pretender to the French throne, lived there from 1886 to 1894, and held Court in his suite. Queen Emma, Regent of the Netherlands, stayed in 1895, with the fourteen-year-old Queen Wilhelmina, for a private visit of sight-seeing and shopping, although their departure from Brown's, by the wish of Queen Victoria, was made something of an official occasion, in an open landau, with postilions and scarlet-clad outriders. In the 1920s Queen Wilhelmina was staying once more at Brown's, with her small daughter Princess Juliana; and during the Second World War it was in room Number 36 of Brown's that the Dutch Government in exile declared war on Japan.

During the First World War Queen Elizabeth of Belgium lived there with her family for a while, and King Albert would join her from time to time, when he could take leave from the Western Front.

Haile Selassie of Ethiopia fled to Brown's in 1936, King Zog of Albania in 1939. King George II of the Hellenes, exiled in 1924, with the rise of Venizelos, lived at Brown's until 1935, when the Greek monarchy was restored, and during these years Brown's was the official court of the Greek royal family.

Alexander Graham Bell stayed there while he was perfecting his invention of the telephone. It was the choice of Cecil Rhodes when he was in London and also of Rudyard Kipling.

At the beginning of the century, Brown's became a private limited company. For many years it was controlled by the Bon family but in 1948 it was acquired by Trust Houses Limited. With all the changes, the quality of Brown's has survived, together with its tradition of preserving the privacy of its guests. As David Tennant says in his booklet about Brown's, ' . . . it has been and will continue to be a cherished tradition of Brown's never to disclose the names of these guests. When they enter the hotel they can be assured of privacy as complete as if it were their own home . . .'

Throughout the nineteenth century, there were a number of

places of worship in Mayfair which have now disappeared. Keith's Mayfair Chapel – sometimes called the Curzon Chapel – survived until 1899, but there were other proprietary chapels, the most fashionable at one time being the Berkeley Chapel, built about 1750, in the current style, with a cupola and Doric porch. It stood at the corner of Charles Street and Chesterfield Street, until it was pulled down in 1907, and here Sidney Smith, who afterwards lived at Number 33 Charles Street, was appointed morning preacher for a time, attracting large and aristocratic congregations by his pungent rhetoric.

The average salary for a morning preacher at this time was £50 a year and for an evening preacher £65. The proprietors knew the importance of a good organist, and he also usually commanded about £50 a year.

Many Victorians recalled the Berkeley Chapel as a comfortable old place, with its gallery and cushioned seats, a reminder of the easy-going Georgian days, but Dr Lee of Lambeth, who was incumbent from 1856 to 1858, had other views.

'It was coloured inside and out by what London painters term "a warm drab", he said, 'and upholstered throughout with pink velvet and heavy hangings on brass rods. Its prominent ornament was a very handsome highly polished and useful stove which greatly dwarfed the undersized communion table. The chapel, however, had an aristocratic and eminently select congregation – peers and peeresses, and their offspring . . . There was a rich odour of human nature throughout the place and the congregation fanned itself or used smelling salts. The preacher's manners were those of a very superior person, and he appeared ever conscious of having been made so.'*

There was another fashionable chapel in Albemarle Street during Regency times. This was St George's, opposite the Royal Institution, a proprietary chapel, comfortable and warm, where at one time evening service was held at nine o'clock, so that the congregation had time to dine first and arrived in evening dress. This came down in 1906, just before the Berkeley Chapel.

St Mark's, North Audley Street, was originally a chapel of ease of St George's, Hanover Square. It was first built by Sir John Deering in 1828 and intended for the artisans living in the small streets and tenements of Mayfair just south of Oxford Street, but it was rebuilt in 1878 by Sir Arthur Blomfield, after the humble dwellings near by

* Quoted by H. R. T. Brandreth in *Dr Lee of Lambeth*.

had been cleared away and replaced by fashionable and expensive flats. He retained the Ionic front and designed a Byzantine interior, and the church became as fashionable as the neighbourhood.

The Gothic Christ Church, Down Street, was not built until 1865, its parish including Shepherd Market.

The Duke of Westminster owned a private chapel in Park Street, which was pulled down in 1882, and he then built St Mary's in Bourdon Street, designed by Sir Arthur Blomfield, which was demolished in 1961. C. R. Cockerell's Hanover Chapel, standing between Hanover Street and Princes Street, in Regent Street, had been part of Nash's plan for the street, but it was pulled down in 1897. St Anselm's in Davies Street, opened in the following year, had an even shorter life, for it was demolished in 1938.

The beautiful Jesuit Church of the Immaculate Conception in Farm Street is Mayfair's only Roman Catholic church, and was built in 1844, the first permanent Jesuit church in London after Catholic emancipation had been granted in 1829.

There was little room left in Mayfair by this time and Farm Street was the best spot available. It was an obscure back street, deriving its name from Hay Hill Farm, and the site of the church was a little lane known as Berkeley Mews.

The foundation stone was laid in 1844 by Father Lythgoe, Superior of the English Jesuits, and the architect was J. J. Scoles, who built it in the decorated Gothic style of the fourteenth century. Five years later, on the Feast of St Ignatius, 31 July 1849, the church was opened under the title of the Immaculate Conception.

The Farm Street façade was copied from the west front of Beauvais Cathedral and the east window from that of Carlisle Cathedral, representing, like the east window of St George's, Hanover Square, the theme of the root of Jesse.

Pugin designed the magnificent altar and reredos. The walls of the sanctuary are lined with dark green marble and alabaster and the marble communion rail is inset with panels of lapis lazuli; and the side chapels and altars are as beautiful, lavishly decorated and in marked contrast to the austere simplicity of the surviving Anglican churches in Mayfair.

In 1851 Cardinal Manning was received into the Roman Catholic Church at Farm Street and said his first mass. In 1940 the church was damaged by enemy bombing and a third of the roof was destroyed, but the lights of the great east window had already been taken down and packed away for safety and the altar vessels and other ornaments were mainly rescued. The services and the pastoral work of the church were not interrupted and during the 1950s the church received a new roof and the damaged west front was redesigned.

In 1966 it became a parish church, with the right to administer the sacrament of baptism.

Close by, overlooking a corner of the garden which was once the St George's burial-ground, is St George's School. This was originally St George's School of Instruction and Industry, founded in 1804 and occupying rented accommodation in South Street, but in 1898 the present attractive red-brick school was built and the children of St George's in South Street moved here along with the children from General Stewart's charity school near by, which he had founded in 1742, at the time that he bequeathed the land on which St George's, Hanover Square, was built. Today the school ranks as a Voluntary Junior Mixed and Infants Primary Church of England school.

Opposite the Church of the Immaculate Conception stands an old house bearing the date 1757, but farther along on this side of Farm Street a delightful looking old house which had become derelict has just been demolished.

When the Mayfair Chapel was pulled down in 1899 the last great mansion of Mayfair was built on the site. This was Sunderland House, a wedding present to Consuelo Vanderbilt from her father, on her marriage to the Duke of Marlborough. It was a house in the style of the French Renaissance, which would have looked far better if it had been set, in the grand manner, in the midst of landscaped gardens, instead of rising abruptly from the pavement of Curzon Street and being hemmed in at the back by the shops and narrow lanes of Shepherd Market.

As a private house it had a very short span, for the marriage was an unhappy one, ending in divorce. The building was badly damaged during an air-raid of the Second World War but it is still standing and today is the large office-block known as Lombard House, the headquarters of Lombard, the banking house.

The King's Weigh House Chapel in Duke Street was built in 1891 for the Congregationalists, and it was here that Maude Royden preached for many years, while the Christian Science Church in Curzon Street, facing down Half Moon Street, is the most recent of the Mayfair churches, having been built in 1912.

XV

The Nineteenth Century

All through the nineteenth century Mayfair was 'the most aristocratic of addresses', its inhabitants a close-knit society which wielded
great power both socially and politically. Many of the houses were
by this time out of date, but the residents did not move westwards,
as the wealthy inhabitants of Bloomsbury did. Instead they rebuilt
and modernised their houses and stayed comfortably where they
were, close to the Park and Piccadilly, St James's and Westminster.
In some cases houses were gutted and entirely rebuilt, but mostly it
was a case of porches being added, in imitation of the new Cubitt
houses in Belgravia, and bow-windows replacing the flat, eighteenth-
century sashes. Drainage was overhauled and the 1880s saw the
installation of the first bathrooms; while in the smaller streets, slums
were cleared away and blocks of expensive red-brick flats arose.

Much of the delicate Regency and Georgian furniture was now
considered out of fashion, while French furniture was thought
'vulgar', because of its bright gilding. If not discarded, this English
and French furniture was rudely jostled and overshadowed by the
cumbersome, heavily carved and over-elaborated pieces which became so popular after the Great Exhibition of 1851. There was ad-
verse criticism of it even at the time, by the more discerning, but the
majority liked it well enough and bought it, while Pugin's Medieval
Court in Hyde Park sparked off the Gothic revival.

There was a craze for sombre brown paint in hallways and even beautiful mahogany doors were sometimes covered with paint. Drawing-rooms in Mayfair, as elsewhere, were overcrowded with armchairs and occasional tables, sociables and whatnots. Foot-stools and cushions, bell-pulls and firescreens were covered with embroidery and every table had its bobble-fringed cover. Wallpapers were smothered in pattern and then hidden by pictures. The velvet and brocade curtains were dark and heavy and more light was excluded by the Nottingham lace and Madras muslin close against the windows.

However, with the work of William Morris and his friends during the 1860s and the spread of the aesthetic movement in the 1870s and 1880s, the standard of interior decoration gradually improved, and the next generations began to see with new eyes and appreciate all over again the quality of the furniture their grandparents had held in such little regard, and its value rose in the salerooms.

Early in the nineteenth century, by which time the old Tyburn Lane had become the handsome but still rural Park Lane, there was more building here of houses both large and comparatively small. Regency terraces were built between the existing large mansions, some with their backs to the Park, so that their bow-fronted, first-floor drawing-rooms at the back of the house had a view over the Park.

Later the new Victorian palaces arose. Aldford House, close to old Grosvenor House, was built in 1896 by Alfred Beit, the South African millionaire. It was a long, low, rambling building, unlike anything else that had ever been seen in Mayfair, and it was called a number of things, from a transplanted African lodge to a glorified bungalow; but the stables alone cost £10,000 and the winter garden was full of exotic tropical flowers, with a large pond for good measure. Alfred Beit did not live long to enjoy his new house, for he died in 1906, and the house was then bought by the Honourable Frederick Guest, but in 1931 it was sold for development and the present block of flats, Aldford House, built on the site.

Barney Barnato built himself a French château but died before it was finished, and Sir Edward Sassoon lived in it for a few years, before it was demolished. R. W. Hudson, who made his fortune in soap, built himself the medieval Stanhope House, with the ground-floor windows and the oriel windows above a riot of beautifully carved stone-work, like a house on the Grand Canal in Venice. It still stands at the corner of Stanhope Street, close to the Dorchester Hotel, and is now partly occupied by a branch of Barclay's Bank.

At the southern end of Park Lane a row of smaller terrace houses was built, but they all came down in 1956, for the building of the Hilton Hotel.

Park Lane, by the end of the century, was lined with houses, great and small, and of those which existed before the new building of the mid-nineteenth century, the one where Disraeli lived throughout his married life still survives. This is Number 29, at the corner of Upper Grosvenor Street, formerly Number 2 Grosvenor Gate, a large Regency house with its front door in Upper Grosvenor Street and its curving first-floor balcony overlooking the Park; and here Mary Anne had lived with her first husband, Wyndham Lewis.

During the 1820s she was writing: 'Wyndham has promised me a beautiful house in town, and this is to be made very pretty.' They took possession in 1827 and Mary Anne was delighted, for she now had two drawing-rooms and two boudoirs of her own. If only Wyndham had been freer with his money, she would have made it 'one of the prettiest houses in the world', but she was contented enough with her red, gold and white drawing-rooms and her blue boudoir.

That year they gave a grand ball at the new house and Mary Anne, describing it all to her brother John, wrote:

> My company were most of the first people in London. The Duke of Wellington said it was like fairy land, the best ball he had been at this season . . . the Duchess appears so very kind and amiable and expressed so much admiration of all she saw . . . the balustrades of the staircase were entwined with wreaths of flowers, the whole of the balcony (which goes all round the house) was enclosed as if making part of it, a crimson carpet at the bottom, the whole lined with lampshades all the way round.

Wyndham Lewis died suddenly, in 1838, of a heart-attack. Benjamin Disraeli had been a close friend of them both for several years, having first met Mary Anne at the Bulwer-Lyttons', when Edward and his tempestuous Rosina were still together, living at Number 36 Hertford Street.

Disraeli was no stranger to Mayfair. Before he won his first seat in Parliament, in 1837, he had written *Vivian Grey* and several other novels, which were published by his father's friend and publisher, John Murray II. In 1832, when he was twenty-six, he had had a passionate love affair with Clara Bolton, and then, after a few months, with Lady Henrietta Sykes, living not far away from the Wyndham

Lewis house, in Upper Grosvenor Street. Clara, furious at being supplanted, told all, or nearly all, to Henrietta's husband, Sir Francis; but when Henrietta drove round to Clara's house in King Street, St James's to give her a piece of her mind, she found Sir Francis's carriage outside and discovered that they were deeply involved in a love affair of their own. It was checkmate but the affair between Henrietta and Disraeli petered out and Henrietta, after a brief romance with Lord Lyndhurst, fell in love with Daniel Maclise, the Irish artist who was a friend of both Disraeli and Charles Dickens. By this time Henrietta and her husband had moved to a house in Park Lane, and here Sir Francis found Henrietta and Maclise in bed together one day. He contemplated divorce but his own reputation was none too sound and a few years later Henrietta was dead.

Disraeli was looking for a rich wife and in Mary Anne he was singularly fortunate, for not only had she been left a wealthy widow, but they fell genuinely in love with each other. In August 1839 they were married at St George's, Hanover Square, and despite the fact that she was ten or eleven years older than Disraeli, the marriage remained blissfully happy, until her death in 1872.

During all these years, the house in Park Lane remained their London home, and from her balcony Mary Anne could watch all that went on in the Park – the flirtations, intrigues, assignations and manoeuvrings among Mayfair society, during their daily rides and drives – for during the London season, from autumn until Christmas and from May to July, they were all living on each other's doorsteps and the darkest of secrets could not be hidden for long.

After Mary Anne's death, the house and her money reverted to the Wyndham Lewis family. Disraeli moved to Whitehall Gardens for a time, but for the last three months of his life he was living at Number 19 Curzon Street, where he died in 1882. The house was not far from where Horace Walpole's friends Mary and Agnes Berry, had been living, at Number 8, until the middle of the century, the last sister dying in 1852.

Within the Mayfair boundaries, life remained assured and prosperous throughout the century, as the Empire rose to its zenith and Great Britain established herself as the workshop of the world. Plebeian red blood, it is true, now mingled freely with the patrician blue, but it was the red blood of millionaires, which could not be gainsaid, for this was increasingly a commercial and material age, when the fortunes that were being made in commerce and industry were dazzling.

A few people, living on inherited incomes which were still large, could afford to deplore the assault on their aristocratic traditions, but more were prepared to enjoy the advantages which great wealth was able to bring. And when the opportunity offered, they married it with few misgivings.

Life was very comfortable, and well into the nineteenth century many residents continued the leisurely ways of the eighteenth, into which they had been born. When they drove through London be-wigged and liveried footmen attended them, riding on the board behind the chariot or coach. They disliked the idea of travelling in railway trains. No omnibuses were allowed to penetrate their quiet streets and no costermongers or street traders ever ventured near, except for the muffin men and the lavender-sellers and itinerant musicians, whom they loved, for they were part of the slow-moving world into which they had been born. They disliked change and even resisted the first attempts at gas-lighting, which they considered too garish and modern. It had been installed in Pall Mall in 1807, but Grosvenor Square held out until 1842, clinging to their old flam-beaux, lamps and candles.

They abhorred any hint of radicalism and after the Reform Bills they closed their ranks. Some, knowing full well that never in human history has a society subsisting on inherited wealth and other people's labours survived for more than a few generations, were prepared to accept what was coming, but most turned a blind eye and hoped for the best, compromising with their doubts by supporting innumer-able charities. Yet they knew that as the star of the middle classes rose, their own would inevitably decline. It was a change that could not be withstood. The days of their stately isolation, in their own private world of Mayfair, were numbered.

H. G. Wells saw it happening. 'The hand of change rests on it all, unfelt, unseen; resting for a while, as it were half-reluctantly, before it grips and ends the thing for ever.'

Yet as late as 1928 Ralph Nevill, in his book *Romantic London*, re-calls Charles Street in the 1870s and 1880s, when it was 'full of carriages and fine horses during the season and a dignified butler and two footmen stood ready at almost every door to receive visitors coming to pay calls'.

With the development of Bayswater and Belgravia, the traffic conditions in Park Lane grew increasingly chaotic – and more so after Victoria Station was opened in 1860, for as public transport was not allowed in the Park, Park Lane was the only direct link between north and south. At the narrower, Piccadilly end, the traffic jams were one of the sights of the town, as cabs and carriages, growlers and hansoms, tradesmen's vans and costermongers' barrows fought to extricate themselves from the herds of cattle and flocks of sheep which also used the road, on their way to market, and the horse-buses running from Victoria to Paddington Station.

In 1871, when Hamilton Place was opened up, a new channel was carved out for this end of Park Lane, and at the apex of the triangle formed by the old and new Park Lane and Piccadilly the Thorney-croft fountain was placed, a characteristically Victorian piece of symbolism, with the figures of the three Muses forming its base, three marble statues of Shakespeare, Milton and Chaucer above, and surmounting it all a gilded, bronze-winged figure of Fame, blowing her own trumpet, one foot poised on a globe.

The population of the country was increasing very quickly. Trains were bringing more people into London each day. They were visiting the West End, enjoying the theatres, the hotels and the restaurants. Even the shops were changing. With the patenting in 1850 of Singer's sewing-machine, the ready-made clothing business was soon under way. For the seamstresses, endless hours of hand-sewing were merely replaced by equally long hours of drudgery at a sewing-machine, but new shops for women's clothing opened in Mayfair.

In 1866 Redmayne and Company of Numbers 19 and 20 New Bond Street and Number 35 Conduit Street were advertising made-up skirts for walking. Mrs Washington Moon, a Ladies' and Children's Outfitter who, in 1851, was proudly displaying her Royal Warrant, moved from Regent Street to New Burlington Street.

Mrs Addley Bourne, Family Draper, Jupon and Corset Manu-facturer to the Court and Royal Family, was established in 1860 at Number 37 Piccadilly, opposite St James's Church, selling under-clothes, corsets and a variety of crinolines, including inflatable ones made of rubber tubes. Six years later she was advertising 'A thousand crinolines at Half-Price . . . commencing at 5/11, usually 10/6 . . . Beautiful shapes but a little dusty . . . offered for a short time during stock-taking.'

She was canny, for like all good dressmakers, she sensed that fashion was about to change. Charles Worth had arrived in London in 1837, when he was a boy of twelve, to become an apprentice at Swan and Edgar's, and a few years later departed for Paris, to try his fortune as a designer of women's clothes. By the 1860s he was rapidly becoming a dictator of women's fashions in Paris and was growing tired of the crinoline. And very soon after Mrs Bourne's sale, crinolines were on their way out.

The National Linen Company moved from Fleet Street to Number 130 New Bond Street and Fenwick's came down from Newcastle upon Tyne to New Bond Street in 1891.

In Oxford Street there were two shops specialising in clothes for servants, and in Regent Street several shops which supplied ready-made mourning clothes, available at short notice, including Jay's General Mourning House.

Department stores such as Bourne and Hollingsworth, John Lewis, D. H. Evans and Peter Robinson were established in Oxford Street. They bought in bulk and were able to sell cheaply to the flocks of women who, by the end of the century, were coming to London by train or horse-bus for a day's shopping.

It was in 1875 that Arthur Lazenby Liberty opened his shop in Regent Street, for the sale of Japanese prints and Chinese porcelain, thereby putting the aesthetic movement firmly on its feet, for among his customers were William Morris, Carlyle, Ruskin, Charles Keen, G. F. Watts, Burne-Jones, Leighton, Millais, Alma Tadema, Whistler and Dante Gabriel Rossetti.

The arcade linking Old Bond Street to Albemarle Street was opened in 1879 and became the Royal Arcade after Queen Victoria had patronised H. W. Bretell, hosier and shirt-maker, from whom she bought her riding shirts, knitting wool and large, plain linen handkerchiefs, and Goodyear's, the florists, which is now established in Brook Street, next door to Claridge's.

In South Street, only a few yards down from Park Lane, are two memorial plaques, one on each side of the road. They both commemorate women whose lives spanned the Victorian years, and for close on half a century they lived nearly opposite each other. Both represent an important facet of social history and yet it would be difficult to find two women whose lives, though contemporary, were more sharply contrasted in every aspect.

On the south side of the street, the plaque commemorates Florence Nightingale, who lived in a house on the site for the last fifty years of her life. She was born in 1820, so was in her mid-thirties when she left the luxury of her parents' home to superintend the *Establishment for Gentlewomen During Illness*, which had been opened in Harley Street. A year or two later, she accepted the challenge of the Crimea and the calamity of Scutari.

Back in England, she worked ceaselessly for the cause of the sick.

Her work inspired Henri Dunant to begin the Red Cross movement and establish the Geneva Convention; and it also hastened the founding of the British Army Medical School. She then turned her attention to the second part of her life's work – the founding of the first training school for nurses at St Thomas's hospital.

By this time, in the early 1860s, she was almost a permanent invalid and had established herself in the little house at Number 10 South Street, living almost as a recluse, although her mental energies never flagged. She kept in touch with her nursing school, wrote lectures for the nurses and entertained them at South Street. By 1865 she was agitating for the reform of the Poor Law and an improvement in the condition of workhouse infirmaries; and in her *Notes on Hospitals*, first published in 1859, she had some hard words for women who wore their crinolines when they were nursing. She also published *Notes on Nursing for the Labouring Classes*, which in its day had as great a circulation as *Mrs Beeton's Cookery Book*, which came out about the same time. Miss Nightingale advocated the blessings of fresh air and it was from this time, in the 1860s, that a few Victorians began to open their windows, pull back all the velvet and Nottingham lace, and let air and light into their stuffy, over-furnished rooms.

She had her prejudices. She had no time for inoculation or vaccination, the first idea of which had been brought back from Turkey by Lady Mary Wortley Montagu a century earlier, nor for Lord Lister's antiseptic treatment of wounds after surgery, but she was a great woman, and during the wars which were to come thousands of soldiers were to benefit and be thankful for the work to which she dedicated herself.

The nature of her ill-health was never defined. Sir George Pickering, in his book *Creative Malady*, has suggested that it was a psycho-neurosis induced by her determination to get her own way, particularly with the British Army and the Medical School. When she was thwarted she became ill, so that in effect she was daring the Army to cause her death. When her family tried to persuade her to lead a more social life, the same symptoms developed. But left alone, she was able to work.

Physically she was strong. She endured the terrible hardships of the Crimea without flinching, and she lived to be ninety. Three years before her death she was given the Order of Merit, and she was also given the Freedom of the City of London, the first woman ever to receive it, but by that time she was too old and blind to realise the great honour that had been paid to her.

Number 15 South Street, across the road, still stands, a charming little brick Georgian house on the corner of Rex Place, neat and attractively simple, having three storeys and a basement, with a balcony in front of the drawing-room window on the first floor. Here for almost the same fifty years as Florence Nightingale across the road, lived Catherine Walters – known to the world, as her memorial plaque records – as Skittles, the last of the Victorian courtesans.

Catherine was born in 1839, in the slums of the Mersey river front, the third of five children. Her father was a 'tide waiter' on the river, but though, unlike many of his neighbours, he was in regular work, he was a drunk. The children received little or no education and brought themselves up as best they could, in a world that was rough, hard and ugly. Little is known of Catherine's childhood in Liverpool, but she seems to have earned her first few coppers setting up the skittles in a pub skittle-alley near her home. She may also have helped in a livery stable, or even have been a circus rider for a time, for somehow or other she learnt to ride and developed a love and understanding of horses and a skill in handling them which was altogether exceptional. Added to this, she was beautiful, with lovely blue eyes and red-gold hair, and had a superb figure. And by the time she was twelve she had learnt to swear as fluently as anyone on the river front, in a Liverpool accent which she never completely lost.

She was practically illiterate and was faced with a life of drudgery in the Liverpool slums. The only alternative, and the most practical way of survival in reasonable comfort, was prostitution, for she had realised very early the power that she could exercise over men.

A young businessman brought her to London and set her up in a small house at Fulham. Who he was or what became of him no one knows, but Skittles was soon savouring the delights of gaslit London's night-life during the 1850s – the suppers at Cremorne and the dancing at the Argyll Rooms, where young men came to look for partners. These were built on the spot where the old Piccadilly Hall of the seventeenth century had once stood, in Great Windmill Street.

Admission to the main floor of the Argyll Rooms, with its glittering mirrors and chandeliers, was a shilling, but the gallery, with its alluring, shadowy alcoves and crimson velvet seats, its dim lighting and soft music, drifting up from the orchestra below, was more expensive. Here an occasional young man from Mayfair would sometimes drop in, but mostly it was the place for clerks and shop assistants, undergraduates and young subalterns, who disdained the street traders of the Haymarket and the Burlington Arcade but could not afford the expensive brothels like the one Kate Hamilton ran off Leicester Square during the 1860s. Kate was too fat and too ugly to continue as a practising member of her profession, for she weighed twenty stone by this time. Her establishment was approached by a long tunnel, with two janitors keeping watch at the street end, ready to give warning of a police raid, and she presided on a platform from where she could see all that was going on, dressed in the lowest of evening gowns and sipping champagne from midnight till dawn.

Skittles was no ordinary prostitute. She had taste and dressed simply. She was a romantic and despite her lack of education was very intelligent. She had tact and sensitivity and learnt to be a good listener. She also had an irresistible zest for living and a sense of humour, and she never took herself too seriously.

When Mayfair returned to London for the season, part of the social round was the daily parade in Hyde Park, where they rode or drove. The fashionable time for this parade varied, but during the 1860s it was from noon until about two o'clock in the afternoon. At the beginning of the century, none but members of society would have presumed to take part in the parade, but early in Victorian times the first courtesans began to show themselves. The owners of the Mayfair livery stables took to selecting young girls, who were both beautiful and skilled horsewomen, to ride their horses in the Park and thus display their paces to prospective customers. That the girls displayed themselves at the same time and often acquired rich lovers into the bargain was all part of the game.

The 'pretty horse-breakers' became part of the Hyde Park ritual – the despair of the young women of society who were looking around for husbands and the delight of the hunted, who were more interested in less permanent liaisons.

The girls appeared every day except Sundays. Then there was no riding or driving in the Park and the courtesans vanished, for this was the place for the church parade, from Stanhope Gate to the Achilles statue, when families from Devonshire House and Crewe House, Apsley House, Dorchester House, Grosvenor House and all the other Mayfair mansions in the squares and terraces strolled in stately decorum from the morning services at St George's, the Grosvenor Chapel and the other places of worship, to meet and exchange greetings with their friends.

The religious observance of Sunday exerted a power over people's way of behaving and thinking which is almost incomprehensible to most of the current generation, and even as late as the Boer War there was no fighting on Sundays.

Skittles met the owner of a livery stable in Bruton Mews who recognised her amazing skill in horsemanship, as well as her good looks and beautiful figure. He arranged for her to be dressed in the best riding-habit London could make, so tightly fitting that she was naked beneath it, and he provided her with his best mounts and most expensive little phaetons. Her part of the bargain was to ride and drive in the Park to advertise his wares. What happened in between times was no concern of his.

Skittles looked outstandingly beautiful when she arrived in Hyde Park, adopting an expression of expensive aloofness, choosing the least frequented parts of the Park and showing always her consummate skill. Within a few weeks she had made her first important conquest – none other than Lord Hartington, heir to the Duke of Devonshire. He was twenty-eight and Skittle twenty-two. To the fury of Lottie, the Duchess of Manchester, who was deeply attached to the shy young Hartington and had taken him under her wing, intending to mould his political career, he fell deeply in love with Skittles for a time and she, with too much heart for a professional courtesan, loved him in return.

He took her nearly everywhere, unashamedly showing her to his friends. They were perturbed. Could he possibly be intending marriage? Catherine looked beautiful, behaved well and dressed like a duchess, but when she opened her mouth it was disastrous, and the thought of her presiding one day at Devonshire House, where the gorgeous Georgiana had reigned not so many years before, was insupportable.

Suddenly Hartington came to his senses and departed to America, ostensibly to visit the scenes of the American Civil War. He did not leave Catherine destitute. He and his mightily relieved family arranged for an annuity to be paid to her from the Devonshire estates; but she was badly shaken.

It was the summer of 1862. Rotten Row was deserted and in Mayfair the shutters were up and the furniture shrouded in dust-sheets. The German watering-places had become fashionable for summer visitors from both London and Paris and here Catherine decided to go for a spell. She chose Ems and before many days had passed she had captured the heart of Aubrey de Vere Beauclerk, who was staying there with his young wife. The Beauclerk family was descended from the Duke of St Albans, son of Charles II and Nell

Gwynn, and Beauclerk showed no lack of the family tradition. He left his wife, who had to make her own way home, and took Catherine first to Italy and then, at her request, to America. Here it was she who left him, and it was his turn to return home alone, to his forgiving wife.

Catherine unwisely sought out Hartington, hoping for a reconciliation, but he had completely recovered from his few weeks of infatuation; and she knew in her heart that she never could have undertaken the social duties and responsibilities of a future Duchess of Devonshire. They quarrelled but parted without malice.

Hartington returned to London and appeared, with no warning or explanation, at one of Lottie's tea parties at her house in Great Stanhope Street. She received him without comment at his long absence, and the friendship was resumed from the point where Catherine had interrupted it, as though she had never been. And it continued for the next thirty years, until the Duke of Manchester died and Lottie was free to marry him.

Catherine went to Paris and quickly established herself under the protection of the elderly Achille Fould, Napoleon III's Minister of Finance. She rode each day in the Bois, as she had ridden a year or two earlier in Rotten Row. She met the Emperor and the leaders of Parisian society during the gay, glittering sixties, when Worth was dressing the Empress Eugénie, the elegant Princess Metternich and anyone else who could afford to pay for his lovely and wildly expensive dresses. Guerlain was enticing them with his subtle scents. Sarah Bernhardt was rising to fame. Offenbach was enchanting them with the hauntingly sweet melodies and delicious banalities of *La Belle Hélène* and *La Grande Duchesse* and the tinsel-bright boulevard world was chuckling delightedly at the blatant wantonness of the can-can.

Catherine also met some of the famous courtesans of the Second Empire – La Barucci, La Piava and the outrageously flamboyant Cora Pearl, all of whom paraded the Bois in their splendid coaches, attended by liveried footmen, and were established in their vast, ornate and sumptuously furnished mansions.

She managed to learn a little French but was never fluent. At the British Embassy she met the young Wilfrid Scawen Blunt, who fell passionately in love with her, but after a few days she broke off the affair, determined never again to become emotionally involved but to concentrate on her chosen career of courtesan. He was distraught for a time but eventually came to understand her point of view, and they remained warm friends all their lives, even after his marriage.

Catherine was increasingly drawn to England and each winter she crossed from France to hunt with the Quorn. Some of the women members objected, but Catherine was such a superb horsewoman and behaved with such discretion, always staying quietly at the Haycock Inn at Wansford for the season, that the Master refused to forbid her the field.

During the World Exhibition, held in Paris in 1867, she met one of its most illustrious visitors, Edward, the Prince of Wales, but this was also the year that Achille Fould died. Catherine returned to England and settled in the house she had already bought for herself in Chesterfield Street, still going to Leicestershire each winter for the hunting.

During these years of the middle sixties she had been reading and educating herself, and she had also learned a great deal from Achille Fould, who had been an unfailingly good friend to her. She acquired poise and had become a good conversationalist; and in Chesterfield Street she established a salon. As she moved into her late thirties, she rode less in Hyde Park, preferring the company of intelligent men and good conversation to the tedious triviality of the fashion parade.

Her Sunday afternoon tea parties became a feature of Mayfair life and among her visitors were Gladstone, who had been introduced to her by Wilfrid Blunt, and Bertie, the Prince of Wales, who was probably her lover for a time.

Gladstone had become Prime Minister in 1861, when the new Liberal party came into being and the Whigs died. Mayfair was suspicious of his liberalism but even more concerned about the indiscretion of his friendship with Skittles, although she always maintained, and is to be believed, that it was purely platonic. Gladstone had a passion for saving fallen women, but his enemies said he was interested only in those who were young and beautiful. 'He managed to combine his missionary meddling with a keen appreciation of a pretty face,' sneered Henry Labouchère.

One of Gladstone's successful reclamations was the beautiful Laura Bell. Ten years older than Catherine, she had been, in her day, a famous London courtesan. As a girl she had worked at Jay's General Mourning House in Regent Street, and here the Nepalese Envoy had seen her and been overcome by her unusual loveliness. He had set her up in a house in Wilton Crescent and before he returned to India a few years later she had extracted a quarter of a million pounds from him, but to avoid a scandal and maintain the Empire's good name, the British Government had reimbursed him.

Unblushingly, Laura joined the Hyde Park parade, sometimes riding, sometimes driving in her phaeton, with a small tiger sitting proudly behind, wearing a tall cocked hat and yellow and black striped waistcoat. Her prize was Captain Augustus Frederick Thistlethwaite. They married in 1857 and lived at Number 15 Grosvenor Square, but Thistlethwaite was soon appalled by her extravagance. They quarrelled and she took to the bottle. It was Gladstone who reformed her, and by the late 1860s she had found God and become an ardent Salvationist. She opened a mission for fallen girls at her home in Grosvenor Square, which both Gladstone and his wife visited from time to time. The end of the story was not so happy for Captain Thistlethwaite. Always eccentric, he gradually grew odder. He had a disconcerting habit of shooting his revolver at the ceiling, when he wished to summon a servant, instead of pulling the bell, and one day he shot himself instead of the ceiling. So in 1887 the widowed Laura sold the house in Grosvenor Square and retired to a cottage in Hampstead for her remaining years.

How much effect Gladstone's reforming zeal had on Skittles no one can say, but they became warm friends and he always wrote to her on her birthday and sent her a small gift.

The year 1870 and the Franco–Prussian war saw the end of the gay life in Paris for many years to come. Eugénie fled to England, living for a time at Claridge's – and, perhaps, for the first few days, at Brown's – before settling at Chislehurst, and the deposed Emperor joined her, after his ignominious surrender to the Prussians, though he was already a sick man and survived for only another three years.

The end of the Second Empire in France meant the end of the wealthy courtesans. One or two went over to the Prussians. La Barucci died during the siege of Paris. Cora Pearl stayed in Paris and nursed the sick and wounded for a time. Then she came to London to join the Emperor's cousin, Prince Napoleon, but the Grosvenor Hotel refused to accommodate her and she ended up in Dublin. Later she returned to France, but in 1886, having grown old and ugly, she died in poverty.

England watched the fate of France from the security of her increasing wealth and vast Empire, which was reaching the zenith of its power, and gave a home to her refugees. She could afford to be generous. For the rich and the rising middle classes life had never been better; and although the poor were growing poorer, life in Mayfair seemed unchanging.

In 1872 Skittles moved to Number 15 South Street, where

Gladstone and Bertie were still regular visitors, until Bertie's attentions were diverted by the advent of Lily Langtry. Life for Skittles was very pleasant. She had plenty of money and was still receiving her annuity from the Devonshire estates. She had kept her looks and her figure and still hunted with the Quorn, although her nose was put a little out of joint when the Empress Elizabeth of Austria visited England and followed the same hunt, for the Empress was a superb horsewoman, perhaps the first serious rival Skittles had ever encountered on the field.

Morally society was no better and no worse than it had ever been. Queen Victoria and the middle classes had a strict moral code and Dr Willett Cunnington, in his book *The Art of English Costume*, makes the point that 'the Victorian prudery, once well established, served as a kind of regulator by which a constant but safe emotional pressure could be maintained; its practical value in the general improvement of behaviour has not received the credit it deserved now that we no longer, we think, require this ingenious refinement of sex-appeal'.

With the increasing influence of the Prince of Wales and the Marlborough House group, that refinement, which too often has been dismissed as hypocrisy, was gradually whittled away, and many society girls became as promiscuous as the courtesans, although behaving with the outward decorum decreed by the Court.

In the result, the courtesans began to lose the battle for the possession of the young aristocrats and had to adopt subtler means than the Hyde Park parade for the pursuit of their profession.

With the approach of middle-age, Catherine began to feel the first signs of arthritis. Gradually she gave up riding and then had to forgo her new sport, roller-skating, the craze which had gripped London society for a short time during the 1870s, well before the bicycling fashion of the 1890s.

Bicycling was at first a very exclusive pastime, confined to the very rich.

'When the vogue began,' writes Ralph Dutton, in his book *The Victorian Home*, 'bicycles were treated much as if they had been horses. The machine was sent in the charge of a footman to Battersea Park or Regent's Park, whither the owner would drive in her carriage. Arrived at her destination, she would leave her victoria and with a good deal of ceremony mount her machine, and ride gracefully round and round on the broad smooth roads. The exercise over, the bicycle was handed back on the return of the footman, and the lady would return home as she had come. The simple pleasure of bicycling entailed at that time a good deal of work on the part of a devotee's staff.'

But Lottie, the new Duchess of Devonshire, and her friends practised cycling in the large courtyard of Devonshire House, still sheltered from the public gaze by its high brick wall, despite the addition of the golden gates. She had at last married the faithful Hartington, two years after the death of her first husband, the Duke of Manchester, and a year after Hartington had become the 8th Duke of Devonshire, on the death of his father in 1891. The wedding had taken place very quietly at the new Christ Church, Down Street.

By this time Kitchener had become a member of Catherine's circle of friends at South Street and a regular visitor at her Sunday afternoon tea parties.

Across the road, Florence Nightingale was still working feverishly from her invalid couch, for the amelioration of the lot of the poor and the sick. Sometimes she would put in twenty hours work in a day, and at one stage, when Cabinet Ministers wished to consult her, she said that she could spare them not more than fifteen minutes each of her precious time, while Gladstone was denied even that. He had only to cross the street to find a warm welcome from Catherine, and when he died, in 1889, she mourned for him sincerely.

Despite the infiltration of commercial wealth into the aristocratic exclusiveness of Mayfair, life went on with the same degree of seclusion. Class is difficult to define and few families searching for an unblemished record could fail to find a few serious blots, so even the most aristocratic die-hards of Mayfair came to accept the new order of things philosophically and enjoyed the new sources of wealth. By 1900 one in ten of the population were domestic servants and of the two million women between the ages of fifteen and twenty-five who were in employment, domestic service accounted for more than a third, so that life for their masters and mistresses remained very comfortable. As late as the 1880s ladies riding in the Row, in top-hats and immaculately tailored habits, were accompanied by grooms. The fashionable time for the parade had moved to half past five in the afternoon, for the dinner hour was tending to grow later each year and was soon to be eight or half past eight.

There were some interesting if short-lived clubs in Mayfair during Catherine's lifetime, among them the Cosmopolitan Club, which met at Number 30 Charles Street. It had first been founded in 1851 by Sir Robert Monier and met at his rooms at Number 49 New Bond Street, but as it grew in numbers it moved to the house in Charles Street, which had been the studio of G. F. Watts, before he moved to little Holland House in Kensington.

The members included Layard, the archaeologist of Nineveh and Babylon, G. F. Watts, Ruskin, and – by the sixties – Laurence Oliphant, Speke, the discoverer of the source of the Nile, Tennyson, Millais, Lord Leighton, Thackeray, Anthony Trollope, Froude and the 2nd Lord Lytton, but the club was wound up in 1903, when the house needed repair and funds were too low to meet the expense.

Bulwer, the 1st Lord Lytton, had lived in Charles Street for a short time, after he had separated from Rosina, and it was here that he fitted up his drawing-room as a facsimile of a room he had seen at Pompeii, and made the air heavy with the scent of a smoking pastille, rising from a model of Vesuvius, but by 1839 he was on the move again, and before he died, in 1873, he had had eleven addresses in Mayfair, the last being Number 12 Grosvenor Square, only a few doors away from the Thistlethwaites.

There were no clubs for women in Victorian times and until around the 1880s women in society did not dine in public either at a restaurant or the public dining-room of a hotel, but a first step was taken in 1875 with the establishment of the Albemarle Club, 'for the accommodation of both ladies and gentlemen', which was held at the Albemarle Hotel; and it was here that the Marquess of Queensberry, a descendant of Old Q's heir, left the abusive note for Oscar Wilde which led to Wilde's trial and downfall.

By the time the old Queen died, in 1901, Catherine was confined to a bath-chair and her eyesight was failing, but she still retained her elegant, slim figure and, wearing a thick black veil over her still beautiful face, was wheeled out each day by an attendant for her visit to Hyde Park.

Throughout the short span of the Edwardian era she still held her Sunday afternoon tea parties, but while the social life of Mayfair reached its peak of luxury and extravagance, her own circle of friends grew smaller every year.

The new Duke and Duchess of Devonshire entertained lavishly and were close friends of King Edward and Queen Alexandra. This was still the London of hansoms, growlers and horse-buses, although the twopenny tube was running between Shepherd's Bush and the Bank by 1902. The first motor taxi arrived in 1903, but hansoms and growlers remained until 1914, when the horses were impounded for active service. Motor-buses arrived in 1904 and by 1911 the old horse-buses were nearly all off the road.

It was the London of the great musical comedies – *The Merry Widow, The Chocolate Soldier, The Arcadians, The Dollar Princess* and *The Belle of Mayfair* – and of the Gilbert and Sullivan operas at the Savoy. Gordon Selfridge opened his mammoth store in Oxford Street. The Piccadilly Hotel was built on the site of the old St James's Hotel and Restaurant. The Ritz opened in 1905.

For Mayfair and the rich, and also for the middle classes, life was fun. For the poor it was grim. The voice of social conscience was heard increasingly and the King, who was a kindly man, lent a sympathetic ear to many a worthy cause, but the problem was too enormous for patchwork cures, and in the meantime life was sweet for those with the means to enjoy it.

The annual return from the country to Mayfair went on each season attended by a company of nurses and nursemaids, butlers, footmen, coachmen, boot-boys, cooks, housemaids and parlour maids.

Early in the nineteenth century Disraeli, in his novel *Sybil*, had described the two nations of rich and poor into which the country was divided, 'between whom there is no intercourse and no sympathy, who are as ignorant of each other's habits, thoughts and feelings, as if they were dwellers in different zones or inhabitants of different planets; who are formed by a different breeding, are fed by a different food, are ordered by different manners, and are not governed by the same laws.'

The same held true during the early years of the twentieth century and despite the shock of the Boer War, which most people thought would be over in a few weeks but which dragged on for more than two and a half years, there were many who still could not believe that the Empire was vulnerable and their comfortable way of life could ever change. They refused to see the signs or listen to the warnings.

Catherine, alone in her comfortable little house in South Street, was puzzled and saddened by it all. In 1908 the Duke of Devonshire died and Lottie moved to Grosvenor Square, the famous Waterloo House, Number 44, which the Harrowby family had just vacated, and here she installed its first bathroom. Edward VII died in 1910 and so did Florence Nightingale, and by the following year Lottie, the double duchess, was dead.

Catherine lived on all through the First World War, little knowing, even then, that it was the beginning of the end of the old Mayfair and the world she had known for close on half a century.

She had known and liked the Kaiser. 'I have two letters he wrote me and he also gave me his photograph and a jewelled sunshade,' she wrote to Wilfrid Blunt. 'The latter I have sold to get some money for the poor wounded men.'

The Empress Eugénie, the last surviving player in the drama of Paris in 1870, lived on until 1920, dying in Madrid at the age of ninety-four. And a month later Catherine, now eighty-one and the last of the Victorian courtesans, died in her home in Mayfair.

XVI

Mayfair Today

After the shock and carnage of the First World War, life in Mayfair was never the same. A million young Englishmen had died, among them many heirs to titles and fortunes, and after the years of terrible destruction came the days of reckoning and the slump. As the world struggled to extricate itself from the distress of the twenties and early thirties came the Second World War, bringing in its aftermath even graver problems and conflicts.

The residents of Mayfair, burdened with ever-increasing taxation and death duties, found their houses too big and too expensive to run and there were few, if any, servants to maintain them. Moreover, with the advent of the motor-car at the turn of the century, the week-end habit had developed, and the days of the large town houses were numbered.

Devonshire House was the first casualty, in 1925, and behind the block of offices which rose in its place the eight-storey Mayfair Hotel was built, on part of the garden site. Grosvenor House came down in 1926, Dorchester House and Aldford House in 1931, Chesterfield House in 1932, Brook House in 1933. Lansdowne House was truncated in 1935 and Londonderry House was demolished in 1963.

Elsewhere in Mayfair a steadily increasing number of houses were put up for sale or to let between the wars. Hanover Square was already commercial. In Grosvenor Square the houses began to look derelict. In 1937 the eastern side of Berkeley Square and several of the houses adjoining it in Bruton Street were pulled down for the building of the flats of Berkeley Square House.

It all happened very quickly and when people realised what was being lost it was too late – and yet there were far too many houses for them all to be preserved.

These were the years when the night-clubs of Mayfair became so popular. The Embassy, still flourishing, was established in Old Bond Street, a favourite club of the late Duke of Windsor, when he was Prince of Wales, and equally fashionable for luncheon or dinner as well as later in the evening. Close by in Grafton Street, Hutch was singing at Chez Victor during the late 1920s, and next door, at the Grafton Galleries, Paul Whiteman first came to fame; and Uncle's in Albemarle Street was another fashionable spot.

By 1931 half the houses in Grosvenor Square were empty and the Grosvenor Estate began to redevelop it with blocks of flats, six to eight storeys high, planning to keep the square architecturally uniform, but long before they had completed the scheme the Second World War broke out. The Americans who already had their Embassy at Number 1, now took over many of the flats for their Forces' personnel and when the war was over the whole of the west side of the square was pulled down for the vast American Embassy, a long and comparatively low building, designed by Eero Saarinen, which fits in admirably with the rest of the buildings in the square. Even the Waterloo house and the Duchess of Kendal's house have now gone, but they had been sadly altered by Victorian residents and their façades had lost much of their eighteenth-century charm. So the only reminder of the dramas which once took place in Number 44 is the little pub behind it, in Adam's Row, which is called the Waterloo Dispatch and carries the sign of a messenger on horseback, bearing the famous news. It is a neat, attractive little place, with chairs and tables set out on a low veranda during the summer.

The rebuilding of Grosvenor Square is now complete and it is as well-bred looking as it ever was, if rather austere, all neo-Georgian red brick with white stone-facings. On the east side, between Grosvenor Street and Brook Street, are the buildings of the Canadian High Commission, the Royal Canada Navy and Canadian defence departments. On the north side is the Europa Hotel, a seven-storey building which was opened in 1964, and on the south side the Britannia Hotel and the Indonesian Embassy, with blocks of flats in between.

The old garden has been laid out formally and many of the plane trees cut down to clear a broad avenue for the approach to the Sir William Reid Dick memorial statue of President Franklin D. Roosevelt, which went up in 1948.

All that is left of the old days is the dark little Georgian house in the north-east corner, almost in Brook Street, where John Adams lived from 1785 to 1788.

In 1919 the 8th Earl of Berkeley, who had no children and was the last of the line, sold his Berkeley estate to Lord Bearsted's Samuel Estates, Ltd. This valuable twenty acres had remained almost intact since the 5th and last Lord Berkeley of Stratton had left it first to Anne Egerton and then to the 5th Earl of Berkeley, but during the depression of the 1920s Lord Bearsted sold out to developers and it was at this time that the east side of Berkeley Square came down and the large block of flats was built. In 1941 the garden was thrown open to the public, the responsibility for its maintenance being transferred from the residents to the Westminster City Council.

Several of the houses on the west side, including the Clermont Club at Number 44, have now come under a preservation order, although they are occupied by clubs or businesses. A few of the beautiful houses in Hill Street have been demolished and replaced by blocks of flats but most have been preserved and are now occupied by businesses, publishers, property companies or clubs. In Charles Street the story is the same. Many of the Georgian façades are there but the houses are property companies, music publishers, architects' offices and the like. Number 46, once the home of Lord Revelstoke, is now the headquarters of the English Speaking Union, and 19A is the Burmese Embassy. Number 16, Mrs Ronald Greville's house, is the Guards Club.

In Piccadilly, Swan and Edgar, rebuilt in 1924 at the time of the rebuilding of Nash's Regent Street, survives and flourishes. The Edwardian Piccadilly Hotel is still there. The Albany Chambers are as secluded and exclusive as they ever were. The Royal Academy at Burlington House was never busier, with its summer and winter exhibitions, and in the winter of 1974-5 held the exhibition to celebrate the bicentenary of the birth of William Turner, who in the days of the Regency had exhibited some of his work at the Egyptian Hall which stood nearly opposite.

The Burlington Arcade looks more alluring than ever, with its newly painted bright pink ceiling.

Albemarle Street, where Lord Clarendon's great house once stood, still has an uninterrupted view across Piccadilly to the dip of St James's Street and the old red-brick Tudor palace.

In the western part of Piccadilly there are more survivals. Along this stretch, opposite the Green Park, men less than a century ago used to stroll leisurely, arm-in-arm, dressed in tall silk hats and frock-coats, for from Down Street to Hamilton Place the houses had nearly all become clubs; and one of the last of the strollers was the elderly Disraeli, leaning on the arm of his kind old friend, Lord Rowton.

Cambridge House is still the Naval and Military Club, and next door is the America Club. Number 105, which Cubitt rebuilt for the Marquess of Hertford and which became the Green Park Hotel for a time, before it was re-established in Half Moon Street, is now the headquarters of the Arts Council of Great Britain, and Number 106 is still the St James's Club. Numbers 111 to 112 are now the nine-storey Park Lane Hotel, with its grand, pillared porch, built between the wars, and Number 116 is the Athenaeum Court Hotel. Number 127 is the Cavalry Club and the Royal Air Force Club is next door, at Number 128.

Beyond this all is change. Piccadilly Terrace has disappeared and the new Park Lane, which was widened at the end of the last century, is now wider still, the fountain having been taken away to make more room. The narrow neck of Old Park Lane is lined on the east with the vast Hilton Hotel and the Londonderry House Hotel, next door to each other, and on the west side, reaching over to Hamilton Place, is the Inn On The Park. And west again the mighty Inter-Continental has risen on the site of Piccadilly Terrace, where once there were so many members of the Rothschild family living that it was known as Rothschild Row.

There are a few Regency houses left in Park Lane, but they are all, including Disraeli's old house, used as offices; down at the Piccadilly end, Number 17, on the corner of Brick Street, is another Regency house which has survived amidst all the new building and is now the headquarters of the W.R.V.S.

Oxford Street is, as it ever was, a street of shops catering for every-one, rich and poor, and Regent Street, despite the rebuilding, still retains the wide, sweeping curve of Nash's plan.

Bond Street is still exclusive and elegant. The jewellers, Asprey and Tessier, still maintain their traditions, as does the firm of Philip Antrobus, which was established at Number 11 New Bond Street, in 1815. Cartier's, at Number 175 New Bond Street, first came to

Mayfair in 1903. The Paris house was founded by Louis François Cartier in 1849 and it was the future Edward VII who suggested to Cartier's grandson, that he establish a London house in conjunction with Jean and Gaston Worth, son of the great Charles, who had died in 1895. Jean and Gaston had opened their first London establishment in Grosvenor Street in 1900 and three years later Worth and Cartier were in Old Burlington Street, but in 1909 Cartier's moved to New Bond Street, with Pierre's younger brother Jacques in charge.

Jacques Cartier designed his own jewellery and in 1921 opened his own workshop, which today occupies the upper floors of the Bond Street premises. Most of the Cartier jewellery is still designed and made here, under the guidance of his eldest son Jean-Jacques and his grandson Jacques.

In the days of the ruling Indian princes, Cartier's designed much of their fabulous regalia, as well as the jewellery of Europe's millionaires, but the days of glittering tiaras and diamond necklaces have gradually faded. While maintaining their standards of impeccable workmanship, Cartier's have adapted much of their work to simpler tastes and smaller pockets. Today, as well as producing exquisite jewellery and hand-made watches which are among the finest in the world, they make relatively inexpensive jewellery which suits so much of contemporary taste and means.

There are more than twenty goldsmiths and silversmiths in Bond Street today, including S. J. Phillips, where many a Crown jewel from some long-departed European Court may be found, and the Bond Street Silver Galleries at Number 112 New Bond Street, where a number of firms exhibit their matchless silver-work. The street has distinguished picture galleries, such as Agnew's, Frank Partridge and the Cooling Galleries, shops selling the finest of china and porcelain, exquisite linen and lovely clothes, shoes and handbags of the softest leather, and the beautiful antique shops.

At Number 34 is Sotheby's, which was founded in 1744, specialising at first in the sale of old books. The firm moved here from Wellington Street half a century ago, occupying the premises of the old Doré gallery, where Gustave Doré's pictures used to be regularly exhibited: and since the end of the Second World War, Sotheby's sale-rooms, with their unpretentious entrance, have helped to make London the centre of the world market for the sale of works of art.

And to help maintain the prestige and elegance and world-wide reputation of Bond Street is the Bond Street Association, which deals with all the problems which arise in regard to traffic congestion, maintenance and trading policies, as do the Oxford Street and Regent Street Associations.

If you look up above the shop-windows as you walk down Bond Street you can see that many old buildings have survived, as for example at Elizabeth Arden's, Number 20 New Bond Street, where the exterior of the upper floors of this splendid Georgian house are little changed.

East of Bond Street little remains of old Mayfair. The survivals are all to the west. One of the surprises is Avery Row, winding down from Brook Street to the eastern end of Grosvenor Street, a narrow, shabby and forgotten little street where once the Tyburn river flowed. And leading from it, with an entrance in Bond Street, between Brook Street and Grosvenor Street, is Lancashire Court, a twisting maze of old shops, pubs and cafés, which has mysteriously survived.

In the Royal Arcade, Brettell's are still selling beautiful shirts, as they did to Queen Victoria, and if you look down the Arcade towards Albemarle Street, you can still catch the feel of Georgian Mayfair, for the houses on the western side of the street, as far up as the Albemarle street frontage of Brown's Hotel, have hardly changed at all in appearance.

In the streets leading westwards from Bond Street to Grosvenor Square and Berkeley Square, the great houses are now occupied by exclusive couturiers and expensive showrooms of business houses, and these with the beautiful shops of North and South Audley Street, Mount Street and Davies Street and their blocks of flats above, are impeccably maintained.

The northern part of Davies Street was not built until about 1890, when the old Grosvenor market at the top of South Molton Street was demolished for the extension of Davies Street to Oxford Street, but at its southern end, opposite Mount Row, still stands one of the first houses ever to be built on Sir Richard Grosvenor's estate, at the time that Grosvenor Square was being planned. This is Bourdon House, built about 1723, for William Bourdon, on land leased from the Grosvenor estate. Though designed in the Palladian tradition, it was different from the houses in the square, for this was essentially a country house, set in fields and market gardens. It was smaller and simpler in concept, although it stretches back a long way and is far larger than might appear at a first glance.

There is a carved stone pediment over the neat doorway and a delightful fanlight. The house has two floors above the ground floor and basement, which is protected by an iron railing, and at the side is a small paved courtyard enclosed by a brick wall and wrought-iron gateway. Two or three of the front windows are still blocked, a relic of the days of the monstrous window-tax, which was first imposed in 1696, on the number of windows a house possessed, and was not repealed until 1851.

Inside, the house has a feeling of intimacy and comfort, for the rooms are comparatively small and beautifully proportioned, several of them almost square. They are panelled, the window-seats are wide and some of the shutters and cornices beautifully carved or moulded.

The main staircase, rather narrow for eighteenth-century hoops, reaches only to the first floor, but from the landing small doors lead to the upper part of the house and a labyrinth of small rooms, as in Bell Finch's house in Berkeley Square. They are approached by a narrow spiral staircase, which can be seen through the small glass dome which gives light to the first-floor landing.

After the demolition of Grosvenor House in 1926, the Grosvenors made Bourdon House their London home and the late 2nd Duke of Westminster lived here until his death in 1953. It is now occupied by Mallett's, the antique dealers of Number 40 New Bond Street, who have preserved it beautifully and furnished it with some of their incomparable furniture, so that it still has the feel of a country house and has changed hardly at all in two hundred and fifty years.

In South Audley Street, opposite the Grosvenor Chapel, Purdey's, the gunsmith, is still in business. Here kings and princes, the aristocracy and the big game-hunters have bought their guns for generations, and through the windows, above the blue paint which almost covers them, you can see, as you pass by, the trophies of many a hunt, for the walls of the main showroom are lined with the heads of tropical game.

Farther along, on the opposite side, at Number 19 South Audley Street, is the magnificent china shop of Thomas Goode and Company, which the founder of the firm first opened in 1827 at Number 15 Mill Street, Hanover Square, and moved to its present site in 1845. His son rebuilt the shop in 1876, displaying here the finest china, porcelain and glass of the day, particularly of Minton ware, and the two famous Minton elephants, standing seven feet high, with their howdahs and carved wooden plinths, are still to be seen in the windows, on permanent display.

It is a quiet, beautiful shop, where exquisite craftsmanship is displayed in a properly elegant setting, and like so many of Mayfair's shops, the customers come from all over the world. The firm, still in the hands of the Goode family, have also a smaller showroom at Number 2 Old Bond Street, the two establishments housing between them what is considered to be the finest collection in the world of Royal Worcester, Minton, Royal Doulton, Royal Crown Derby, Wedgwood and Spode bone china and Stuart, Royal Brierley, Webb, Edinburgh and Waterford crystal glass, as well as continental glass and contemporary table-ware.

Heywood Hill's bookshop in Curzon Street, established between the wars next door to Trumper's, the Court hairdresser, is as well-known and loved as Bumpus's, which after many moves since its foundation in 1790, has settled happily in Mount Street.

The Curzon cinema, first built between the wars and rebuilt in 1963, is in the true Mayfair tradition, for as well as showing first-class, intelligent films, it is supremely comfortable, its armchair seats roomy enough for the most long-legged of clients.

Mayfair also has its own theatre, occupying part of the building of the Mayfair Hotel.

The old Lansdowne Passage, running between the gardens of Lansdowne and Devonshire House, and along which the highway-man once escaped, is still there, though it has been closed for many years, but the new Lansdowne Passage, linking Berkeley Street with Fitzmaurice Place, runs alongside it, at a higher level, lined on either side with bright little shops and coffee-bars. And that brings us back to Curzon Street and the arched entrance into Shepherd market.

When Consuelo, the Duchess of Marlborough, was living in Sunderland House, backing on to the market, she said she was living in a slum, but Shepherd market has never been that. Disraeli, describing it in 1847 in his novel *Tancred*, wrote of 'a cluster of small streets, of little houses frequently intersected by mews, which here are numerous and sometimes gradually rather than abruptly terminating in a ramification of these mysterious regions. Sometimes a group of courts develops itself, and you may even chance to find your way into a small market place. Those, however, who are accustomed to connect these hidden residences of the humble with scenes of misery and characters of violence, need not apprehend in this district any appeal to their sympathies, or any shock to their taste. All is extremely genteel; and there is almost as much repose as in the golden saloons of the contiguous palaces . . .'

This was fair comment and the market is very much the same today, though its residents would not thank Disraeli for calling them genteel. It is busy, flourishing and friendly, without being in the least self-conscious of its age and the strange circumstance of its survival, so close to modern Piccadilly. It has shops of all kinds, including a number of antique shops, and an abundance of places for eating and drinking, from pubs to cafés and restaurants, Tiddy Dol's Eating House, with its eighteenth-century décor, offering traditional English food, as well as musical entertainment and dancing. And since no traffic can penetrate the narrow, winding streets of the market, it is a happy place in which to stroll or take a drink at one of the pavement cafés and watch the world go by.

As the small, tightly-knit circle of English aristocratic society disintegrated and the mansions of Mayfair gradually ceased to be private residences, hundreds of flats were built for the resident population, and there also remained the large stabling in the mews. Although a motor-car takes up as much room as a horse, it does not need an ostler or a coachman, and there was still their accommodation available. It was after the First World War that the fashion for adapting mews to modern living accommodation began. It has been going on ever since and today there are some extremely attractive mews cottages in Mayfair which are used as private residences, some of them of a considerable size. Culross Street, for example, off Park Lane, once a large mews, is entirely composed of these adaptations, and very attractive and fashionable they are.

Mayfair today is a place of luxury hotels and elegant shops, of exclusive restaurants and amusing clubs, the best known being perhaps the large Playboy Club in Park Lane, and it is still probably the most fashionable and expensive part of London in which to live. As well as the physical remains of the eighteenth century in the beautiful houses in many of the streets between Bond Street and Park Lane, an intangible personality has survived. There is a feeling of easygoing luxury in the shops and restaurants, a sense of gaiety which is stronger than the inevitable nostalgia for Mayfair's past glories.

It is a place where you can enjoy yourself. In the early 1920s Curzon House became the residence of the future King George VI and his bride, while their house in Piccadilly was being prepared for them. Today it is the Curzon House Club, one of London's most exclusive gaming clubs, furnished in the grand manner of the eighteenth century, with its wide and magnificent staircase rising from the left of the entrance hall, carpeted in the favourite deep crimson. The White Elephant Club, at Number 28 Curzon Street, is housed in a much smaller eighteenth-century house, only a few doors away from the house where Disraeli lived for his last few years and died, in 1881.

It has more than a dozen night-clubs, many of them established in old Mayfair houses, and the eating opportunities, which are international, include the incomparable Mirabelle Restaurant. The Mirabelle was opened at Number 56 Curzon Street in 1936, under the management of Erwin Schleyen, before passing into the ownership of the De Vere Hotels and Restaurants Group. It is here that distinguished European restaurants hold their Gastronomic Festivals, and at the latest, in 1975, Maxim's of Paris took up residence for a fortnight.

There are Austrian, French, Japanese, Spanish and Turkish restaurants in Mayfair, as well as the English ones, including Scott's in Mount Street, while most of the big hotels, in addition to their splendid food, offer dancing and cabaret each evening.

Adaptation is the key to survival, and by constantly adjusting its way of life, keeping where possible the best of the old world and at the same time accepting the best of the new, Mayfair has triumphantly ridden the storm of change and there is nowhere in the world quite like it.

BOOKS CONSULTED

Adburgham, Alison, *Shops and Shopping 1800–1914*, Allen & Unwin, 1964.

Andrews, Allen, *The Royal Whore*, Hutchinson, 1971.

Blyth, Henry, *Skittles*, Rupert Hart-Davis, 1970.

Boswell, James, *Life of Samuel Johnson*, 1791.

Boyle's Court Guide, 1802.

Burnet, Gilbert, *History of My Own Time*, 1832 edn (Smith).

Chancellor, E. B., *Private Palaces of London*, Kegan Paul, 1908.

Chancellor, E. B., *The Squares of London*, Kegan Paul, 1907.

Clinch, George, *Mayfair and Belgravia*, Truslove and Shirley, 1892.

Coke, Lady Jane, *Letters to Mrs. Eyre, 1747–1758*, Sonnenschein and Co., 1899.

Coke, Lady Mary, *Letters and Journals*, Kingsmead Reprints, 1970.

Colby, Reginald, *Mayfair*, Country Life, 1966.

Creevey Papers (edited John Gore), 1793–1838, Batsford, 1963.

Dasent, Arthur, *Piccadilly*, Macmillan, 1920.

Dasent, Arthur, *A History of Grosvenor Square*, Macmillan, 1935.

Dickens, Charles, *Little Dorrit*, Chapman & Hall, 1862.

Doran, John, *A Lady Of The Last Century*, Bentley and Son, 1873.

Evelyn, John, *Diary*, 1818.

Falk, Bernard, *The Berkeleys of Berkeley Square*, Hutchinson, 1944.

Frost, Thomas, *The Old Showmen and the London Fairs*, Tinsley Brothers, 1874.

Gatty, Charles, *Mary Davies and the Manor of Ebury*, Cassell and Co., 1921.

Hamilton, Anthony, *Memoirs of Count Gramont*, John Grant, 1908.

Hardwick, Mollie, *Mrs. Dizzy*, Cassell, 1972.

Heal, Sir Ambrose, *The London Furniture Makers, 1600–1840*, Batsford, 1953.

Hobhouse, Hermione, *Lost London*, Macmillan, 1971.

Holden, A. N. and Co., *14 Stanhope Gate*, Boulton and Paul, 1947.

Johnson, B. H., *Berkeley Square to Bond Street*, John Murray, 1952.

Knight, Charles, *London*, Charles Knight and Co., 1841.

La Roche, Sophie, *Sophie In London, 1786*, Jonathan Cape, 1933.

Mitchell and Leys, *A History of the English People*, Longmans, 1951.

Mitchell and Leys, *A History of London Life*, Longmans, 1958.

Nevill, Ralph, *Mayfair and Montmartre*, Methuen, 1921.

Nevill, Ralph, *Romantic London*, Cassell, 1928.

Nevill and Jerningham, *Piccadilly to Pall Mall*, Duckworth, 1908.

Ogg, David, *England in the Reign of James II and William III*, Oxford Paperbacks, 1967.

Pennant, Thomas, *Account of London*, 1791.

Pepys, Samuel, *Diary*, 1825.

Robinson, Mary (Perdita), *Memoirs*, Lippincott, 1894.

Walford, E., *Old and New London*, Cassell, 1893.

Walpole, Horace, *Memoirs and Portraits, 1751*, Batsford, 1963.

Weeton, E., *Journal of a Governess* (Vol. 2: 1811–1825), O.U.P., 1939.

Wheatley, H. B., *A Short History of Bond Street, Old and New*, Fine Art Society, 1911.

Wilson, Harriette, *Memoirs*, Eveleigh Nash, 1909.

Wraxall, Sir N. W., *Historical Memoirs of His Own Times*, Richard Bentley, 1836.

Wright, Lawrence, *Clean and Decent*, Routledge and Kegan Paul, 1960.

Index